Wireshark® 101
Essential Skills for Network Analysis
2nd Edition

*Always ensure you have proper authorization
before you listen to and capture network traffic.*

Protocol Analysis Institute, Inc
59 Damonte Ranch Parkway, #B340
Reno, NV 89521 USA
www.packet-level.com

Chappell University
info@chappellU.com
www.chappellU.com

To arrange bulk purchase discounts for sales promotions, events, training courses, or other purposes, please contact Chappell University (*info@chappellU.com*).

Book URL: *www.wiresharkbook.com*
13-digit ISBN: 978-1-893939-75-2
10-digit ISBN: 1-893939-75-8

(Version 2.0a)

Distributed worldwide for Chappell University through Protocol Analysis Institute, Inc. Protocol Analysis Institute, Inc. is the exclusive educational materials developer for Chappell University.

For general information on Chappell University or Protocol Analysis Institute, Inc., including information on corporate licenses, updates, future titles, or courses, contact the Protocol Analysis Institute, Inc., at *info@wiresharkbook.com*.

For authorization to photocopy items for corporate, personal, or educational use, contact Protocol Analysis Institute, Inc., at *info@wiresharkbook.com*.

Trademarks. All brand names and product names used in this book or mentioned in this course are trade names, service marks, trademarks, or registered trademarks of their respective owners. Wireshark and the "fin" logo are registered trademarks of the Wireshark Foundation.

Limit of Liability/Disclaimer of Warranty. The author and publisher have used their best efforts in preparing this book and the related materials used in this book. Protocol Analysis Institute, Inc., Chappell University, and the author(s) make no representations or warranties of merchantability of fitness for a particular purpose. Protocol Analysis Institute, Inc., and Chappell University assume no liability for any damages caused by following the instructions or using the techniques or tools listed in this book or related materials used in this book. Protocol Analysis Institute, Inc., Chappell University, and the author(s) make no representations or warranties that extend beyond the descriptions contained in this paragraph. No warranty may be created or extended by sales representatives or written sales materials. The accuracy or completeness of the information provided herein and the opinions stated herein are not guaranteed or warranted to produce any particular result and the advice and strategies contained herein may not be suitable for every individual. Protocol Analysis Institute, Inc., Chappell University, and author(s) shall not be liable for any loss of profit or any other damages, including without limitation, special, incidental, consequential, or other damages.

Copy Protection. In all cases, reselling or duplication of this book and related materials used in this training course without explicit written authorization is expressly forbidden. We will find you, ya know. So don't steal or plagiarize this book.

Acknowledgments

There are many people who were directly and indirectly involved in building the concept of this lab-based book in its first and second edition. Your time and patience (through never-ending revisions and updates) are truly appreciated.

Lanell Allen
Jim Aragon
Brenda Cardinal
Tobias Clary
Gerald Combs
Joy DeManty
John Gonder
Jennifer Keels
Jill Poulsen
Erin Shirley
Kayla Smith
John Wright

I would especially like to thank Jim Aragon for his meticulous technical and grammatical expertise. Jim, you did another great job on this edition—you are still my "style guru!" <grin>

Special thanks to the following individuals who offered encouraging quotes for readers beginning their Wireshark journey or honing their skills with this book.

Lanell Allen, Wireshark Certified Network Analyst™
Richard Bejtlich, Chief Security Officer, Mandiant
Sake Blok, Wireshark Core Developer and SYN-bit Founder
Anders Broman, Wireshark Core Developer and System Tester at Ericsson
Loris Degioanni, Creator of WinPcap, Founder and CEO at Draios
Betty DuBois, Chief Detective of Network Detectives and Certified Wireshark University Instructor
Tony Fortunato, Senior Network Performance Specialist, The Technology Firm
Lionel Gentil, iTunes Software Reliability Engineer, Apple, Inc.
John Gonder, Cisco Academy Director, Las Positas College
Jennifer Keels, CNP-S, CEH, Network Engineer
Gordon "Fyodor" Lyon, Founder of the open source Nmap Security Scanner project
Steven McCanne, CTO and Executive Vice President, Riverbed

As always, my sincere thanks to the **Wireshark Core Developers** and Gerald Combs who have built Wireshark into an indispensable tool. The current list of core developers can be found at *wiki.wireshark.org/Developers*.

If I've missed anyone in this acknowledgments section, I apologize sincerely.

Dedication

This book is dedicated to
my Mom and Dad.
I miss you both.

About this Book

Who Should Read this Book?

This book is written for beginner analysts. This book provides an ideal starting point whether you are interested in analyzing traffic to learn how an application works, you need to troubleshoot slow network performance, or determine whether a machine is infected with malware.

Learning to capture and analyze communications with Wireshark will help you really understand how TCP/IP networks function. As the most popular network analyzer tool in the world, the time you spend honing your skills with Wireshark will pay off when you read technical specs, marketing materials, security briefings, and more.

This book can also be used by current analysts who need to practice the skills contained in this book.

In essence, this book is for anyone who really wants to know what's happening on their network.

What Prerequisite Knowledge do I Need?

Before you delve into this book (or network analysis in general), you should have a solid understanding of basic network concepts and TCP/IP fundamentals. For example, you should know the purpose of a switch, a router, and a firewall. You should be familiar with the concepts of Ethernet networking, basic wireless networking, and be comfortable with IP network addressing, as well.

There are a few spots in this book where you will need to access the command prompt to set a path to an application directory or to run basic command-line tools such as *ipconfig/ifconfig, ping*, or *tracert/traceroute*. If you are unfamiliar with these tools, there are plenty of resources on the Internet to show you how they work on various platforms.

You will find a *Network Analyst's Glossary* at the back of the book. This glossary covers many of the terms and technology mentioned in the book. For example, if you aren't familiar with WinPcap when it's discussed in the book, just flip to the *Network Analyst's Glossary* to learn more.

What Version of Wireshark does this Book Cover?

This book was written using several Wireshark 2.x.x versions. If you are still stuck in the world of Wireshark 1.x, it's time to update your version. Wireshark 2 offers numerous advantages over the earlier versions, such as a native install for Macintosh users, Intelligent Scrollbar, much better graphs, a related packet column and more.

Where Can I Get the Book Trace Files?

Probably your first step should be to download the book trace files and other supplemental files from *www.wiresharkbook.com*. Click the Wireshark 101 book link and download the entire set of supplemental files for this Second Edition book.

The book supplemental files are available in *.zip* format. Create a folder on your local system and unzip the files into that folder.

If you have questions regarding the book or the book web site, please send them to *info@wiresharkbook.com*.

Where Can I Learn More about Wireshark and Network Analysis?

Download or watch Laura's free four-part Wireshark 101 course online at the All Access Pass portal (*www.lcuportal2.com*).

For more information on the All Access Pass and other training options, visit Chappell University at *www.chappellU.com*.

Foreword by Gerald Combs

What's happening on the network?

This is one of those small questions with large answers. For many people it's an important question, particularly when network problems impact lives and livelihoods.

The first time I saw someone analyze a network they used an oscilloscope. It was the 1980s and network analysis tools were scarce. I blame hair bands.

The oscilloscope was all we had on hand in our university lab and it showed us the square-ish electrical pulses that bounced up and down and made up the Ethernet frames flying around our network. It was a very narrow, limited view of the network, but it was fascinating.

A few years later at a different university I had to troubleshoot the network for our IT department. By then we had better tools such as tcpdump and a Sniffer which gave us packets instead of pulses. It was still daunting at first because our network was a zoo of different technologies: Ethernet, FDDI, token ring, IPX, DECnet, IP, AppleTalk, and more.

It didn't make much sense at first, but it was still fascinating. You could see what was in each message going across the network along with all the clever methods that people had devised to let computers talk to each other. That fascination turned into a passion which is still going strong.

Later on I had to answer the question, *"What's happening on the network?"* at an ISP. The nice tools to which I had grown accustomed were unavailable and I felt blind.

I started writing a protocol analyzer and released it as an open source application. Thanks to contributions from an amazingly talented team of developers and users, it grew into the world's most popular protocol analyzer.

I think everyone should have a fundamental understanding of computer networks. They are a vital part of modern society, and as such it's important to know how they work.

It's also important to know that Wireshark won't give you this understanding by itself - no tool will. Fortunately, Wireshark has a vibrant ecosystem that surrounds it, from the development team, to the user community, to companies that offer Wireshark-related products and services (including my employer), and to instructors like Laura. The ecosystem is an amazing collection of people who are keenly interested in protocol analysis and equally interested in helping each other. It is an honor to be part of it.

Networks may not make a lot of sense at first (they didn't for me), but that's OK. Laura can help you understand how they work (and how they often don't). She can give you the understanding you need to get the most out of Wireshark.

What's happening on *your* network?

Gerald Combs
Creator of Wireshark® (formerly *Ethereal*)

Table of Contents

Chapter 0 Skills: Explore Key Wireshark Elements and Traffic Flows

There has been one constant in the network traffic aspect of my career, which started in 1998: packet analysis with Ethereal, later renamed to Wireshark.

The Air Force Computer Emergency Response Team (AFCERT), where I learned the trade, was an early adopter of the first versions of the tool. Today, I couldn't imagine doing protocol inspection without Wireshark, and the project has only improved over time.

Richard Bejtlich
Chief Security Officer, *Mandiant Corporation*

Quick Reference: Key Wireshark Graphical Interface Elements

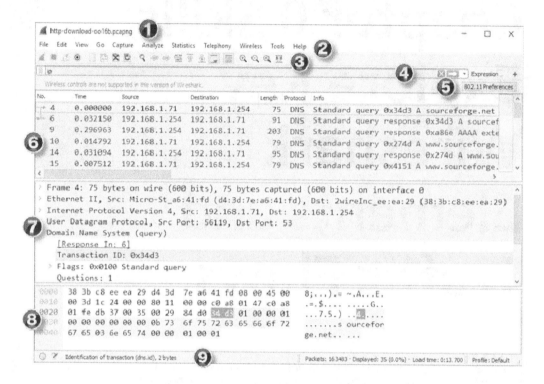

(1) **Title bar** – trace file name, capture source, or "The Wireshark Network Analyzer"
(2) **Main menu** – standard menu
(3) **Main toolbar** – learn to use this set of icon buttons!
(4) **Display Filter and Filter Expressions area** – focus on specific traffic
(5) **Wireless toolbar** – define 802.11 settings
(6) **Packet List pane** – packet relationship indicator and summary of each frame
(7) **Packet Details pane** – dissected frames
(8) **Packet Bytes pane** – hex and ASCII details
(9) **Status Bar** – access to the Expert, annotations, packet counts, and profiles

0.1. *Understand Wireshark's Capabilities*

Knowing what Wireshark can do will help you determine if it is the right tool for the job.

Wireshark is the world's most popular network analysis tool with an average of over 1 million downloads per month. Wireshark is also ranked #1 in the world as a security tool[1]. Named one of the "Most Important Open-Source Apps of All Time"[2], Wireshark runs on Windows, Mac OS X, and *NIX. Wireshark can even be run as a Portable App[3].

Wireshark is a free open source software program available at *wireshark.org*. When run on a host that can see a wired or wireless network, Wireshark captures and decodes the network frames, offering an ideal tool for network troubleshooting, optimization, security (network forensics), and application analysis. Captured traffic can be saved in numerous trace file formats (defaulting to the *.pcapng* format).

Wireshark's decoding process uses dissectors that can identify and display the various fields and values in network frames. In many instances, Wireshark's dissectors offer an interpretation of frame contents as well—a feature that significantly reduces the time required to locate the cause of poor network performance or to validate security concerns.

The open source development community has created thousands of dissectors to interpret the most commonly seen applications and protocols on networks. A core set of Wireshark developers is led by Gerald Combs, the original creator of Ethereal (Wireshark's development name prior to May 2006). As an open source project, Wireshark's source code is open to anyone for review or enhancement.

Wireshark can be used to easily determine who the top talkers are on the network, what applications are currently in use, which protocols are supported on a network, whether requests are receiving error responses, and whether packets are being dropped or delayed along a path. In addition, numerous filters can be applied to target a specific address (or address range), application, response code, conversation, keyword, etc.

The Wireshark installation package includes numerous tools used to capture packets at the command line, merge trace files, split trace files, and more.

Based on SLOCCount (Source Lines of Code Count), created by David A. Wheeler, Wireshark has over 2.4 million total lines of code (SLOC)[4] and the total estimated cost to develop Wireshark is over $95 million.

---

[1] SecTools.Org: Top 125 Network Security Tools, *sectools.org*.

[2] eWEEK/eWEEK Labs, May 28, 2012, see *www.eweek.com/c/a/Linux-and-Open-Source/The-Most-Important-OpenSource-Apps-of-All-Time/5/*

[3] See *portableapps.com* to learn more about this platform and to download the Portable App launcher. Download the Wireshark portable application from *www.wireshark.org*.

[4] See *www.wireshark.org/download/automated/sloccount.txt* for the current SLOCCount estimates.

The following is a quick list of some tasks that can be performed using Wireshark.

General Analysis Tasks

- Find the top talkers on the network
- See network communications in "clear text"
- See which hosts use which applications
- Baseline normal network communications
- Verify proper network operations
- Learn who's trying to connect to your wireless network
- Capture on multiple networks simultaneously
- Perform unattended traffic capture
- Capture and analyze traffic to/from a specific host or subnet
- View and reassemble files transferred via FTP or HTTP
- Import trace files from other capture tools
- Capture traffic using minimal resources

Troubleshooting Tasks

- Create a custom analysis environment for troubleshooting
- Identify path, client, and server delays
- Identify TCP problems
- Detect HTTP proxy problems
- Detect application error responses
- Graph IO rates and correlate drops to network problems
- Identify overloaded buffers
- Compare slow communications to a baseline of normal communications
- Find duplicate IP addresses
- Identify DHCP server or relay agent problems on a network
- Identify WLAN signal strength problems
- Detect WLAN retries
- Capture traffic leading up to (and possibly the cause of) problems
- Detect various network misconfigurations
- Identify applications that are overloading a network segment
- Identify the most common causes of poorly performing applications

Security Analysis (Network Forensics) Tasks

- Create a custom analysis environment for network forensics
- Detect applications that are using non-standard ports
- Identify traffic to/from suspicious hosts
- See which hosts are trying to obtain an IP address
- Identify "phone home" traffic
- Identify network reconnaissance processes
- Locate and globally map remote target addresses
- Detect questionable traffic redirections
- Examine a single TCP or UDP conversation between a client and server
- Detect maliciously malformed frames
- Locate known keyword attack signatures in your network traffic

Application Analysis Tasks

- Learn how applications and protocols work
- Graph bandwidth usage of an application
- Determine if a link will support an application
- Examine application performance after update/upgrade
- Detect error responses from a newly installed application
- Identify which users are running a particular application
- Examine how an application uses transport protocols such as TCP or UDP

 # WARNING

Before you capture your first packet, ensure you have permission to listen to the network traffic. If you are an IT staff member, obtain written permission to listen to network traffic for troubleshooting, optimization, security, and application analysis. Consult a legal specialist to understand your local and national laws regarding packet capture on wired and wireless networks.

0.2.   Get the Right Wireshark Version

Since you may move from one location to another, from one computer to another, and from one operating system to another, it's best to know on what systems you can install Wireshark. Wireshark runs on most of the commonly used operating systems, including Windows, Mac OS X, and *NIX systems.

All OS versions of Wireshark can be obtained from *www.wireshark.org*. Click the **Download** button and the site will recognize the operating system you are running and highlight the version of Wireshark that is most appropriate for that operating system.

TIP

If you are really new to Wireshark, consider downloading, installing, and using either the Windows or Apple OS X version—these are the simplest processes since they only require running an executable installation file.

As of Wireshark version 2, the Windows and Apple OS X installation processes are quite simple since these versions of Wireshark are available with an installer program.

Binary packages are available for most *NIX distributions. If a binary package is not available for your platform you can download the source and build it yourself. Refer to the Wireshark documentation (*www.wireshark.org/docs/wsug_html/*).

Wireshark also comes preinstalled on a number of forensic tool distributions, such as Kali Linux (*www.kali.org*), although it may not be the latest Wireshark version.

The complete list of operating system requirements is available at *www.wireshark.org/docs/wsug_html_chunked/ChIntroPlatforms.html*.

0.3. *Learn how Wireshark Captures Traffic*

Understanding how Wireshark captures traffic will affect how you use Wireshark's features. In this section we refer to the elements depicted in Figure 1.

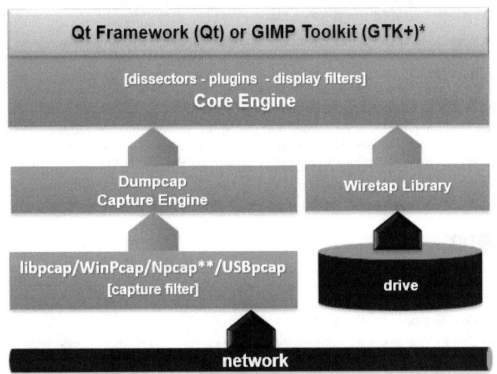

* GTK support will eventually be discontinued in Wireshark v2.

** Early releases of Wireshark v2 do not include Npcap — visit Npcap.org for more information.

Figure 1. How Wireshark handles traffic from a live capture or from a saved trace file.

The Capture Process Relies on Special Link-Layer Drivers

When your computer connects to a network, it relies on a network interface card (such as an Ethernet card) and link-layer driver (such as an Atheros PCI-E Ethernet driver) to send and receive packets.

Wireshark also relies on network interface cards and link-layer drivers to pass up traffic for capture and analysis. For capturing, you can use either WinPcap or Npcap (special link-layer drivers) on Windows hosts. Libpcap is the special link-layer driver used on *NIX hosts and Apple OS X. USBpcap is used to capture communications to and from local USB ports.

When you start capturing traffic with Wireshark, a tool called Dumpcap is launched in the background to do the actual capturing. Frames are passed up from the network, through one of these special link-layer drivers directly into Wireshark's Capture Engine. If you applied a capture filter (only capturing broadcast traffic for example), the frames that pass through the capture filter are passed up to the Capture Engine. Capture filters use Berkeley Packet Filtering (BPF) syntax.

For more information on filtering out (excluding) or filtering in (passing on to Wireshark) specific traffic types, refer to *Reduce the Amount of Traffic You have to Work With* on page 120.

The Dumpcap Capture Engine Defines Stop Conditions

The Dumpcap capture engine defines how the capture process runs and the stop conditions. For example, you can set up a capture to save frames to a set of 50 MB files and automatically stop after six files have been written. We refer to these files as trace files.

The current default trace file format is *.pcapng* (packet capture, next generation).

TIP

The .pcapng format offers the ability to save metadata with a file. For example, you can save trace file and packet annotations (comments) inside your trace file. We will look into this process in Chapter 7.

The Core Engine is the Goldmine

The Capture Engine passes frames up to the Core Engine. This is where Wireshark's power becomes evident. Wireshark supports thousands of dissectors that translate the incoming bytes into human-readable format frames. The dissectors break apart the fields in the frames and often perform analysis on the content of those fields.

For more information on how Wireshark dissectors work, see *Dissect the Wireshark Dissectors* on page 65.

The Qt Framework Provides the User Interface

As of Wireshark version 2, the Qt (pronounced either "Q-T" or "cute") framework is the preferred option to provide the cross-platform interface for Wireshark. With very few exceptions, you can move seamlessly from a Wireshark system running on one platform to a Wireshark system running on another platform with no problems. The basic interface elements are essentially the same.

The GTK+ Toolkit is Being Phased Out

The GTK+ (GIMP Toolkit) was the primary graphical toolkit until Wireshark version 2 was released. Although the early releases of Wireshark version 2 still include the option to install the GTK configuration of Wireshark, this option is being phased out. Now is the time to become familiar with and embrace the Qt framework.

The Wiretap Library is Used to Open Saved Trace Files

The Wiretap Library is used for the input/output functions for saved trace files. When you open a trace file (whether captured with Wireshark or another analysis tool), the Wiretap Library delivers the frames to the Core Engine.

TIP

The Wiretap Library understands the most commonly used trace file formats. If you receive a trace file in a format that the Wiretap Library doesn't support, consider examining the capture tool or process to determine if .pcap or .pcapng formats are available and perform the capture process again.

For more information on the Wiretap Library, see *Open Trace Files Captured with Other Tools* on page 52.

0.4.   *Understand a Typical Wireshark Analysis Session*

Although each analysis session is a bit different, there are some basic steps that you may want to perform during each analysis session.

The following is a checklist of the most common tasks performed during an analysis session. Consider using this basic task checklist when you open a trace file.

✓   Determine who is talking in the trace file
    See *Find Out Who's Talking to Whom on the Network* (Page 229)

✓   Determine what applications are in use
    See *List Applications Seen on the Network* (Page 239)

✓   Filter on the conversations of interest
    See *Filter on a Single TCP or UDP* Conversation (Page 169)

✓   Graph the IO to look for drops in throughput
    See *Graph Application and Host Bandwidth* (Page 242)

✓   Open the Expert to look for problems
    See *Identify TCP Errors* (Page 249)

✓   Determine the round trip time to identify path latency
    See *Use Filters to Spot Communication Delays* (Page 186)

Each of these tasks is covered in this book.

TIP

Now is the time to start your own checklist of tasks. As you go through the labs in this book, note the tasks that you'd like to repeat each time a trace file comes in. As with many skills, practice will pay off.

0.5. Differentiate a Packet from a Frame

You will see both terms used in the world of protocol analysis. The term "packet" is often used as a blanket term to describe anything sent across a network, but there is a definite difference between these two terms.

Recognize a Frame

The term "frame" is used when referring to the communication from the Media Access Control (MAC) layer header (such as an Ethernet header) through the MAC trailer. All communications between devices use frames. We don't spend a lot of time troubleshooting or analyzing Ethernet frames, however. There's not a lot to analyze in an Ethernet header or trailer and Ethernet technology is fairly well implemented and not often the problem. In the world of wireless technology, however, there is a lot going on in the WLAN header—enough to focus on during a troubleshooting session.

You will not always see the Ethernet trailer when analyzing traffic. Some operating systems do not support capturing the trailers on Ethernet networks.

Just to make this more confusing, Wireshark adds a "Frame" section to provide extra information about all actual frames. When you look inside the Packet Details pane, you will see this Frame section at the top. If you expand that section, you will see time, coloring and other information added to the actual frame by Wireshark.

The actual frame begins with the second line, labeled "Ethernet II." Wireshark's Frame section only contains information about the frame (metadata). It does not contain any of the actual contents of the frame.

Figure 2 indicates the beginning and ending of the actual frame as well as the Frame section that contains the metadata.

Recognize a Packet

A packet is the stuff that sits inside a MAC frame. In TCP/IP communications, a packet begins at the IP header and ends just before the MAC trailer. People often refer to network analysis as "packet analysis"—this naming is due to the fact that the majority of analysis tasks begin at the IP header. Figure 2 indicates the beginning and ending of the packet.

Recognize a Segment (and Watch for Ambiguities)

This term is the catalyst for many arguments regarding network terminology. A TCP *data* segment consists of application bytes preceded by a TCP header. The "data" may include an HTTP header or just contain data. The confusion with this term arises when you examine the establishment of a TCP connection. During this time, each TCP peer shares its Maximum Segment Size (MSS) value. In this instance, the term segment is used to define the receive *data segment size*, not including the TCP header. Figure 2 indicates the beginning and ending of the TCP segment.

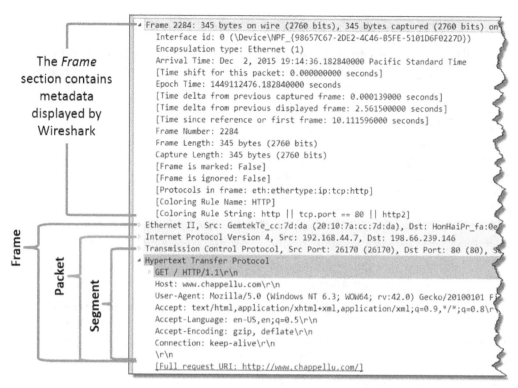

The *Frame* section contains metadata displayed by Wireshark

Frame

Packet

Segment

Figure 2. It is best to learn and use the proper terminology whenever possible.

In this book, we use the term "frame" when focusing on the MAC header in communications, or when referring to a value in the **No.** column (frame number column) in the Packet List pane.

Since Wireshark often refers to frames as packets in various menus, we will use Wireshark's terminology in those cases. For example, the File menu contains an option to "Export Specified Packets" even though it is actually exporting frames.

0.6. Follow an HTTP Packet through a Network

To be a good analyst, you must know TCP/IP very well. Also key to communications analysis is a solid understanding of how packets travel through a network and how the traffic is affected by various network devices.

Let's look at a network path that includes a client, two switches, one standard router, a router that performs Network Address Translation (NAT) and a server.

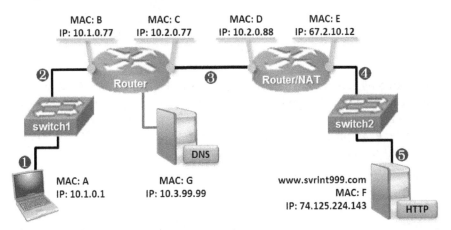

Figure 3. How will these devices affect the format of the frame along the path?

In Figure 3, our client sends an HTTP GET request for the main page on the HTTP server. We've used simple letters to represent the MAC addresses (aka hardware addresses) of the devices.

To know how devices affect the contents of the frame, we will look at how this frame is altered as it travels through switches, routers, and even a router/NAT device.

TIP

There are many times when you will need to capture at more than one location. For example, when you want to know how a device affects the contents of a frame, you need to capture the frame both before and after it travels through the device. You may also want to capture traffic at two locations to determine which internetworking device is dropping packets.

Because capturing at multiple locations is a common analysis task, you should have Wireshark (or at least Dumpcap) loaded on more than one laptop or be prepared to capture using port spanning or a full-duplex tap. We will cover these capture options in Chapter 2.

Point 1: What Would You See at the Client?

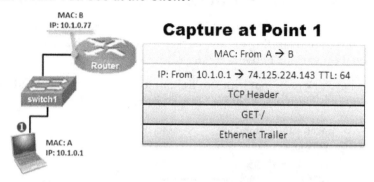

All devices can only send to the hardware address of local machines in MAC headers. This MAC header will be stripped off by the first router along the path—these MAC headers are only temporary and are used to get the packet to the next hop along a path. In the IP header example above, the packet is addressed from 10.1.0.1 (client) to 74.125.224.143 (server).

Analyst View: At this point, the Ethernet header of our client's GET request is addressed to the local router's MAC address (B).

Point 2: What Would You See on the Other Side of the First Switch?

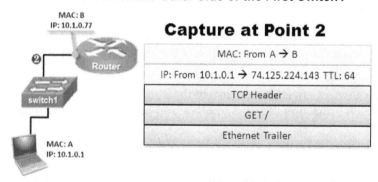

True switches[5] do not affect the contents of the frame. Switch 1 would simply look at the destination MAC address (MAC address B) to determine if that host is connected to one of the switch ports.

When the switch finds the switch port associated with MAC address B, the switch forwards the frame out the appropriate switch port.

Analyst View: We would see a frame that matches the frame we saw at point 1.

---

5   A true switch does not offer any routing functionality. The only purpose of a true switch is to learn what machines are connected to it (based on MAC addresses) and forward traffic accordingly.

Point 3: What Would You See on the Other Side of the Router?

Capture at Point 3

MAC: From C → D
IP: From 10.1.0.1 → 74.125.224.143 TTL: 63
TCP Header
GET /
Ethernet Trailer

MAC: C
IP: 10.2.0.77

MAC: D
IP: 10.2.0.88

Router   ❸   Router/NAT

Upon receipt of the frame, after checking to make sure the frame isn't corrupt and that the frame is addressed to the router's MAC address, the router strips off the Ethernet header.

The router examines the destination IP address in the packet (it is now considered a packet, not a frame) and consults its routing tables to see if it knows what to do with the packet. If the router does not know how to get to the destination IP address (and it doesn't have a default gateway to send the packet to), the router will drop the packet and send a message back to the originator indicating there is a routing problem. We can capture these error messages with Wireshark and detect which router is unable to forward our packets to the destination.

If the router has the information required to forward the packet, it decrements the IP header Time to Live (hop count) field value by 1 and applies a new Ethernet header to the packet before sending it on to the router/NAT device.

Analyst View: We would see a new Ethernet header (from C to D) and an IP header Time to Live value that has been decreased by 1.

Point 4: What Would You See on the Other Side of the Router/NAT Device?

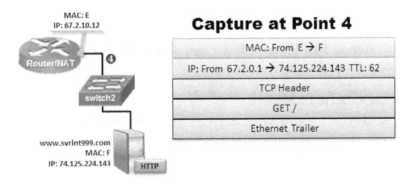

MAC: E
IP: 67.2.10.12

Router/NAT   ❹

switch2

www.svrint999.com
MAC: F
IP: 74.125.224.143   HTTP

Capture at Point 4

MAC: From E → F
IP: From 67.2.0.1 → 74.125.224.143 TTL: 62
TCP Header
GET /
Ethernet Trailer

The router/NAT device goes through the same routing process as the previous router before forwarding the packet. Additionally, the router/NAT device changes the source IP address (network address translation) and source port number while making note of the original source IP address and source port number. The router/NAT device associates this information with the newly assigned outbound IP address and port number.

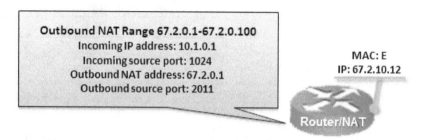

Analyst View: We would see a new Ethernet header (from E to F) and an IP header Time to Live value that has been decreased by 1. In addition, we would see that the source IP address and source port number has changed.

Point 5: What Would You See at the Server?

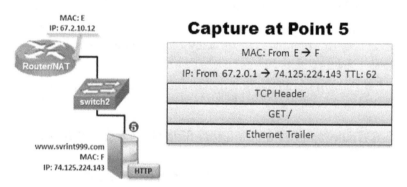

At this point we should see the same frame that we saw at Point 4. Remember, switches should not alter the contents of a frame.

Where You Capture Traffic Matters

If you capture at Point 1, 2, or 3, you cannot determine the MAC address of the server. Likewise, if you capture at Point 3, 4, or 5, you cannot determine the MAC address of the client. If you capture at point 5, you cannot tell the actual IP address of the client, either.

Beware of Default Switch Forwarding

Remember, switches forward frames based on MAC address. If you'd connected a Wireshark system to either of the switches in Figure 3, you would not have seen any of the traffic between our HTTP client and HTTP server. The switches would only forward broadcast, multicasts, and traffic destined to your Wireshark system's MAC address down your port[6].

Switches do not alter the MAC addresses or the IP addresses of the traffic, but they can be a major roadblock in network analysis.

Consider the example shown in Figure 4. We loaded Wireshark on the machine connected to switch port 1. We have a problem if we want to listen to the traffic between the two other devices on the network. The switch is not going to forward this down our port—it's not addressed to our MAC address.

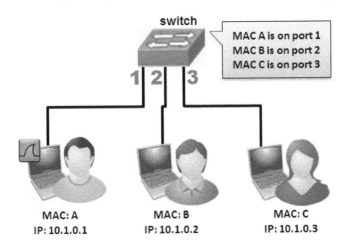

Figure 4. Switches can affect the amount of traffic you see.

It is this limitation that causes us to figure out other methods for listening in on network traffic. We will look at our options in *Identify the Best Capture Location to Troubleshoot Slow Browsing or File Downloads* on page 103.

 TIP

Plan and test your capture methods in advance. It's not a fun process to start testing capture methods when all hell breaks loose on the network and users, their managers, your manager, and the CEO are pounding on your office door or encroaching in your cubicle air space. Be prepared—be practiced.

---

[6]   One other item can be sent down your switch port—traffic to an unknown MAC address. If all goes well, this should rarely happen. We have resolution processes to ensure we know target MAC addresses and we should only see MAC addresses that are in use on the network.

0.7. Access Wireshark Resources

Eventually you will hit a problem that you just can't solve. Whether it is a problem in Wireshark functionality or packet structures, you can find assistance in several key places on the Internet.

Use the Wireshark Wiki Protocol Pages

Wireshark offers support through a series of Wiki protocol pages.

Visit *wiki.wireshark.org* to see all the Wiki information related to Wireshark. You can also add the protocol or application name to the URL for assistance on a protocol. For example, you can type *wiki.wireshark.org/Ethernet*[7].

You can also get to these pages by right-clicking on any protocol displayed inside a frame, as shown in Figure 5. Wireshark detects the protocol selected and launches the related Wiki page.

---

[7]   Note that the URL is case sensitive. If you browse to wiki.wireshark.org/ethernet (all lower case), you will see a message indicating that "This page does not yet exist."

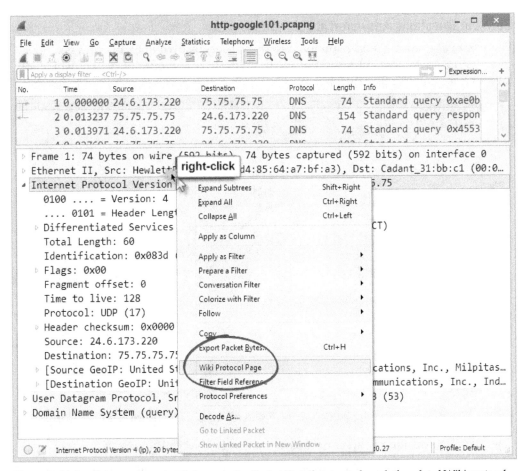

Figure 5. Right-click on any protocol shown in the Packet Details pane to launch the related Wiki protocol page. [http-google101.pcapng]

Get Your Questions Answered at *ask.wireshark.org*

There is a very active Q&A forum for Wireshark users (shown in Figure 6). Visit *ask.wireshark.org* to pose your questions to the Wireshark community. You must register for a free account to post a question here.

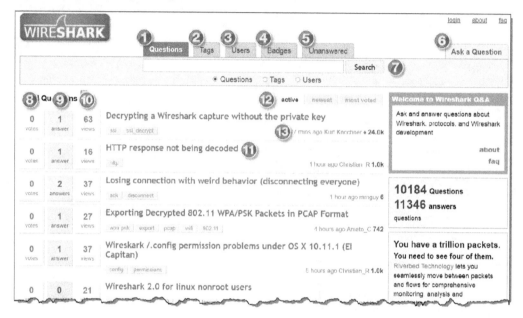

Figure 6. Use the Search function (7) to look for key words related to your question at ask.wireshark.org.

The following lists the key areas on *ask.wireshark.org*.

(1)   **Questions tab** – Click to return to the All Questions page (shown above).

(2)   **Tags tab** – Click to see the list of tags related to questions – click on tags related to your topic of interest to see if there is helpful information there.

(3)   **Users tab** – Click to see the users who participate in the Q&A forum – this area also includes their status in badge colors, counts, and administrative status (diamonds).

(4)   **Badges tab** – Click to see how many contributors have achieved recognition for their participation in the Q&A forum.

(5)   **Unanswered tab** – Click to see questions that are still considered unanswered. Unfortunately, many Q&A participants do not mark questions "answered" even though they have been.

(6)   **Ask a Question tab** – Click to ask your question. If you don't have a free account here yet, your question will be saved as you create an account and log in with your new credentials.

(7)   **Search area and button** – Search for the topic you are interested in first. This is a great place to start.

(8)   **Vote count** – Forum users can vote on (like/unlike) questions.

(9)   **Answer count** — This number indicates how many answers have been submitted to a question.

(10) **View count** — This number indicates how many times a question has been viewed. This is a great indicator to determine how "hot" a topic is.

(11) **Question title (hyperlink) and tags** — Click on the question title to jump to the question page. The tags indicate the topic(s) covered in the question.

(12) **Jump to buttons** — Click on any of these buttons to jump to the list of active questions, newest questions, or questions that have the most votes.

(13) **Question activity age and contributor information** — This area indicates how old a question is (based on last activity such as answer, comment, or even just posting the question), who contributed to the question most recently, and information about that last contributor. The contributor information includes the Karma level (level of acquired trust in the forum) and their administrative levels.

For more information on the Q&A forum, visit *ask.wireshark.org/faq/*.

Note: During the initial development of this book, we pulled up the most active questions and the hottest topics on the Q&A Forum. That list, along with years of experience teaching Wireshark techniques and analyzing network traffic, led to the skills covered in this book.

0.8. Analyze Traffic Using the Main Wireshark View

You don't always need to do a deep dive into the traffic to understand what's going on. A quick look at the main Wireshark window may be all you need to find the cause or culprit.

Open a Trace File (Using the Main Toolbar, Please)

When launched, Wireshark displays a Start Page. Although there are many functions available on the Start Page, the fastest way to navigate in Wireshark is through the main menu, main toolbar, and keyboard shortcuts. Click the **File Open** button on the main toolbar (circled in Figure 7). Open *http-google101.pcapng* (available at *www.wiresharkbook.com*).

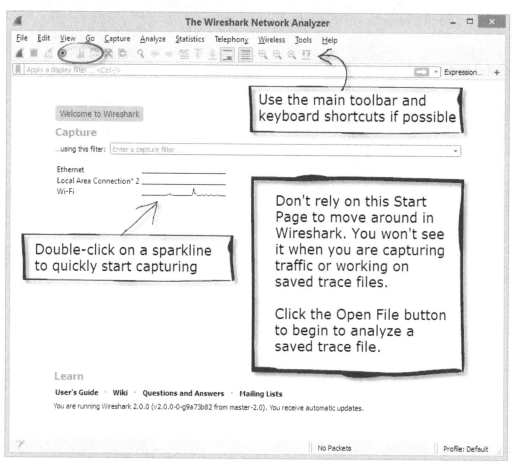

Figure 7. The Start Page appears when you launch Wireshark. Whenever possible, use the main toolbar and keyboard shortcuts to navigate in Wireshark.

TIP

As of Wireshark version 2, the list of keyboard shortcuts is available under Help | About Wireshark | Keyboard Shortcuts. See *Learn the Keyboard Shortcuts* on page 24.

This trace file contains the traffic between a client and the *www.google.com* server when someone opens the main web site page. If you capture your own traffic to *www.google.com*, it may look quite different. Your traffic will contain different MAC and IP addresses and you may have some elements of the Google site cached (on disk). In the case of cached content, you will load portions of the web site page from disk—you will not see the cached content being sent from the server in the trace file.

We will work with this trace file as we explore the various elements of the Wireshark main view.

Launch a Capture with Sparklines

Sparklines illustrate the traffic level seen on available interfaces. Double-click on a sparkline to quickly launch a capture on that interface.

Know When You Must Use the Main Menu

We all know how to use menus. The key is *when* to use the main menu (Figure 8) and *where* to find what you're looking for. Many of Wireshark's functions are available through the right-click method or the main toolbar (also referred to as the icon toolbar).

Figure 8. All functions in the Go and Capture menu items can be done faster using the main toolbar.

The following list highlights the reasons you may need to use the main menu instead of the main toolbar.

File—open file sets, save subsets of packets, export SSL session keys and objects

Edit—change preferences, clear marked/ignored packets, and time references

View—view/hide toolbars and panes, edit the **Time** column setting, reset coloring

Analyze—create display filter macros, see enabled protocols, save forced decodes

Statistics—build graphs and open statistics windows for various protocols

Telephony—perform all telephony-related functions (graphs, charts, playback)

Wireless—perform Bluetooth and WLAN functions (devices, statistics)

Tools—access the Lua scripting console and jump to resources

Help—check for updates, access Wireshark folder information and shortcut list

Again, this list focuses on things you need in the main menu. Become an efficient analyst by finding the fastest ways to perform tasks.

Use the Main Toolbar Whenever Possible

You can work very efficiently by clicking on the buttons on the main toolbar to open files and access filters, coloring rules, and preferences. In this book we use most of the key functions on the main toolbar. These functions are listed in Figure 9.

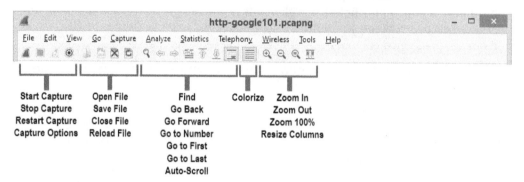

Figure 9. Become familiar with the main toolbar functions – this is the fastest way to work in Wireshark.

Learn the Keyboard Shortcuts

Under Help | About Wireshark | Keyboard Shortcuts, you will find the list of shortcuts available. In addition, right-clicking on many pop-up windows in Wireshark will bring up a list of keyboard shortcuts applicable to that window.

Shortcut availability is based on your version of Wireshark and the operating system on which you installed Wireshark.

The following lists keyboard shortcuts for Windows:

Shortcut	Name	Description
Ctrl+Shift+C	As Filter	Copy this item as a display filter
Ctrl+W	Close	Close this capture file
Ctrl+Left	Collapse All	Collapse all packet details
Ctrl+1	Color 1	Mark the current conversation with its own color.
Ctrl+2	Color 2	Mark the current conversation with its own color.
Ctrl+3	Color 3	Mark the current conversation with its own color.

Ctrl+4	Color 4	Mark the current conversation with its own color.
Ctrl+5	Color 5	Mark the current conversation with its own color.
Ctrl+6	Color 6	Mark the current conversation with its own color.
Ctrl+7	Color 7	Mark the current conversation with its own color.
Ctrl+8	Color 8	Mark the current conversation with its own color.
Ctrl+9	Color 9	Mark the current conversation with its own color.
Ctrl+Shift+A	Configuration Profiles…	Manage your configuration profiles
F1	Contents	Help contents
Ctrl+Alt+1	Date and Time of Day (1970-01-01 01:02:03.123456)	Show packet times as the date and time of day.
Ctrl+Shift+D	Description	Copy this item's description
Ctrl+Shift+E	Enabled Protocols…	Enable and disable specific protocols
Ctrl+Right	Expand All	Expand packet details
Shift+Right	Expand Subtrees	Expand the current packet detail
Ctrl+H	Export Packet Bytes…	Export Packet Bytes…
Ctrl+Shift+F	Field Name	Copy this item's field name
Ctrl+N	Find Next	Find the next packet
Ctrl+F	Find Packet…	Find a packet
Ctrl+B	Find Previous	Find the previous packet
Ctrl+Home	First Packet	Go to the first packet
Ctrl+G	Go to Packet…	Go to specified packet
Ctrl+Shift+D	Ignore All Displayed	Ignore all displayed packets
Ctrl+D	Ignore/Unignore Packet	Ignore or unignore this packet
Ctrl+End	Last Packet	Go to the last packet
Ctrl+Shift+M	Mark All Displayed	Mark all displayed packets
Ctrl+M	Mark/Unmark Packet	Mark or unmark this packet

Ctrl+Shift+N	Next Mark	Go to the next marked packet
Ctrl+Down	Next Packet	Go to the next packet
Ctrl+.	Next Packet in Conversation	Go to the next packet in this conversation
Ctrl+Alt+N	Next Time Reference	Go to the next time reference
Ctrl+0	Normal Size	Return the main window text to its normal size
Ctrl+O	Open	Open a capture file
Ctrl+K	Options…	Capture options
Ctrl+Shift+P	Preferences…	Manage Wireshark's preferences
Ctrl+Shift+B	Previous Mark	Go to the previous marked packet
Ctrl+Up	Previous Packet	Go to the previous packet
Ctrl+,	Previous Packet in Conversation	Go to the previous packet in this conversation
Ctrl+Alt+B	Previous Time Reference	Go to the previous time reference
Ctrl+P	Print…	Print…
Ctrl+Q	Quit	Quit Wireshark
F5	Refresh Interfaces	Refresh interfaces
Ctrl+R	Reload	Reload this file
Ctrl+Shift+L	Reload Lua Plugins	Reload Lua plugins
Ctrl+Shift+F	Reload as File Format/Capture	Reload as File Format/Capture
Ctrl+Space	Reset Colorization	Reset colorized conversations.
Ctrl+Shift+R	Resize Columns	Resize packet list columns to fit contents
Ctrl+R	Restart	Restart current capture
Ctrl+S	Save	Save this capture file
Ctrl+Shift+S	Save As…	Save as a different file
Ctrl+Alt+3	Seconds Since 1970-01-01	Show packet times as the seconds since the UNIX / POSIX epoch (1970-01-01).

Ctrl+Alt+4	Seconds Since Beginning of Capture	Show packet times as the date and time of day.
Ctrl+Alt+5	Seconds Since Previous Captured Packet	Show packet times as the seconds since the previous captured packet.
Ctrl+Alt+6	Seconds Since Previous Displayed Packet	Show packet times as the seconds since the previous displayed packet.
Ctrl+T	Set/Unset Time Reference	Set or unset a time reference for this packet
Ctrl+E	Start	Start capturing packets
Ctrl+E	Stop	Stop capturing packets

Master the Filter Toolbar

We use display filters to pull the "needle out of the haystack." When you have thousands or hundreds of thousands of packets to look through, use display filters to see traffic that is related to the task at hand. For example, if you are troubleshooting someone's web browsing session, you can use a display filter to remove email sessions or virus update traffic from view.

Figure 10 highlights the purpose of each section of the filter toolbar.

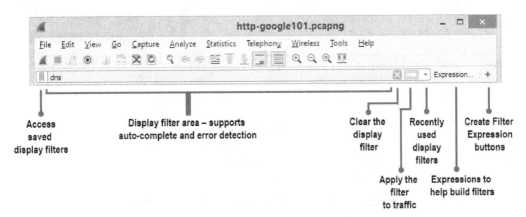

Figure 10. Learn to use the display filter toolbar to save time analyzing traffic.

Summarize the Traffic Using the Packet List Pane

Wireshark has three panes (windows)—the Packet List pane, the Packet Details pane, and the Packet Bytes pane.

The Packet List pane is the top pane, as shown in Figure 11.

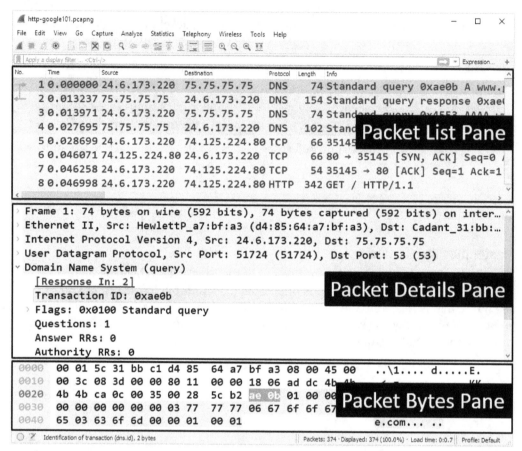

Figure 11. When you select a frame in the Packet List pane, the Packet Details pane and Packet Bytes pane provide additional information on the selected packet. [http-google101.pcapng]

Scroll through the Packet List pane to see which hosts are communicating, the protocols or applications in use, and general information about the frames. Wireshark colors the frames based on a set of coloring rules. For more information on coloring rules, see *Identify Applied Coloring Rules* on page 199.

You can add columns to the Packet List pane and sort on any column. This sorting ability can help you find similar packets or large delays in the trace file. By default, the Packet List pane is sorted by the frame number column ("**No.**" column on the far left side).

Figure 12 shows the Packet List pane of *http-google101.pcapng*. Each packet in the trace file contains information in the default columns listed below.

- **Number ("No.") column** — Each frame is assigned a number. By default, traffic is sorted on the **No.** column from low to high. You can sort the Packet List pane by clicking on the desired column heading. If you change the sort order and want to return to the default look of the Packet List pane, sort on this column.

  To the left of the No. column is the Related Packets Indicator which depicts the relationship between packets in a stream and requests/responses. The Related Packets Indicator is only active for the stream (or conversation) in which the currently selected packet resides.

- **Time column** — By default, Wireshark shows when each frame arrived compared to the first frame in the **Time** column. We will use this column to find delays in *Detect Latency Problems by Changing the Time Column* on page 89.

- **Source and Destination columns** — The **Source** and **Destination** columns show the highest layer address available in each frame. Some frames only have a MAC address (ARP packets, for example), so those MAC addresses will be displayed in the **Source** and **Destination** columns. In Figure 12, we see that all of our frames have IP addresses shown in the **Source** and **Destination** columns.

- **Protocol column** — Wireshark displays the last dissector applied to the frame. This is a great place to look if you're trying to figure out what applications are in use. In Figure 12, we see DNS, TCP, and HTTP listed in this column.

- **Length column** — This column indicates the total length of each frame. We can easily detect if an application uses itty bitty stinkin' packet sizes by looking at this column.

- **Info column** — This column provides basic information about the frame. Look at this column as you scroll through this trace file. You will see many DNS queries and responses, many HTTP GET requests, and data packets as the user loads the main Google page.

- **Intelligent Scrollbar** — Although this is not a column, it is important to mention this important feature of the Packet List pane. The Intelligent Scrollbar provides a miniature view of the traffic coloring seen in the trace file. We will examine the Intelligent Scrollbar in *Navigate Manually on the Intelligent Scrollbar* on page 213.

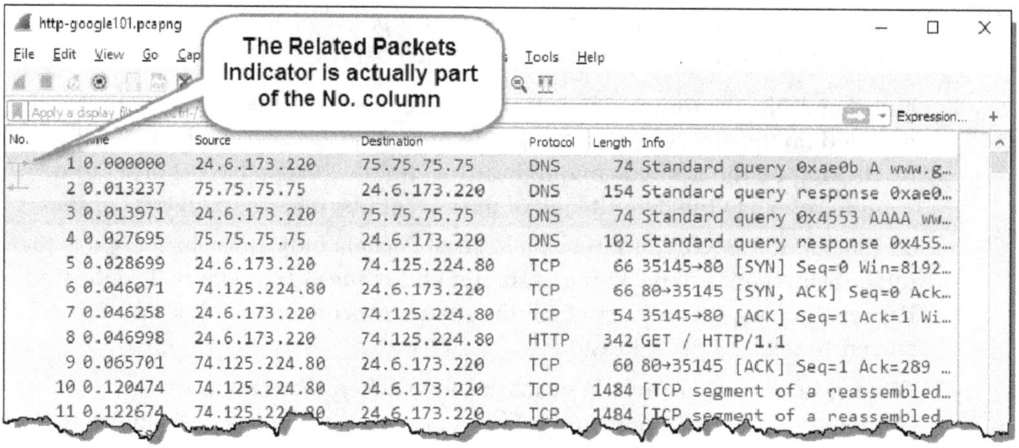

Figure 12. The seven default columns of the Packet List pane. [http-google101.pcapng]

Related Packets Indicator

To the left side of the No. column, you will see the Related Packets Indicator. The Related Packets Indicator depicts the relationship between packets in a stream (also referred to as a conversation).

The Related Packets Indicator only shows the relationship of packets in the same stream as the selected packet. For example, if you select a DNS query packet, the Related Packet Indicator will connect this packet to the associated DNS response is (if it exists in the trace file). If you select a frame in a TCP stream, you may see more interesting information, such as the checkmark indicating the packet that has been acknowledged by the selected packet.

Try this with *http-google101.pcapng*. Click on frame 1 and you will notice the Related Packets Indicator links frame 1 with frame 2. Frame 1 is a DNS query and frame 2 is the associated response. Click on frame 6 and you will see a line indicating the start of the stream and a checkmark next to frame 5 indicating that the selected frame is acknowledging frame 5. Figure 13 depicts many of the Related Packets Indicator markings.

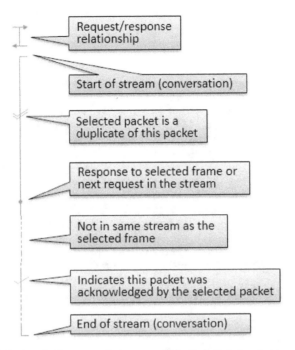

Figure 13. The Related Packets Indicator can help you quickly find related packets.

Sort Columns in the Packet List Pane

As mentioned earlier, you can sort the Packet List pane by clicking on the desired column heading. For example, if you click on the **Protocol** column heading when viewing *http-google101.pcapng*, Wireshark reorders the frames as DNS, HTTP, and TCP (ascending alphabetically), as shown in Figure 14.

Click the Number ("**No.**") column heading once to reorder the Packet List pane in its original order (from low to high).

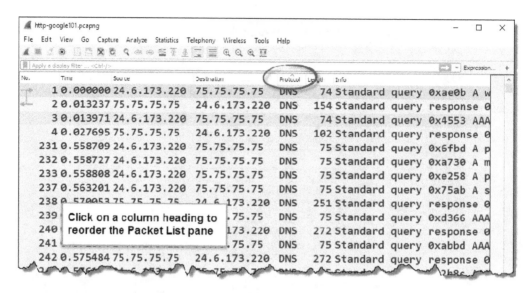

Figure 14. Click once on any column heading to sort from low to high – click again to sort from high to low. [http-google101.pcapng]

Reorder the Columns

You can change the location of columns by clicking and dragging on a column heading to move it left or right. In Figure 15 we moved the **Time** column to the right.

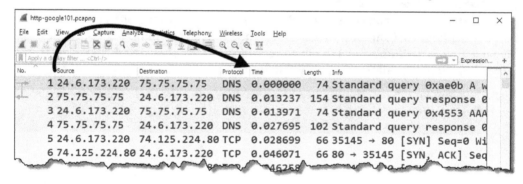

Figure 15. Just click and drag column headings left or right to reorder columns. [http-google101.pcapng]

Right-Click on Column Headings to Hide, Display, Rename, and Remove Columns

Right-click on any column heading to view your options in a drop-down menu. Click on column names to toggle them on and off, as shown in Figure 16[8].

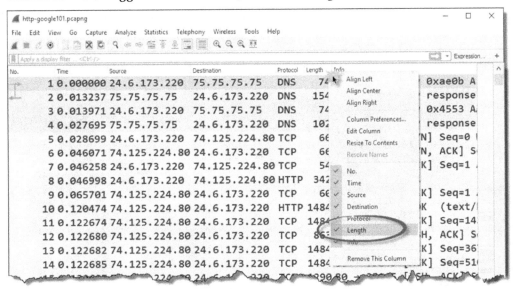

Figure 16. Right-click on any column heading to view the column options menu. When you do not want to see a column, simply uncheck the column on the list. [http-google101.pcapng]

Select **Remove This Column** to remove it from the list, if desired.

---

8   We hid columns at various points in this book to enable us to show more information contained in other columns.

Right-Click in the Packet List Pane to View Available Options

Many of Wireshark's windows and views support right-click functions. Right-click on any packet in the Packet List pane to see what's available, as shown in Figure 17.

In this book, we use this right-click functionality to apply filters, colorize traffic, reassemble traffic (follow streams), force Wireshark to dissect something in a different way, and more.

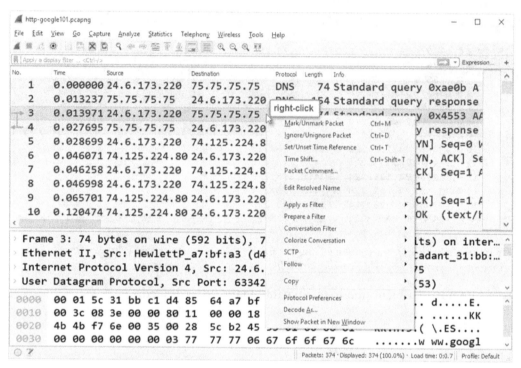

Figure 17. Right-click on any packet in the Packet List pane to see the available functions.
[http-google101.pcapng]

Use Packet Coloring to Your Advantage

Wireshark contains a set of default coloring rules to help you identify the traffic types and spot network problems faster. You can easily change these coloring rules and create additional coloring rules to alert you to unusual traffic. We will work with coloring rules in *Identify Applied Coloring Rules* on page 199.

Dig Deeper in the Packet Details Pane

When you click on a packet in the Packet List pane, Wireshark shows the details for that packet in the Packet Details pane (the middle pane). The Packet Details pane shows the power of Wireshark's dissectors.

As mentioned earlier, the Frame section is not part of a packet as it travels through a network — Wireshark adds the Frame section for additional information about the frame, such as when the frame arrived, what coloring rule is applied to the frame, the frame number, and frame length, as seen in Figure 18.

As you move through the Packet Details pane, click on the ⟩ indicators to expand sections of the frames. Alternately you can use right-click to expand an entire frame (**Expand All**) or expand just one collapsed section (**Expand Subtrees**).

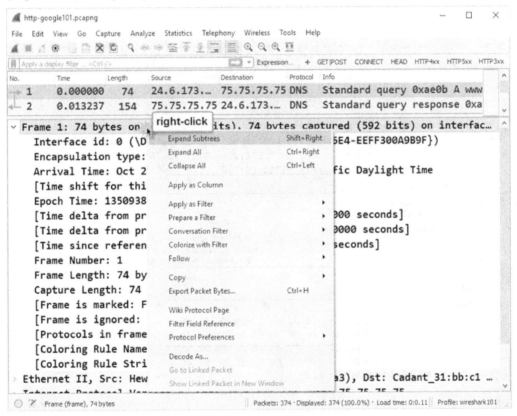

Figure 18. The Frame section includes metadata such as arrival timestamp, frame number, and dissectors applied to the frame. [http-google101.pcapng]

Get Geeky in the Packet Bytes Pane

This is the "geek pane." The Packet Bytes pane shows the contents of the frame in hex and ASCII formats, as shown in Figure 19. If the frame doesn't have any readable strings, the ASCII portion will look like a bunch of junk. We may look at this pane when Wireshark sees "data" in a frame.

When you highlight a field in the Packet Details pane, Wireshark also highlights the location of that field and the bytes contained in that field in the Packet Bytes pane. Wireshark also indicates the field directly under your cursor when you hover over the bytes area.

If you don't want to see the Packet Bytes pane, simply drag it to the bottom of the window. Drag your cursor up from the bottom to bring it back.

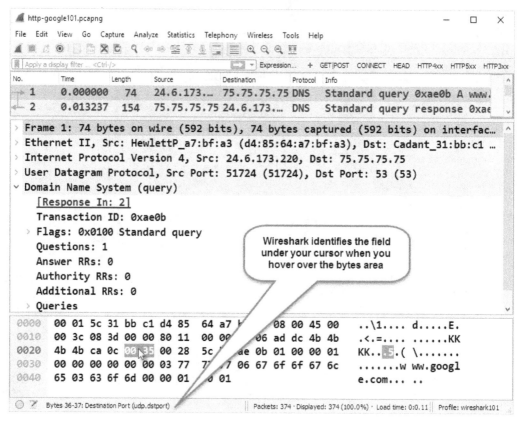

Figure 19. The Packet Bytes pane shows ASCII strings contained in the packet. [http-google101.pcapng]

Pay Attention to the Status Bar

The Status Bar consists of two buttons and three columns. These columns can be resized as necessary.

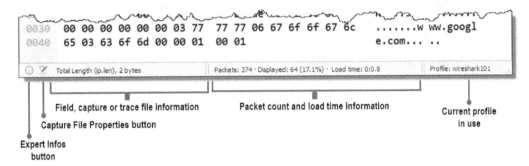

Figure 20. The Status Bar content changes depending on what you click on in the Packet List pane, Packet Details pane, or Packet Bytes pane. [http-google101.pcapng]

Find Problems with the Expert Information Button ⬤

The first button is the **Expert Information** button. This button is colored to show you the highest level of information contained in the Expert Information window. The Expert Information window can alert you to numerous network concerns seen in the trace file as well as packet comments. We will work with the Expert Information window in *Use the Expert Information Button on the Status Bar* on page 249.

Add Notes to a Trace File with the Annotation Button ✏

The second button is the trace file **Annotation** button. Click this button to add, edit, or view a trace file comment. The trace file now has to be saved in *.pcapng* format to preserve the comment.

First Column: Get Field, Capture, or Trace File Information

The information shown in the first column (to the right of the **Annotation** button) changes depending on what is highlighted in the panes above it or if you are running a live trace file. In Figure 20, we see a (plain English) field name, the corresponding display filter field name, and the field length[9]. Click around inside the Packet Details pane to see the contents of this first column change.

Second Column: Get Packet Counts (Total and Displayed)

When you open a saved trace file, the second column indicates the total number of packets in the file, the number and percentage of packets currently displayed (in case we applied a display filter), the number and percentage of marked packets (packets we marked as "of interest"), and the amount of time required to load the trace file. During a live capture, this column displays the number of packets captured, displayed, and marked.

---

[9]   This will be an important feature when you create display filters later in this book.

In Figure 20, we can see that *http-google101.pcapng* contains 374 packets and we have applied a display filter. Only 64 packets match the display filter.

Third Column: Determine the Current Profile

The third column indicates your current profile. Figure 20 indicates that we are working in a profile called *Wireshark101*. Profiles are created so you can customize your Wireshark environment.

For more information on profiles, refer to *Customize Wireshark for Different Tasks (Profiles)* on page 81.

There are two things you can do to improve efficiency using Wireshark.

First, try right-clicking on various packets, fields, and windows in Wireshark to determine if right-click functionality is available. Many tasks are *only* available when you right-click. Other can just be performed faster using the right-click method.

Second, get to know Wireshark's main toolbar and use that whenever possible.

Although Wireshark launches with the Start Page, once you leave the Start Page, you don't return to it unless you close a trace file or restart Wireshark. Use the main toolbar and the right-click method to work with trace files instead of returning to the Start Page.

▢ Lab 1: Use Packets to Build a Picture of a Network

When you are analyzing traffic, try to get a feel for the network layout from what you can learn in the packets. Who is sending the packets? Who are the targets? What are their MAC and IP addresses? If multiple hosts talk through a device, it is likely a router. Switches are transparent, but you must assume that clients go through switches to reach a router.

In this lab you will examine the MAC and IP addresses to build a picture of a portion of a network. In addition, you will look at the **Protocol** column to determine what applications are running on various hosts. Red text (visible in ebook versions only[10]) indicates that we just learned this information from the current frame.

Launch **Wireshark,** click the **File Open** button ▢ on the main tool bar and double-click on *general101.pcapng* to open this file.

Frame 1

```
Frame 1: 134 bytes on wire (1072 bits), 134 bytes captured (1072 bits) on interface 0
Ethernet II, Src: Cadant_31:bb:c1 (00:01:5c:31:bb:c1), Dst: IPv6mcast_01 (33:33:00:00:00:01)
Internet Protocol Version 6, Src: fe80::201:5cff:fe31:bbc1, Dst: ff02::1
```

Examine the Packet List pane. Frame 1 uses IPv6. Look in the Ethernet and IP headers for this frame in the Packet Details pane (shown below). This appears to be an IPv6 multicast (note the *IPv6mcast* designation in the destination Ethernet address field).

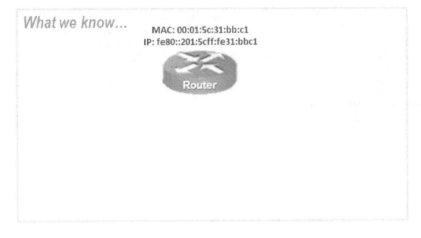

---

10   For those of you reading the paperback book version, you will need to open the trace file in Wireshark to see the colors. Printing color books is still cost-prohibitive, so the paperback is in black and white. However, the ebook version is in color.

Frame 2

```
Frame 2: 60 bytes on wire (480 bits), 60 bytes captured (480 bits) on interface 0
Ethernet II, Src: Cadant_31:bb:c1 (00:01:5c:31:bb:c1), Dst: Broadcast (ff:ff:ff:ff:ff:ff)
Address Resolution Protocol (request)
```

Frame 2 is an ARP packet. Look inside the Ethernet header then inside the ARP portion of the packet. This ARP request is sent to locate the MAC address of the Target IP Address.

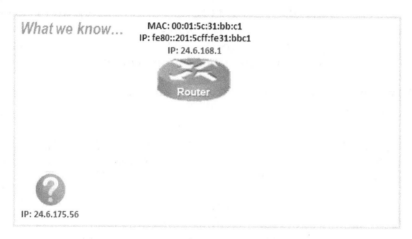

Frame 3

```
Frame 3: 66 bytes on wire (528 bits), 66 bytes captured (528 bits) on interface 0
Ethernet II, Src: HewlettP_a7:bf:a3 (d4:85:64:a7:bf:a3), Dst: Cadant_31:bb:c1 (00:01:5c:31:b
Internet Protocol Version 4, Src: 24.6.173.220, Dst: 216.168.252.157
Transmission Control Protocol, Src Port: 41865, Dst Port: 80, Seq: 0, Len: 0
```

Frame 3 is a TCP handshake packet to the HTTP port. Again, look in the Ethernet header and IP header to build your picture of the network. Since the target has not responded, we really can't say the target is there. We will mark it with a question mark until we see it talk on the network.

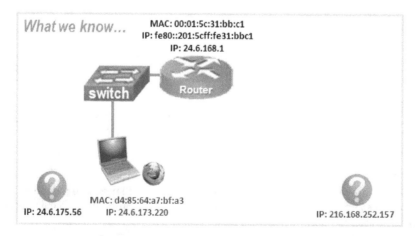

Frame 4

```
Frame 4: 66 bytes on wire (528 bits), 66 bytes captured (528 bits) on interface 0
Ethernet II, Src: Cadant_31:bb:c1 (00:01:5c:31:bb:c1), Dst: HewlettP_a7:bf:a3 (d4:85:64:a7:b
Internet Protocol Version 4, Src: 216.168.252.157, Dst: 24.6.173.220
Transmission Control Protocol, Src Port: 80, Dst Port: 41865, Seq: 0, Ack: 1, Len: 0
```

Frame 4 is the reply to frame 3. We can now draw in the new HTTP server in our diagram. Look at the source MAC address in frame 4. It comes from the router, not the source server.

Remember that routers strip off the received MAC header and apply a new MAC header. The new MAC header contains the address of the router's interface on this network as the new source MAC address and the address of the next hop destination device as the new destination MAC address. This is how a router forwards a packet. On your local network, you may see traffic from many different IP addresses come from the MAC address of the local router.

Frame 5 finishes the TCP 3-way handshake.

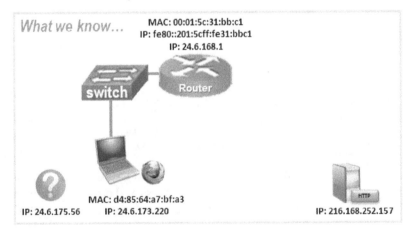

Frame 6

```
Frame 6: 152 bytes on wire (1216 bits), 152 bytes captured (1216 bits) on interface 0
Ethernet II, Src: HewlettP_a7:bf:a3 (d4:85:64:a7:bf:a3), Dst: Broadcast (ff:ff:ff:ff:ff:ff)
Internet Protocol Version 4, Src: 24.6.173.220, Dst: 255.255.255.255
User Datagram Protocol, Src Port: 17500, Dst Port: 17500
```

Frame 6 is a Dropbox LAN Sync Discovery Protocol (DB-LSB-DISC) packet from our client. This packet is sent to the broadcast address.

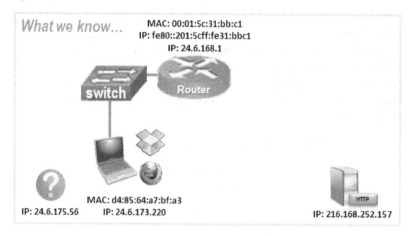

Frame 7

```
Frame 7: 66 bytes on wire (528 bits), 66 bytes captured (528 bits) on interface 0
Ethernet II, Src: AsustekC_19:9e:19 (c8:60:00:19:9e:19), Dst: Cadant_31:bb:c1 (00:01:5c:31:b
Internet Protocol Version 4, Src: 24.6.169.43, Dst: 199.59.150.9
Transmission Control Protocol, Src Port: 58403, Dst Port: 80, Seq: 0, Len: 0
```

Frame 7 is another TCP handshake packet, but we have a new source and destination. We can now draw in a new source MAC and IP address and a new destination IP address. We must wait for the target to send a packet before we say it is definitely there.

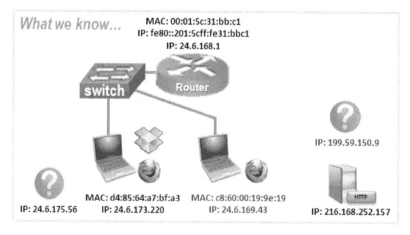

Frame 8

```
Frame 8: 66 bytes on wire (528 bits), 66 bytes captured (528 bits) on interface 0
Ethernet II, Src: Cadant_31:bb:c1 (00:01:5c:31:bb:c1), Dst: AsustekC_19:9e:19 (c8:60:00:19:9
Internet Protocol Version 4, Src: 199.59.150.9, Dst: 24.6.169.43
Transmission Control Protocol, Src Port: 80, Dst Port: 58403, Seq: 0, Ack: 1, Len: 0
```

Frame 8 is the answer from the HTTP server (199.59.150.9). We now know that this server is talking on the wire. Frame 9 is the final piece of the TCP handshake.

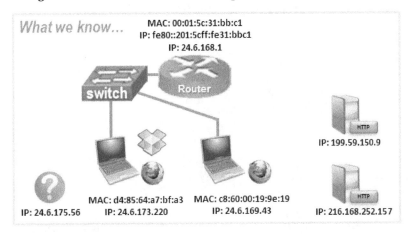

Frame 10

```
Frame 10: 66 bytes on wire (528 bits), 66 bytes captured (528 bits) on interface 0
Ethernet II, Src: AsustekC_19:9e:19 (c8:60:00:19:9e:19), Dst: Cadant_31:bb:c1 (00:01:5c:31:b
Internet Protocol Version 4, Src: 24.6.169.43, Dst: 107.21.109.41
Transmission Control Protocol, Src Port: 58405, Dst Port: 443, Seq: 0, Len: 0
```

Frame 10 indicates that the other local host is trying to connect to another server. This time the target is port 443, the HTTPS port.

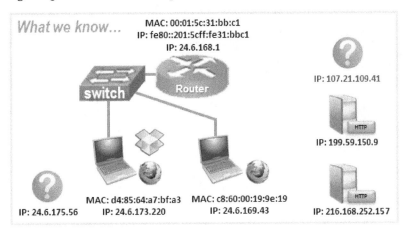

Frame 11

```
Frame 11: 66 bytes on wire (528 bits), 66 bytes captured (528 bits) on interface 0
Ethernet II, Src: Cadant_31:bb:c1 (00:01:5c:31:bb:c1), Dst: AsustekC_19:9e:19 (c8:60:00:19:9
Internet Protocol Version 4, Src: 107.21.109.41, Dst: 24.6.169.43
Transmission Control Protocol, Src Port: 443, Dst Port: 58405, Seq: 0, Ack: 1, Len: 0
```

Frame 11 is a response from the target. We can now assume the target is running. Frame 12 finishes the TCP handshake and our drawing of the network we discovered just by looking at these first few packets in the trace file.

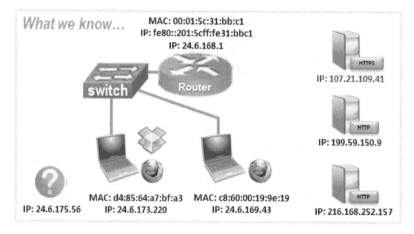

As you can see, lots of different conversations are occurring simultaneously. We can build a picture of the network based on the packets we see. Building an image of a network based on traffic is a common task used in analysis.

0.9. *Analyze Typical Network Traffic*

What is "typical network traffic?" That is a loaded question. Every network is different. They may support different applications and have different network designs. There are, however, some common packets that you'll see during most login procedures and web browsing sessions. There are also some basic TCP/IP resolutions that take place and can usually be seen on the network.

Let's just take a look at what you might see in a typical web browsing process and discuss the types of background traffic that can be seen as well.

Analyze Web Browsing Traffic

Open ***http-google101.pcapng***[11] and follow along as we look at the traffic generated when someone visits *www.google.com*[12].

In a typical web browsing session, your trace file will probably include a DNS request to resolve a host name to an IP address (referred to as an "A" record) [frame 1]. Hopefully a DNS reply will be sent back with at least one IP address associated with that host name [frame 2].

If the client supports both IPv4 and IPv6, you'll see a request to find an IPv6 address (referred to as an "AAAA" record) next [frame 3]. The DNS server will respond with either an IPv6 address or miscellaneous information [frame 4].

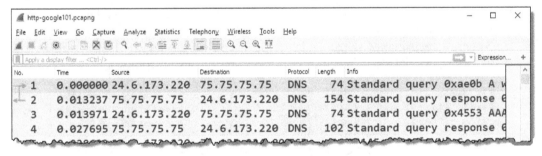

---

[11]   This trace file — and all the other trace files mentioned in this book — are available at *www.wiresharkbook.com*.

[12]   Your own web browsing traffic to *www.google.com* may be quite different. If you had recently accessed the site, your browser will have parts of the Google web site in cache. You won't see those elements being sent from the Google server.

Next we see the TCP three-way handshake between the client and the web server [frames 5, 6, and 7] and then the client's request to GET the main page ("/") [frame 8]. The server acknowledges receipt of the request [frame 9] and sends the OK response [frame 10][13]. Now the server begins sending the main page to the client [frame 11].

```
 5  0.028699 24.6.173.220  74.125.224.80 TCP   66 35145 → 80 [SYN] Seq=0 Win=8
 6  0.046071 74.125.224.80 24.6.173.220  TCP   66 80 → 35145 [SYN, ACK] Seq=0
 7  0.046258 24.6.173.220  74.125.224.80 TCP   54 35145 → 80 [ACK] Seq=1 Ack=1
 8  0.046998 24.6.173.220  74.125.224.80 HTTP  342 GET / HTTP/1.1
 9  0.065701 74.125.224.80 24.6.173.220  TCP   60 80 → 35145 [ACK] Seq=1 Ack=2
10  0.120474 74.125.224.80 24.6.173.220  HTTP 1484 HTTP/1.1 200 OK  (text/html)
11  0.122674 74.125.224.80 24.6.173.220  TCP  1484 80 → 35145 [ACK] Seq=1431 Ac
```

Periodically, the client requests another element of the *www.google.com* page [frame 36] from the same server.

```
35  0.157371 24.6.173.220  74.125.224.80 TCP   54 35145 → 80 [ACK] Seq=289 Ack
36  0.217660 24.6.173.220  74.125.224.80 HTTP  602 GET /images/icons/product/ch
37  0.218226 24.6.173.220  74.125.224.80 TCP   66 35146 → 80 [SYN] Seq=0 Win=8
38  0.221804 24.6.173.220  74.125.224.80 TCP   66 35147 → 80 [SYN] Seq=0 Win=8
39  0.235776 74.125.224.80 24.6.173.220  TCP   60 80 → 35145 [ACK] Seq=29675 A
40  0.236830 74.125.224.80 24.6.173.220  HTTP 1484 HTTP/1.1 200 OK  (PNG)[Unrea
41  0.237959 74.125.224.80 24.6.173.220  TCP  779 80 → 35145 [PSH, ACK] Seq=31
```

In addition, when there is a link on *www.google.com* to another web site, the client will make a DNS query for that next site (as in frames 231, 232, and 233, for example). These DNS queries are triggered when the JavaScript menu bar is loaded. Click on a DNS request and the Related Packets Indicator identifies the DNS responses.

```
231  0.558709 24.6.173.220  75.75.75.75   DNS    75 Standard query 0x6fbd A plu
232  0.558727 24.6.173.220  75.75.75.75   DNS    75 Standard query 0xa730 A map
233  0.558808 24.6.173.220  75.75.75.75   DNS    75 Standard query 0xe258 A pla
234  0.560238 24.6.173.220  74.125.224.80 HTTP  590 GET /images/nav_logo114.png
235  0.561255 24.6.173.220  74.125.224.80 HTTP  952 GET /csi?v=3&s=webhp&action
236  0.561458 24.6.173.220  74.125.224.80 HTTP  576 GET /favicon.ico HTTP/1.1
237  0.563201 24.6.173.220  75.75.75.75   DNS    75 Standard query 0x75ab A ssl
238  0.570053 75.75.75.75   24.6.173.220  DNS   251 Standard query response 0x6
239  0.570888 24.6.173.220  75.75.75.75   DNS    75 Standard query 0xd366 AAAA
```

---

[13]   If you see [TCP segment of a reassembled PDU] instead of OK in frame 10, don't worry. By default, Wireshark reassembles the OK response along with the data being sent to the client. You will work with this setting in Chapter 1.

You can likely see the relationship between the DNS queries and the menu, shown below.

Continue to look through the trace file to get a feel for the traffic that crosses the network when someone opens the main Google page.

Analyze Sample Background Traffic

You will surely see some "background traffic" on your network. Background traffic is generated when automated processes run—no user interaction is required. Background traffic can be seen when Java looks for updates, your virus detection tool looks for updates, Dropbox checks in, IPv6 tries to discover IPv6 routers, and more.

Become familiar with your background traffic so you can recognize it when you are troubleshooting problems. You don't want to waste time troubleshooting a background process that has nothing to do with the problem at hand.

Open *mybackground101.pcapng* to look at the background traffic seen from one of our lab machines. Here is a breakdown of the background traffic on our lab host.

- Starting at frame 1, we see traffic to/from 67.217.65.244 (use an IP address lookup site such as DomainTools.com to check the address and you'll see this is Citrix) – sure enough, this lab host is running GoToAssist, GoToMeeting, and GoToMyPC applets which are all owned by Citrix.
- In frame 25, we see ICMPv6 Neighbor Notifications generated by the IPv6 stack, which is enabled on the lab host (it is a Windows 7 host).
- In frame 27, we see a Local Master Announcement. If we expand the Packet Details pane, we learn that the lab host is called VID02.
- Starting at frame 28, we can see some DNS queries for *javadl-esd-secure.oracle.com*. It looks like our host is updating Java from an Akamai host (we expanded the Packet Details pane to look inside the DNS response for that tidbit).
- Frame 33 tells us that there is an IPv6 router on the network – we see ICMPv6 Router Advertisement packets.
- Frame 83 is a DHCP ACK broadcast onto the network – it indicates the domain is *comcast.net* – yup, that's the ISP serving the lab network.
- Frame 95 is an SNMP get-request to 192. 168.1.105 – we don't see an answer anywhere in the trace file. This is an interesting one. It seems the lab host is configured to look for a network printer by that address – but no such printer exists. (Guess we need to clean off that machine a bit, eh?).

- Starting at frame 96, we learn that our lab host is also running Dropbox – we see some Dropbox LAN Sync Discovery Protocol traffic in there.
- Starting at frame 118, we learn the lab host also runs Memeo for backup – we see some HTTP traffic going to *www.memeo.info* (frame 121 in the expanded HTTP part of the Packet Details) and *api.memeo.info* (frame 134 in the expanded HTTP part of the Packet Details).

This is what a background traffic analysis session feels like — looking through the traffic to define what is "normal." Once we know what is normal, we can look past that to detect what is abnormal.

For example, frame 411 doesn't match the regular traffic we expect to see in a background trace file.

In Figure 21, we see an incoming TCP connection attempt (SYN) which is not expected — this is a client, not a server. In the Packet Details pane, we see the packet is sent to the Secure Shell port (22) — that's a bit of a concern. We also see that Wireshark indicates that something is wrong with the TCP header — there is an unusual value in the Acknowledgment Number field.

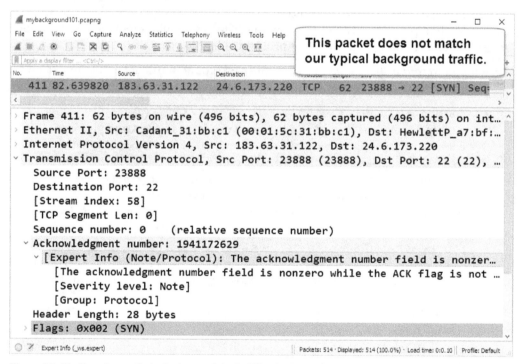

Figure 21. Finding the needle in the haystack isn't difficult if you know the haystack well and can just move it aside. [mybackground101.pcapng]

So who is this 183.63.31.122 host?

Doing a bit of research on the source IP address, we gather the following information:

inetnum:	183.0.0.0 - 183.63.255.255
netname:	CHINANET-GD
descr:	CHINANET Guangdong province network
descr:	Data Communication Division
descr:	China Telecom
country:	CN
status:	ALLOCATED PORTABLE
remarks:	service provider

And, of course, this address popped up at the Internet Storm Center[14] with over 293,000 reports of folks being scanned on port 22 from this host.

Networks can be pretty noisy with various background processes running, but if you can spend some time getting familiar with the "normal" ones, it shouldn't take you long to find the real stinkers.

TIP

In this book you will learn a lot about filtering. Once you learn what is "normal," consider building a filter to remove this normal traffic from view. What is left after filtering out the good traffic may be one or more shiny needles.

---

[14] See *isc.sans.edu/ipinfo.html?ip=183.63.31.122.*

Lab 2: Capture and Classify Your Own Background Traffic

Take a moment and capture your own background traffic as we did in this section. When you complete your capture, perform some research on the resulting trace file to see if you can characterize all the traffic to/from your machine when you are not touching the keyboard.

Step 1:   Close all applications except for Wireshark and any normal background applications that run on your machine.

Step 2:   Click the **Capture Options** ⚙ button on the main toolbar.

Step 3:   Select the interface that indicates active traffic on its sparkline. If you don't see any activity on the sparkline(s), be patient or toggle out to the command prompt to ping another host or browse the Internet to generate some traffic.

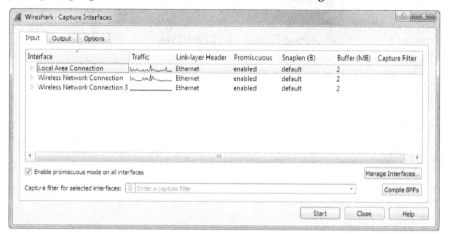

Step 4:   Click **Start**. Let the capture run for at least five minutes (longer if you can wait).

Step 5:   Click the **Stop Capture** button ■ on the main toolbar.

Spend some time going through the trace file to identify the applications that run in the background on your machine. Focus on the **Protocol** column and the **Info** column.

If you don't recognize the application, perform some research on the IP addresses that your system communicates with. Most likely you will also see broadcast or multicast traffic from other hosts on your network.

Step 6:   To save this file, click the **Save** button on the main toolbar, navigate to the target directory, and name your file *background1.pcapng*.

Recognizing your own background traffic will help you remove this from consideration when looking for unusual communications. Consider saving trace files of your "normal" traffic to refer to when troubleshooting.

0.10. Open Trace Files Captured with Other Tools

Although Wireshark is considered the de facto standard in packet capture and analysis tools, there are numerous other tools available. It is important to know which tools can interoperate with Wireshark.

Some traffic capture tools save files in a different file format than Wireshark's default *.pcapng* format. Wireshark uses its Wiretap Library to convert these other file formats into a format that Wireshark can display. For example, if you receive a trace file captured using Sun Snoop (with the .snoop file extension), Wireshark uses the Wiretap Library to perform the input/output function – handing the frames up to Wireshark for analysis.

Click the **File Open** button on the main toolbar. Click on the arrow next to the **Files of type** section. Wireshark lists all the file types recognized, as shown in Figure 22.

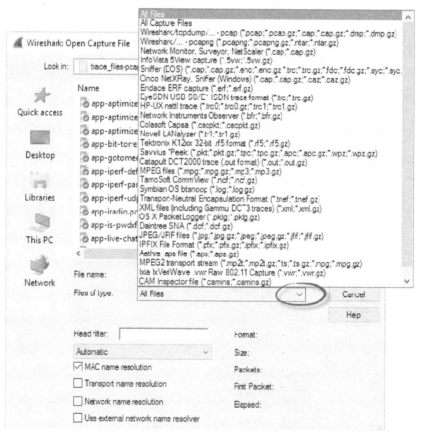

*Figure 22. Click the arrow next to **Files of type** to see all the file formats that Wireshark recognizes.*

TIP

If someone sends you a trace file and Wireshark doesn't recognize the format, first just change the file extension to .pcap (the old default trace file format) and try to open it in Wireshark. If that doesn't work, ask them what #*$&@! tool they used to capture the traffic! Wireshark understands so many formats. It is very unusual to receive a trace file in an unrecognized format.

🖥 Lab 3: Open a Network Monitor .cap File

In this lab you will use Wireshark's Wiretap Library to open a file captured with Microsoft's Network Monitor[15].

Step 1:   Click the **File Open** button 🖳 on the main toolbar.

Step 2:   Navigate to your trace file directory and click on *http-winpcap101.cap*. Wireshark looks inside the trace file to identify what tool was used to capture the traffic, as shown below. Although this file was captured with Microsoft's Network Monitor (NetMon) v3.4, Wireshark marks it as NetMon v2 because that is the format that v3.4 saves in.

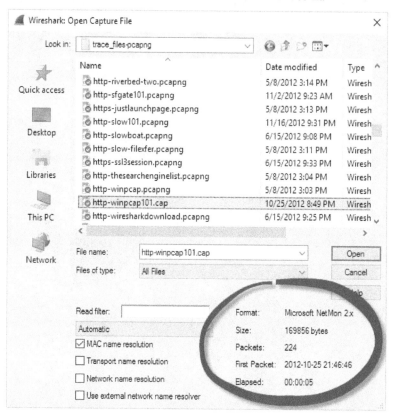

---

15   Microsoft Network Monitor was replaced with Microsoft Message Analyzer, but Message Analyzer can still save trace files in the native Network Monitor .cap format.

Step 3:   Click **Open**. Once the file is open, select **File | Save As** and click the drop-down menu arrow next to **Files of Type**. Select **Wireshark – pcapng (*pcapng;*.pcapng.gz;*.ntar;*.ntar.gz)** and name the file *http-winpcap101.pcapng*.

Wireshark can recognize and open trace files created with most other industry tools. Once open, the fact that this trace file was captured with Network Monitor is transparent to you.

Chapter 0 Challenge

Open *challenge101-0.pcapng* and use the techniques covered in this chapter to answer these Challenge questions. The answer key is located in Appendix A.

We will focus on what you can learn about communications based on the main Wireshark view.

Question 0-1.   How many packets are in this trace file?

Question 0-2.   What IP hosts are making a TCP connection in frames 1, 2, and 3?

Question 0-3.   What HTTP command is sent in frame 4?

Question 0-4.   What is the length of the largest frame in this trace file?

Question 0-5.   What protocols are seen in the **Protocol** column?

Question 0-6.   What responses are sent by the HTTP server?

Question 0-7.   Is there any IPv6 traffic in this trace file?

Chapter 1 Skills: Customize Wireshark Views and Settings

To me, analyzing networks is a bit like practicing a sport like skiing or golf. When you start, it's tough and a bit frustrating, but practice and persistence will make you accomplish amazing things. Remember that becoming a master is a matter of improving your skills, but also of getting the best from your tools. Don't get discouraged if things seem a bit overwhelming at the beginning—you'll improve fast and it's going to be a ton of fun!

Loris Degioanni
Creator of *WinPcap, SteelCentral™ Packet Analyzer* and *SysDig*

Quick Reference: Overview of wireshark.org

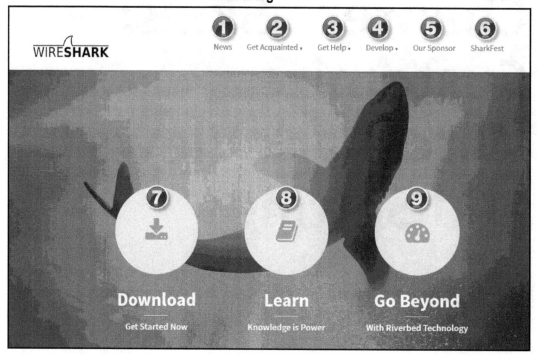

(1) News—General news and events

(2) Get Acquainted—About, Download area and Gerald Combs' blog

(3) Get Help—Q&A Forum, FAQ, documentation, mailing lists, online tools, Wiki page, Bug Tracker

(4) Develop—Get Involved, Developers' Guide, browse the code, latest development builds

(5) Our Sponsor—Launches Riverbed site

(6) SharkFest—All about the yearly Wireshark User and Developer conference

(7) Download—Link to the download page (auto-detects your incoming OS)

(8) Learn—Link to training, documents, videos, and development information

(9) Go Beyond—Link to Riverbed, owner of the Wireshark trademark

1.1. Add Columns to the Packet List Pane

Wireshark contains a default set of columns that provide basic information. If you are focused on a particular issue, however, adding columns can help you quickly detect behavior patterns.

There are two ways to add columns to the Packet List pane—the easy way and the hard way. You should know both methods because sometimes columns can't be created using the easier method.

Right-Click | Apply as Column (the "Easy Way")

The Packet Details pane displays the fields and values contained in the frames. Open a trace file, such as *http-espn101.pcapng* in the example that follows, and right-click on the Internet Protocol section in the Packet Details pane. Select **Expand Subtrees** to see all the fields in the IP header.

To add any field as a column, right-click on the field and select **Apply as Column**, as shown in Figure 23. In this example, we quickly created an IP **Time to Live** (TTL) column.

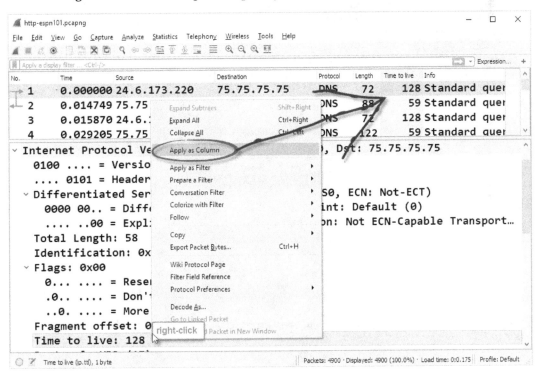

Figure 23. Right-click on any field and select **Apply as Column**. [http-espn101.pcapng]

Edit | Preferences | Columns (the "Hard Way")

If you don't have a packet that contains the desired field for the right-click method, you'll need to use the hard way to build columns. Select **Edit | Preferences | Columns** to see the existing columns, change the order of the columns, and add columns.

Click the **Add** button ⊞ to create a new column entry. On your new column row, double-click the **Title** area and name the column **Time to Live**. Double-click the **Type** area and select **Custom** from the drop-down list. In the **Field Name** area, type `ip.ttl`. Enter the **Field Occurrence** number of 0 to view all occurrences of a field. Now click and drag your column above the Info column and Click **OK** when you are done.

It is much easier to just right-click on an IP TTL field and select **Apply as Column**.

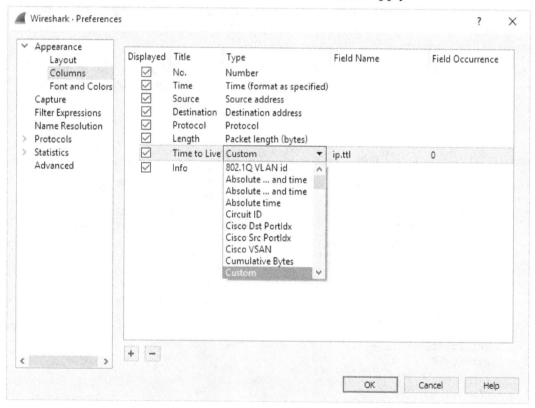

Figure 24. You can add, edit, and rearrange columns in the Preferences window. We clicked and dragged the **Time to Live** *column to place it above the Info column.*

Hide, Remove, Rearrange, Realign, and Edit Columns

You can use the Preferences window to perform functions on your columns, but this is not the fastest way to work with columns. Simply right-click on a column heading in the Packet List pane to specify alignment, edit the column title, temporarily hide (or display) a column, or even delete a column. Click and drag columns left or right to reorder them.

For example, in Figure 25, we are working with *http-espn101.pcapng*. We right-clicked on our new **Time to live** column to view the available column options. If we do not want to use this column again, we can select **Remove This Column**.

TIP

Adding columns to the Packet List pane can save a lot of time when you're comparing traffic characteristics. Be careful of going column-crazy, however. Wireshark will process all displayed *and* hidden columns when it opens a trace file or applies a display filter. If you create and hide 30 different columns, Wireshark is going to be much slower than if you just remove and recreate the columns as you need them.

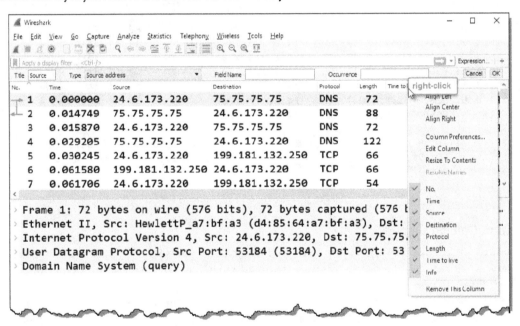

Figure 25. Right-click on a column heading to perform basic column functions. [http-espn101.pcapng]

Sort Column Contents

Columns make the analysis process faster, but there are two other great reasons to create columns: columns can be sorted and column data can be exported.

Click on a column heading once to sort from low to high and click again to sort from high to low. If you have added a column showing the delays between packets, you can sort this column to quickly find the largest delays in the trace file. We will use this technique in *Configure Time Columns to Spot Latency Problems* on page 87.

For example, in Figure 26 we opened *http-espn101.pcapng* and clicked once on the **Time to live** column heading to sort the column from low to high. Scrolling to the top of the trace file, we determined that the lowest TTL value in the trace file is 44.

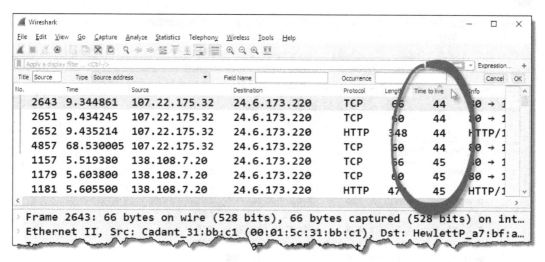

Figure 26. We sorted the Time to live field to find the lowest TTL value in the trace file. [http-espn101.pcapng]

Export Column Data

Another great reason to add columns to the Packet List pane is to export those columns for analysis with another tool. For example, if you added a **Time to Live** column, you can select **File | Export Packet Dissections** and choose **As CSV** (comma-separated value) format. Choose to export only the **Packet summary line** (including the column headings) and you'll end up with a CSV file containing your new column data. You can now open this CSV file in a spreadsheet to manipulate the data further. You will get a chance to practice exporting to CSV format in Lab 30 and Lab 41.

🖥 Lab 4: Add the HTTP Host Field as a Column

During a browsing session, an HTTP client sends requests for HTTP objects to one or more HTTP servers. In each of the requests, the client specifies the name or the IP address of the target HTTP server. This can be very revealing.

Note: All frames from 24.6.173.220 will appear with a black background and red foreground if Wireshark is set to validate IP header checksums. You will ensure this feature is disabled in Lab 5.

Step 1: Click the **File Open** button 🗁 on the main toolbar and open ***http-disney101.pcapng***.

Step 2: First we will hide the Time to Live column (if you created one while following along with the previous section of this book). Right-click the **Time to Live** column heading and uncheck that column in the drop-down menu. If you want to see that column again later, simply right-click on any column heading and click it in the column list to enable it.

Step 3: Scroll down in the Packet List pane and select **frame 15**.

Step 4: The Packet Details pane shows the contents of frame 15. Click the ⟩ in front of Hypertext Transfer Protocol to expand this section of the frame.

Step 5: Right-click on the **Host** line (which contains www.disney.com\r\n) and select **Apply as Column**. Your new **Host** column appears to the left of the **Info** column. You can click and drag the right-hand edge of the column to widen or narrow the column.

Step 6: Click on the **Host** column heading twice to sort the column from high to low.

Step 7: Click the **Go to Top** button ⬆ to jump to the top of the sorted trace file. You can now easily see all the hosts to which the client sent requests, as shown below.

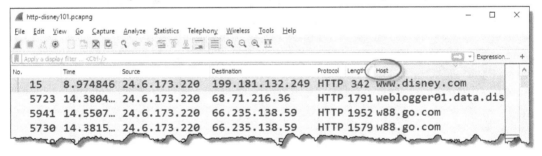

Step 8:   **LAB CLEAN-UP** Right-click on your new **Host** column heading and uncheck it from the column list. If you want to view this column again, right-click any column heading and click on the column name to enable it. Click once on the **No.** column to return to the original sort order.

Adding and sorting columns are two key tasks that can shorten your analysis time significantly. Why go searching through thousands of packets when you can have Wireshark quickly gather and display the information you need?

1.2. Dissect the Wireshark Dissectors

Packet dissection is one of the most powerful features of Wireshark. The dissection process converts streams of bytes into understandable requests, replies, refusals, retransmissions, and more.

Frames are handed up from either the Capture Engine or Wiretap Library to the *Core Engine*. The Core Engine is referred to as the "glue code that holds the other blocks together." This is where the real work begins. Wireshark understands the format used by thousands of protocols and applications. Wireshark calls on various dissectors to break apart fields and display their meanings in readable format.

For example, consider a host on an Ethernet network that issues an HTTP GET request to a web site. This packet will be handled by five dissectors.

The Frame Dissector

The Frame dissector (seen in Figure 27) examines and displays the trace file basic information, such as the timestamp set on each of the frames. Then the Frame dissector hands the frame off to the Ethernet dissector.

```
˅ Frame 9: 346 bytes on wire (2768 bits), 346 bytes captured (2768 bits) on i…
    Interface id: 0 (\Device\NPF_{98657C67-2DE2-4C46-B5FE-5101D6F0227D})
    Encapsulation type: Ethernet (1)
    Arrival Time: Dec 17, 2015 14:19:25.392346000 Pacific Standard Time
    [Time shift for this packet: 0.000000000 seconds]
    Epoch Time: 1450390765.392346000 seconds
    [Time delta from previous captured frame: 0.000199000 seconds]
    [Time delta from previous displayed frame: 0.000199000 seconds]
    [Time since reference or first frame: 0.446373000 seconds]
    Frame Number: 9
    Frame Length: 346 bytes (2768 bits)
    Capture Length: 346 bytes (2768 bits)
    [Frame is marked: False]
    [Frame is ignored: False]
    [Protocols in frame: eth:ethertype:ip:tcp:http]
    [Coloring Rule Name: HTTP]
    [Coloring Rule String: http || tcp.port == 80 || http2]
```

Figure 27. The Frame dissector displays metadata (extra information) about the frame. [http-chappellu101c.pcapng]

 TIP

Every once in a while a dissector bug surfaces. They typically appear as "exception occurred" in the **Info** column of the Packet List pane. If you want to validate the bug, you can search for the protocol as a keyword on the Wireshark Bug Database at *bugs.wireshark.org/bugzilla/*.

The Ethernet Dissector Takes Over

The Ethernet dissector decodes and displays the fields of the Ethernet II header and, based on the contents of the Type field, hands the packet off to the next dissector. In Figure 28, the Type field value 0x0800 indicates that an IPv4 header will follow. Notice that at this point, when we remove the Ethernet frame from the dissection, we are using the term "packet."

```
> Frame 9: 346 bytes on wire (2768 bits), 346 bytes captured (2768 bits) on i...
v Ethernet II, Src: GemtekTe_cc:7d:da (20:10:7a:cc:7d:da), Dst: HonHaiPr_fa:0...
   > Destination: HonHaiPr_fa:0e:a5 (48:5a:b6:fa:0e:a5)
   > Source: GemtekTe_cc:7d:da (20:10:7a:cc:7d:da)
     Type: IPv4 (0x0800)
  Internet Protocol Version 4, Src: 192.168.44.7, Dst: 198.66.239.146
```

Figure 28. The Ethernet dissector looks at the Type field to determine the next required dissector.
[http-chappellu101c.pcapng]

The IPv4 Dissector Takes Over

The IPv4 dissector decodes the fields of the IPv4 header and, based on the contents of the Protocol field, hands the packet off to the next dissector. In Figure 29, the Protocol field value 6 indicates that TCP will follow.

```
> Frame 9: 346 bytes on wire (2768 bits), 346 bytes captured (2768 bits) on i...
> Ethernet II, Src: GemtekTe_cc:7d:da (20:10:7a:cc:7d:da), Dst: HonHaiPr_fa:0...
v Internet Protocol Version 4, Src: 192.168.44.7, Dst: 198.66.239.146
     0100 .... = Version: 4
     .... 0101 = Header Length: 20 bytes
   > Differentiated Services Field: 0x00 (DSCP: CS0, ECN: Not-ECT)
     Total Length: 332
     Identification: 0x074f (1871)
   > Flags: 0x02 (Don't Fragment)
     Fragment offset: 0
     Time to live: 128
     Protocol: TCP (6)
   > Header checksum: 0x4fd8 [validation disabled]
     Source: 192.168.44.7
     Destination: 198.66.239.146
     [Source GeoIP: Unknown]
     [Destination GeoIP: Unknown]
  Transmission Control Protocol, Src Port: 24913 (24913), Dst Port: 80 (80)
```

Figure 29. The IPv4 dissector looks at the Protocol field to determine the next required dissector.
[http-chappellu101c.pcapng]

The TCP Dissector Takes Over

The TCP dissector decodes the fields of the TCP header and, based on the contents of the Port fields, hands the packet off to the next dissector. In Figure 30, the destination port value 80 indicates that HTTP will follow. We will see how Wireshark handles traffic running over non-standard ports in the next section.

```
> Frame 9: 346 bytes on wire (2768 bits), 346 bytes captured (2768 bits) on i...
> Ethernet II, Src: GemtekTe_cc:7d:da (20:10:7a:cc:7d:da), Dst: HonHaiPr_fa:0...
> Internet Protocol Version 4, Src: 192.168.44.7, Dst: 198.66.239.146
v Transmission Control Protocol, Src Port: 24012 (24012), Dst Port: 80 (80), ...
    Source Port: 24012
    Destination Port: 80
    [Stream index: 0]
    [TCP Segment Len: 292]
    Sequence number: 1      (relative sequence number)
    [Next sequence number: 293     (relative sequence number)]
    Acknowledgment number: 1      (relative ack number)
    Header Length: 20 bytes
  > Flags: 0x018 (PSH, ACK)
    Window size value: 256
    [Calculated window size: 65536]
    [Window size scaling factor: 256]
  > Checksum: 0x1a40 [validation disabled]
    Urgent pointer: 0
  > [SEQ/ACK analysis]
  > [Timestamps]
  H------t--- Transfer Pr---- -l-
```

Figure 30. The TCP dissector looks at the port fields to determine the next required dissector.
[http-chappellu101c.pcapng]

The HTTP Dissector Takes Over

In this example, the HTTP dissector decodes the fields of the HTTP packet. There is no embedded protocol or application inside the HTTP packet, so this is the last dissector applied to the frame, as shown in Figure 31.

```
> Frame 9: 346 bytes on wire (2768 bits), 346 bytes captured (2768 bits) on in…
> Ethernet II, Src: GemtekTe_cc:7d:da (20:10:7a:cc:7d:da), Dst: HonHaiPr_fa:0e…
> Internet Protocol Version 4, Src: 192.168.44.7, Dst: 198.66.239.146
> Transmission Control Protocol, Src Port: 24012 (24012), Dst Port: 80 (80), S…
v Hypertext Transfer Protocol
  > GET / HTTP/1.1\r\n
    Host: www.chappellu.com\r\n
    User-Agent: Mozilla/5.0 (Windows NT 10.0; WOW64; rv:42.0) Gecko/20100101 Fi…
    Accept: text/html,application/xhtml+xml,application/xml;q=0.9,*/*;q=0.8\r\n
    Accept-Language: en-US,en;q=0.5\r\n
    Accept-Encoding: gzip, deflate\r\n
    Connection: keep-alive\r\n
    \r\n
    [Full request URI: http://www.chappellu.com/]
    [HTTP request 1/7]
    [Response in frame: 11]
    [Next request in frame: 65]
```

Figure 31. The HTTP dissector does not see any indication that the packet should be handed off to another dissector. [http-chappellu101c.pcapng]

1.3. Analyze Traffic that Uses Non-Standard Ports

Applications running over non-standard ports are always a concern to network analysts, whether the application is intentionally designed to use those non-standard ports or it is attempting to evade identification on a network.

Wireshark uses two basic methods to figure out what dissector to apply to traffic: the static method and heuristic method. In the static method, Wireshark examines the preceding header to determine what logical dissector should be used next. Heuristic dissectors guess at what the next dissector should be.

What Happens When Non-Standard Ports are Used

If an application is running over a non-standard port, Wireshark may apply the wrong dissector to the traffic (using the static method), determine the proper dissector to use and apply it (using the heuristic method), or not apply any dissector (if both methods fail to determine the proper dissector to use).

In Figure 32, we have an FTP communication running over port number 137. Wireshark sees port 137 in use, but the traffic does not match NetBIOS Name Service traffic behavior.

In this case, Wireshark does not continue dissecting the traffic after the TCP dissector. The last dissector applied to the packets is listed in the Protocol column: TCP.

Note: You may want to turn off the coloring ≡ when working with this trace file. The packets were edited with a hex editor and the Ethernet checksums were not recalculated. By default, Wireshark applies the Checksum Errors coloring rule to the packets. You will disable Ethernet checksum validation in Lab 5.

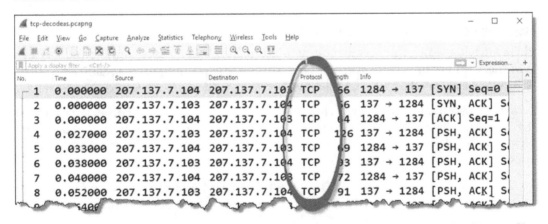

Figure 32. If Wireshark cannot determine   the proper dissector to apply for the application this trace file, it will stop dissecting at TCP. Note that we have turned off coloring while working with this trace file. [tcp-decodeas.pcapng]

How Heuristic Dissectors Work

When Wireshark cannot apply a dissector to data using the simple static method, Wireshark will hand the data off to the first of many available *heuristic dissectors,* as illustrated in Figure 33. Each heuristic dissector looks for recognizable patterns in the data to figure out what type of communication is contained in the packet. If the heuristic dissector doesn't recognize anything, it returns a failure indication to Wireshark. Wireshark then hands the data off to the next heuristic dissector. Wireshark continues to hand the data off to heuristic dissectors until (a) a heuristic dissector returns an indicator of success and decodes the traffic, or (b) Wireshark runs out of heuristic dissectors to try.

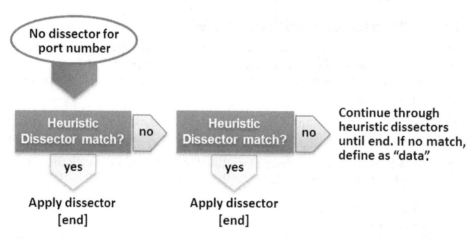

Figure 33. Wireshark applies heuristic dissectors until it is successful or simply marks the undissected bytes as "data".

Manually Force a Dissector on the Traffic

There are two reasons why you may want to manually force a dissector onto traffic: (1) if Wireshark applies the wrong dissector because the non-standard port is already associated with a dissector, or (2) if Wireshark doesn't have a heuristic dissector for your traffic type.

To force a dissector on traffic, right-click on the undissected/incorrectly dissected packet in the Packet List pane and select **Decode As**. In the Value column, select the port you would like to be forcibly dissected. Finally, in the Current column select the desired dissector to be applied to the current trace file.

To remove your manually applied dissector settings, select **Analyze | Decode As** from the Main menu. Select the manual dissector of interest and click the delete button —.

Adjust Dissections with the Application Preference Settings (if possible)

If you know that certain traffic, such as HTTP traffic, runs over a non-standard port on your network, you can add the port to the protocol's preference settings. For example, perhaps you want Wireshark to dissect traffic to or from port 81 as HTTP traffic. Select **Edit | Preferences** ▷ **Protocols | HTTP** and add 81 to the port list, as shown in Figure 34.

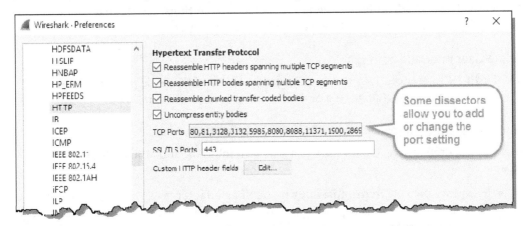

Figure 34. We added port 81 to the list of TCP ports that should be dissected as HTTP traffic.

Not all protocol preferences have configurable port values. If your protocol is not listed in the Protocols section, or your protocol does not allow you to add or change the port setting, you will need to manually force a dissector on the traffic as shown in *Manually Force a Dissector on the Traffic* on page 70.

TIP

You can determine that Wireshark is unable to apply a dissector to some of your frames by selecting **Statistics | Protocol Hierarchy** and looking for "data" under the TCP or UDP sections. You will work with the Protocol Hierarchy window in *List Applications Seen on the Network* on page 239.

1.4. Change how Wireshark Displays Certain Traffic Types

Wireshark is a well-formed piece of clay. Nevertheless, it is in a default state when you install it. Customizing Wireshark will make you and your analysis sessions more effective.

You learned how to add columns using the Preferences settings, but there is so much more you can do. Let's take a look at these key preference settings.

Define User Interface Settings

Select **Edit | Preferences | Appearance** to change many of the basic preferences for your interface here. You will change two of the User Interface settings in Lab 5.

Adjust Capture Settings

Select **Edit | Preferences | Capture** to set a default interface and adjust other capture parameters.

- **Capture packets in promiscuous mode**: If an adapter is capturing in promiscuous mode, that adapter is capturing and passing up packets that are addressed to any hardware address, not just the local hardware address. This is an essential function in network analysis.

- **Capture packets in pcapng format**: The .pcapng format is a newer format for packet capture. Trace files captured directly into .pcapng format include metadata about the capture interface and any capture filter that may have been applied during the capture process.

- **Update list of packets in real time**: Rather than wait for you to stop a capture to view the packets, this setting enables you to begin your analysis of the traffic as packets are being captured.

- **Automatic scrolling in live capture**: This feature scrolls the Packet List pane so the most recently captured packets are always in view. On a busy network, you likely will not be able to do a live analysis as thousands of packets scroll past you on the screen, but this is a nice feature on a quieter network or when filtering is in place.

Typically, you will leave all these items with the default settings.

Define Filter Expression Buttons

You can select **Edit | Preferences | Filter Expressions** to save your favorite display filters as buttons to apply them more quickly to your trace files. There is a faster way to create these buttons, however. We will cover the process of making Filter Expression buttons in *Turn Your Key Display Filters into Buttons* on page 190.

Set Name Resolution Settings

Select **Edit | Preferences | Name Resolution** to view or change the way Wireshark deals with MAC address, port, and IP address resolution.

- **Resolve MAC addresses**: By default, Wireshark resolves the first three bytes of the MAC addresses (the OUI) to friendly names using the *manuf* file in the Wireshark program file directory.

- **Resolve transport names**: Transport names, such as "ftp" instead of port 21 are resolved using the *services* file in the Wireshark program file directory.

- **Resolve network (IP) addresses:** If you want Wireshark to resolve host names (for example, showing *www.wireshark.org* instead of an IP address), enable Network Name Resolution. There are five extra configuration options for resolving network addresses.

    o **Use captured DNS packet data for address resolution**: If enabled, Wireshark examines all the name resolution packets (such as DNS) in the trace file and uses that information to resolve host names. This is an excellent method for resolving names without transmitting any queries onto the network.

    o **Use an external network name resolver**: If enabled, Wireshark will send DNS Pointer (PTR) queries to obtain host names if they can't be obtained from another source, such as the DNS cache, a *hosts* file, or from DNS packets that are already in the trace, not sent by Wireshark. This extra traffic will show up in your trace files and may create extra work for your DNS server (see *Maximum concurrent requests* below).

    o **Enable concurrent DNS name resolution**: This function speeds up the name resolution process by allowing multiple DNS queries to be sent from Wireshark. This is only used if external name resolution is enabled.

    o **Maximum concurrent requests**: This number indicates how many concurrent queries can be sent to the DNS server. Keeping this number low will reduce the load on your DNS server.

    o **Only use the profile "hosts" file**: This is nice option to resolve names of internal hosts that can't be resolved using DNS information. You must create a simple text file called *hosts* that lists IP addresses and names. You can locate the profile directory using **Help | About Wireshark | Folders**. You will learn more about working with profiles in *The Basics of Profiles* starting on page 81.

- **SNMP Resolution Options**: There are several options to resolve SNMP (Simple Network Management Protocol) information contained in trace files. Although Wireshark has some ability to resolve the MIB (Management Information Base) and PIB (Policy Information Base) objects into readable form, you can add additional PIB/MIB modules and paths if desired.

- **GeoIP database directories**: Wireshark can use GeoIP database files to plot IP addresses on a map of the world. You can obtain the *Geo*.dat* files from MaxMind (*www.maxmind.com*)[16]. You will get a chance to enable/disable this feature and use this skill in Lab 32.

You can also set name resolution through **View | Name Resolution**, however this is only a temporary setting. Settings changed in the Preferences window are retained with the current profile.

Set Protocol and Application Settings

Although you can select **Edit | Preferences** ⟩ **Protocols** to view all the protocols and applications that contain editable settings, the right-click method is a faster way to define protocol settings. In Lab 5 you will use the right-click method to view and change several protocol settings:

- *Allow subdissector to reassemble TCP streams*: This setting is enabled by default, but it can cause problems when analyzing HTTP traffic. If an HTTP server answers a client request with a response code (such as 200 OK) and it includes some of the requested data in the packet, Wireshark does not display the response code in the Info column of that response packet. Instead, Wireshark displays "[TCP Segment of a Reassembled PDU]" (Protocol Data Unit). In addition, the HTTP response time measurement will measure from the request to the end of the file download rather than from the request to the response. We would much rather see the response code on the correct packet.

  TCP reassembly *enabled*:

  > Info
  > [TCP segment of a reassembled PDU]

  TCP reassembly *disabled*:

  > Info
  > HTTP/1.1 200 OK

  You can disable the TCP reassembly preference setting until you want to export files that were transferred in an HTTP communication (see *View all HTTP Objects in the Trace File* on page 276).

- *Track number of bytes in flight*: Data bytes that are sent across a TCP connection, but are not acknowledged yet, are considered "bytes in flight." We can configure Wireshark to show us how much unacknowledged data is currently seen in a TCP communication. If the number seems to hit a "ceiling," some TCP setting may be limiting data flow capabilities. When you enable this setting, a new section (shown below) is appended to the TCP header [SEQ/ACK analysis] section in the Packet Details pane. This new field will not be displayed until after the TCP connection is established.

---

[16]   At the time this book was released, the full URL for obtaining the necessary Geo*.dat files was *http://dev.maxmind.com/geoip/legacy/geolite/*. This may change, of course.

```
 v [SEQ/ACK analysis]
    [iRTT: 0.000574000 seconds]
    [Bytes in flight: 1766]
```
Track number of bytes in flight enabled:

- *Calculate conversation timestamps*: This TCP setting tracks time values within each separate TCP conversation. This enables you to obtain timestamp values based on the first frame in a single TCP conversation or the previous frame in a single TCP conversation. When this TCP setting is enabled, a new section (shown below) is appended to the TCP header section in the Packet Details pane.

```
 v [Timestamps]
    [Time since first frame in this TCP stream: 0.010411000 seconds]
    [Time since previous frame in this TCP stream: 0.009710000 seconds]
```

You will work with these settings in Lab 5 and examine their effect on the Wireshark Packet List pane and Packet Details pane.

🖥 Lab 5: Set Key Wireshark Preferences (IMPORTANT LAB)[17]

Wireshark offers several key preference settings to enhance your analysis sessions. In this lab you will use **Edit | Preferences** on the main menu and the right-click method to view and change the preference settings.

These are the settings we will work with in this lab:

- Display filters that Wireshark will remember
- Recently opened files that Wireshark will remember
- Ethernet, IP, UDP, and TCP checksum validations
- TCP *Calculate conversation timestamps* setting
- TCP *Track number of bytes in flight* setting
- TCP *Allow subdissector to reassemble TCP streams* setting

Note: Your Wireshark system should retain all of these settings through the rest of this book with the exception of the TCP *Allow subdissector to reassemble TCP streams* setting, which you will work with during various labs.

Step 1:   Open *http-pcaprnet101.pcapng*.

Step 2:   Select **Edit | Preferences** on the main menu.

Step 3:   Change both the **filter entries** and **recent files** settings to **30**.

These two settings allow you to quickly recall more of your recent filter settings and opened files.

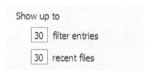

Step 4:   Click **OK**. This automatically applies and saves your settings in this *Default* profile and closes the Preferences window. Next we will use the right-click method to check and change the Ethernet, IP, UDP, and TCP settings.

We will begin by disabling the Ethernet checksum validation (which is enabled by default).

Next, we will ensure IP, UDP, and TCP checksum validations are disabled[18]. These three checksum validations should already be disabled unless you updated Wireshark while retaining previous settings.

---

[17]   The remaining labs in this book assume you have successfully completed this lab.

[18]   Most systems support checksum offloading. If Wireshark obtains a copy of an outbound frame before the checksum values have been calculated, it will mark the checksums invalid. This is a false positive when capturing traffic directly on a host that supports checksum offloading.

Step 5:   With frame 1 selected in the Packet List pane, right-click on the **Ethernet II** section of the Packet Details pane and hover over the **Protocol Preferences** option on the drop-down menu. If this setting is enabled (checked), click on the **Validate the Ethernet checksum if possible** setting to disable it.

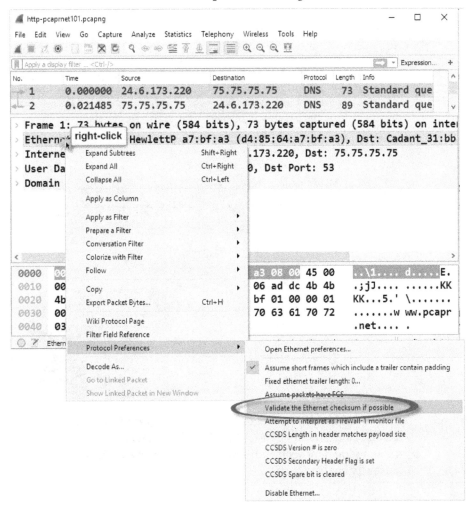

Step 6:   With frame 1 still selected in the Packet List pane, right-click on the **Internet Protocol** section of the Packet Details pane and hover over the **Protocol Preferences** option on the drop-down menu. If this setting is enabled (checked), click on the **Validate the IPv4 checksum if possible** setting to disable it.

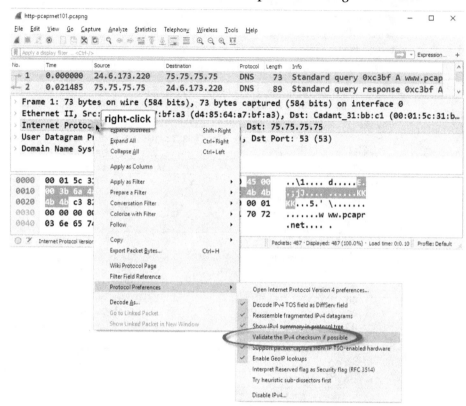

Step 7:   Again, in frame 1, right-click the **User Datagram Protocol** section of the Packet Details pane and hover over the **Protocol Preferences** option from the drop-down menu. Uncheck **Validate the UDP checksum if possible** setting if it is currently enabled.

Step 8:   Select **frame 5** in the Packet List pane. Right-click the **Transmission Control Protocol** section of the Packet Details pane and, under **Protocol Preferences**, disable the **Validate the TCP checksum if possible** setting if it is currently enabled.

Step 9:   Since Wireshark closes the TCP protocol settings menu after you select an option, you must right-click again on the **Transmission Control Protocol** section of the Packet Details pane to review or change the following additional settings.

- Disabled: *Allow subdissector to reassemble TCP streams*
- Enabled: *Track number of bytes in flight*
- Enabled: *Calculate conversation timestamps*

Step 10:   Now let's see how a few of these settings affect the packet displays. Click on frame 8 in *http-pcaprnet101.pcapng*. Expand the **Transmission Control Protocol line**, the **SEQ/ACK analysis**, and **Timestamps** section in the Packet Details pane.

We can see that Wireshark is not validating the TCP checksum and that 287 bytes of data have been sent, but not acknowledged. In addition, we can see that this frame arrived about 20 milliseconds (0.020 seconds) after the first frame of the TCP conversation (also referred to as the TCP stream) and 778 microseconds (0.000778 seconds) after the previous frame of this TCP conversation.

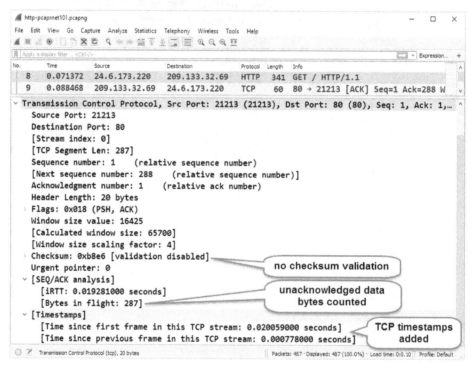

You can easily use the right-click method to change protocol preferences, such as tracking time in each TCP conversation and the number of unacknowledged bytes in a conversation. There are many other application and protocol preference settings that can be set in either the Preferences window or through the right-click method.

1.5. Customize Wireshark for Different Tasks (Profiles)

There are certain customization characteristics that fit troubleshooting tasks while other customized settings may fit network forensics tasks. Profiles enable you to define separate Wireshark configurations for these different analysis processes.

The Basics of Profiles

Profiles are basically directories that contain Wireshark configuration and support files that are loaded by Wireshark when you select to work in each profile. For example, you may create a profile focused on security concerns. This "security profile" may contain filters to display all ICMP traffic or connection attempts traveling in the direction of clients (as opposed to servers) and coloring rules that highlight suspicious traffic that contains known signatures.

Create a New Profile

Right-click on the **Profile** column in the Status Bar and select **New** to create a new profile, name it **Troubleshooting**, and press **Enter**. Click **OK** to begin working with your new profile. All the capture filter settings, display filter settings, coloring rules, columns, and preference settings you set now will be saved in that Troubleshooting profile.

Alternately you can select **Edit | Configuration Profiles...** and click the **Add** + button to create a new profile.[19]

The name of the profile you are working in is displayed in the right-hand column of the Status bar. In Figure 35, we are working in our Troubleshooting profile. Consider creating a different profile for security analysis, WLAN analysis, or any other type of analysis functions you perform.

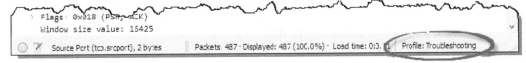

Figure 35. The right column in the Status Bar indicates the profile in use.

TIP

Profiles are a collection of simple text files that define preference settings, capture filters, display filters, coloring rules, and more. If you want to copy part or all of a profile to another Wireshark host, simply copy the profile directory (or the individual files in the profile's directory) to the other host.

---

[19] You can create new profiles based on existing profiles by clicking the **Copy** button in the **Edit | Configuration Profiles** window or right-click on the **Profile** area on the **Status Bar**, select **New**, select an existing profile from the list, and then click the **Copy** button. You will create a new profile based on the *Default* profile in Lab 6.

▢ Lab 6: Create a New Profile Based on the *Default* Profile

Profiles enable you to work with customized settings to be more efficient when analyzing traffic. In this lab you will create a new profile called "*wireshark101*." You will base it on your *Default* profile to ensure any previously created settings will be copied over to your new profile.

Step 1:   Right-click on the **Profile** column in the Status Bar and select **Manage Profiles**. (It does not matter what profile is currently listed in the Profile column.)

Step 2:   Select *Default* from the list of available profiles and click the **Copy** button ▣. Type the name ***wireshark101*** and click **OK**.

Wireshark now displays your new profile in the Status Bar.

In Lab 5 we worked with some key preference settings (such as *Track number of bytes in flight* and *Calculate conversation timestamps*) in the *Default* profile. Since your new profile is based on the *Default* profile, these preference settings are also set in your *wireshark101* profile.

Wireshark remembers the last profile used when it is restarted. To change to another profile, click on the **Profile** area of the Status Bar and select another profile.

1.6. Locate Key Wireshark Configuration Files

Wireshark configuration settings are stored in two places: the global configuration directory and the personal configuration directories. Learning where Wireshark stores settings enables you to quickly alter settings or share individual configurations with other people or other Wireshark systems.

The location of these directories may be different based on the operating system on which Wireshark is installed and where you chose to place Wireshark during the installation process. Select **Help | About Wireshark | Folders** to locate these directories on your system, as shown in Figure 36.

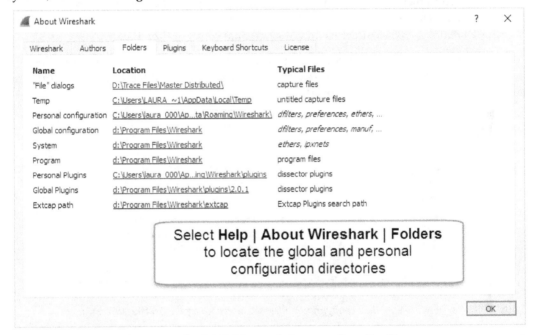

Figure 36. Use **Help | About Wireshark | Folders** *to find your configuration files.*

Your Global Configuration Directory

The global configuration directory contains the default configuration for Wireshark. When you create a new profile (without copying an existing profile), Wireshark pulls the basic settings from the files in the global configuration directory.

The following lists some of the files that may be found in your configuration directories:

- *cfilters* contains the capture filters for a profile.
- *colorfilters* contains the coloring rules for a profile.
- *dfilters* contains the display filters for a profile.
- *io_graphs* contains the default settings for IO graphs. (We will examine IO graphs in *Graph Application and Host Bandwidth Usage* starting on page 242).

- *preferences* contains the settings defined when you select **Edit | Preferences** when those settings do not have their own separate configuration file; this includes name resolution settings, Filter Expression button settings, and protocol settings.

- *recent* contains miscellaneous settings such as column widths, zoom level, toolbar visibility, and the recent directory used for loading trace files.

Your Personal Configuration (and *profiles*) Directory

When you make changes to the *Default* profile or create and customize other profiles, Wireshark stores those changes in your personal configuration directories.

The configuration files for any customized settings made to the *Default* profile reside directly in your personal configuration directory. When you build your first custom profile, Wireshark creates a *profiles* directory in your personal configuration directory.

Inside that *profiles* directory, you will see one directory for each of your custom profiles. Figure 37 shows the directory structure of a Wireshark system that has two custom profiles named *troubleshooting*, and *wireshark101*.

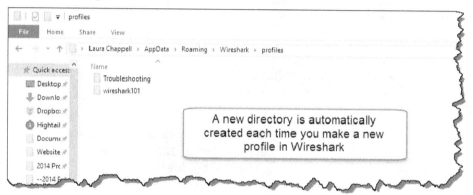

Figure 37. Custom profiles (and their configuration files) are stored under the profiles *directory.*

TIP

Don't be afraid to edit the configuration files. They are just text files that can be altered in a text editor. Now that we've addressed that issue, someday you may open up the *colorfilters* file in a text editor such as Notepad only to see a message that reads, "*# DO NOT EDIT THIS FILE! It was created by Wireshark*" at the top of the file. Disregard that message—there is no reason to avoid editing this file in a text editor. Manual changes will be visible when you reload the profile.

Lab 7: Import a DNS/HTTP Errors Profile

Once you've created that fabulous profile that detects various types of HTTP or DNS problems perhaps, consider installing that profile on your other Wireshark systems. Since Wireshark bases profiles on text files, this is a simple process.

Step 1:   Visit *www.wiresharkbook.com* and download the sample profile (*httpdnsprofile101v2.zip*). This new profile's directory and contents are zipped into a single file.

Step 2:   Select **Help | About Wireshark | Folders**. Double-click on your personal configuration folder to examine the directory structure.

Step 3:   As mentioned earlier, Wireshark creates a *profiles* directory when you build your first custom profile (as you did in Lab 6). If you do not see a *profiles* directory at this point, you can manually create one or return to and complete Lab 6. Open the *profiles* directory.

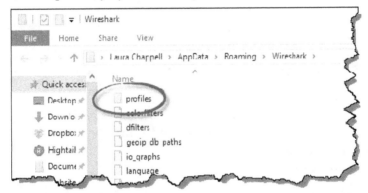

Step 4:   Extract the *httpdnsprofile101v2.zip* file contents into this *profiles* directory. You should see a new directory called *HTTP-DNS_Errors*. Look inside this new directory to see the Wireshark configuration files included in this profile.

Step 5:   Return to Wireshark and click on the **Profile** column on the Status Bar. You should see the new profile listed. Click on the *HTTP-DNS_Errors* profile to examine this new profile.

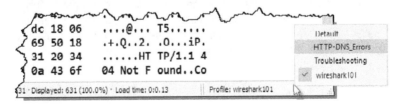

Step 6:   Open **_dns-nmap101.pcapng_** while working in your _HTTP-DNS_Errors_ profile.
You should see some interesting colors in the trace file and two new buttons in
the display filter area.

Step 7:   **LAB CLEAN-UP**   Click the **Profile** column on the Status Bar and select your
wireshark101 profile. You will continue to enhance the _wireshark101_ profile in
upcoming chapters of this book.

Remember that profiles are simply a collection of configuration text files. It is easy to move
single elements of a profile or entire profiles to other machines. If you work with a
troubleshooting team, consider creating common Wireshark profiles that the entire team
can use.

⊘TIP

Some configuration text files, such as the _recent_ configuration file, contain directory paths. This may generate
Wireshark startup errors when you move these types of configuration files to another system that does not have
the same directory paths in place. You could either avoid moving these files to another system or edit the
relevant configuration files to match the directory structure of the target system.

1.7. Configure Time Columns to Spot Latency Problems

Latency is a measurement used to define time delay. As a host sends a request and waits for a reply, there is always some latency. Excessive latency can be caused by problems along a path or at the endpoints.

The **Time** column and **Info** column can be used to detect three specific types of latency—path latency, client latency, and server latency.

The Indications and Causes of Path Latency

Path latency is often referred to as round trip time (RTT) latency because we often measure how long it takes for some packet to be transmitted and the response to be received. Using this measurement process, we can't tell if slow performance is in the outbound or the inbound direction. We just know it is slow somewhere along the path between two devices.

Path latency can be caused by an infrastructure device, such as an enterprise router, that is prioritizing (quality of service) traffic. If your low-priority traffic arrives at such a device when high-priority traffic is flowing through, your lowly traffic may be queued for a bit while the mucky-mucks go flying through.

Path latency and packet loss can also be caused when there is a bandwidth bottleneck on a network. For example, if you connect two heavily-loaded gigabit networks together with a 10 Mbps link, it's like connecting two fire hoses together with a garden hose[20].

On Wireshark, we can see path latency by looking at the first two packets of a simple TCP three-way handshake, as shown in Figure 38. Capture close to the client and watch the client send a SYN packet to the server. How much time goes by before the SYN-ACK? We will look at a trace file that has high path latency in this section.

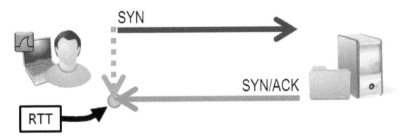

Figure 38. Identify path latency by looking at the round trip time (RTT) between the SYN and SYN/ACK of a TCP three-way handshake.

---

[20] Don't laugh at this one—I've seen this happen before. A slight misconfiguration among the IT team and an energetic intern dragged this network to the ground. It began with big path delays and then deteriorated to monstrous packet loss. I think the intern makes balloon animals at the mall for a living now.

The Indications and Causes of Client Latency

High client latency can be caused by users, applications or a lack of sufficient resources. There is the natural "human-induced" latency (when you wait for a user to click on something on their screen), but there's not much we can do about that. We are looking for client latency problems caused by sluggish client applications.

Of the three latency problems mentioned (path, client and server latency), this is the one that is seen least often. Most applications put the load on the server side of the communications. If, however, you happen to have an application that balances the work load between the client and the server, then we have to consider the client response times.

In Wireshark, client latency is indicated when we see a large delay before a packet from the client (ignoring delays due to user interactions), as shown in Figure 39.

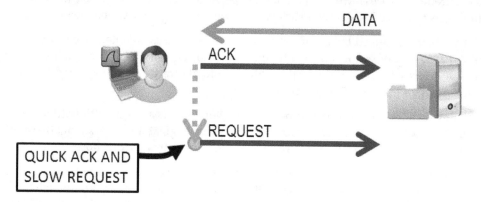

Figure 39. Watch for delays before client requests, but don't worry about delays while we wait for a user to enter something on their keyboard.

The Indications and Causes of Server Latency

Server latency occurs when a server is slow replying to incoming requests. This could be caused by a lack of processing power at the server, a faulty (or poorly written) application, the requirement to consult another server to get the response information (multi-tiered or middleware architecture), or some other type of interference delaying the server responses.

On Wireshark, we can identify server latency by watching a client request heading to the server, a quick acknowledgment from the server, and then a significant wait time before the requested information is received, as shown in Figure 40. Sadly, this is becoming more common on networks as servers are required to support more applications without getting the required upgrades.

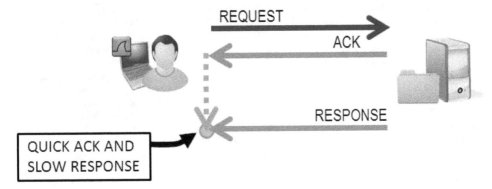

Figure 40. Watch for delays between server ACKs and responses.

Detect Latency Problems by Changing the Time Column Setting

The default **Time** column setting is *Seconds Since Beginning of Capture*. In essence, Wireshark marks the first packet's arrival as 0.000000000. The **Time** column value for each packet after the first one is based on how much later it arrived during the capture process.

To spot high delta times (the time from the end of one packet to the end of the next packet), select **View | Time Display Format | Seconds Since Previous Displayed Packet**. This setting will be retained with the profile in which you are working.

After changing this setting, click the **Time** column twice to sort from high to low to look for large delays in the trace file.

In Figure 41, we opened *http-openoffice101b.pcapng*, set the Time column to *Seconds Since Previous Displayed Packet*, and sorted the **Time** column from high to low. The first packet that appears is a SYN/ACK—the second packet of the TCP handshake. This trace file was taken at the client and this is a perfect indication of path latency.

In essence, this delay before the SYN/ACK packet indicates it took almost ¼ of a second (.226388 seconds) to get to the HTTP server and back. You might as well walk there![21]

```
http-openoffice101b.pcapng                                          —  □  ✕

File  Edit  View  Go  Capture  Analyze  Statistics  Telephony  Wireless  Tools  Help

Apply a display filter ... <Ctrl-/>                                    ▾  Expression...  +

No.    Time        Source           Destination      Protocol  Length  Info
  6    0.226388    150.101.135.12   24.6.173.220     TCP        66  80 → 21458 [SYN, ACK] Seq=0 Ack=
 19    0.207913    150.101.135.12   24.6.173.220     TCP      1514  80 → 21458 [ACK] Seq=10221 Ack=1
144    0.205086    24.6.173.220     150.101.135.12   TCP        54  21458 → 80 [ACK] Seq=1166 Ack=14
 14    0.195098    150.101.135.12   24.6.173.220     TCP      1514  80 → 21458 [ACK] Seq=4381 Ack=11
 43    0.193580    150.101.135.12   24.6.173.220     TCP      1514  80 → 21458 [PSH, ACK] Seq=35041
 25    0.193321    150.101.135.12   24.6.173.220     TCP      1514  80 → 21458 [ACK] Seq=17521 Ack=1
  9    0.193286    150.101.135.12   24.6.173.220     TCP        60  80 → 21458 [ACK] Seq=1 Ack=1166
 32    0.192023    150.101.135.12   24.6.173.220     TCP      1514  80 → 21458 [ACK] Seq=24821 Ack=1
 77    0.190336    150.101.135.12   24.6.173.220     TCP      1514  80 → 21458 [ACK] Seq=71541 Ack=1
117    0.189079    150.101.135.12   24.6.173.220     TCP      1514  80 → 21458 [ACK] Seq=115341 Ack=
 95    0.188946    150.101.135.12   24.6.173.220     TCP      1514  80 → 21458 [ACK] Seq=90521 Ack=1
176    0.188778    150.101.135.12   24.6.173.220     TCP      1514  80 → 21458 [ACK] Seq=175201 Ack=
 58    0.186775    150.101.135.12   24.6.173.220     TCP      1514  80 → 21458 [ACK] Seq=51101 Ack=1
207    0.184125    150.101.135.12   24.6.173.220     TCP      1514  80 → 21458 [ACK] Seq=207321 Ack=
295    0.182731    150.101.135.12   24.6.173.220     TCP      1514  80 → 21458 [ACK] Seq=297841 Ack=
80...  0.181651    150.101.135.12   24.6.173.220     TCP      1514  80 → 21458 [ACK] Seq=8284041 Ack

○ ⁊              Packets: 17483 · Displayed: 17483 (100.0%) · Load time: 0:0.311   Profile: wireshark101
```

*Figure 41. Sort the **Time** column after setting it to Seconds Since Previous Displayed Packet. [http-openoffice101b.pcapng]*

This method is great when you have a single conversation in the trace file, but if you have numerous UDP/TCP conversations, the *Seconds Since Previous Displayed Packet* setting can hide problems.

For example, consider what this column would display if you had five different conversations intertwined in the trace file. The **Time** column is now measuring the delta time between each of the packets with no regard to the fact that there are five different intertwined conversations. We would want to see delays inside the separate conversations.

---

[21]   Ok, walking probably isn't an option—unless you are trying to distract yourself from the ridiculously long wait time you will have trying to download a file from this HTTP server.

Detect Latency Problems with a New TCP Delta Column

In Lab 5, you ensured that the *Calculate conversation timestamps* TCP preference was enabled. In Lab 6, you created your *wireshark101* profile based on the *Default* profile so you should already have this setting in place. Now we will look at how we can create a column based on that preference setting so we can obtain separate delta time values for each TCP conversation.

To add a column for the TCP delta time value, expand a TCP header Timestamps section. Right-click on the **Time since previous frame in this TCP stream** and select **Apply as Column**, as shown in Figure 42. You now have a new column in the Packet List pane.

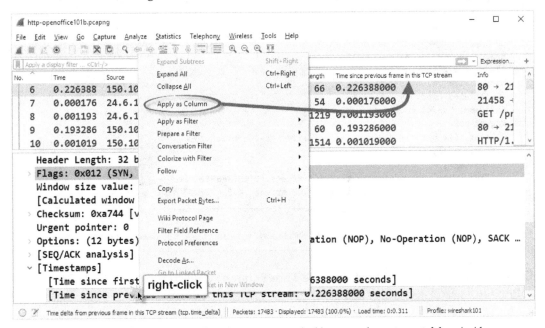

Figure 42. Enable **Calculate conversation timestamps** and add a new column to spot delays inside individual TCP conversations. [http-openoffice101b.pcapng]

This new column name is too long. To rename a column, right-click the column heading and select **Edit Column**. Type the new column name in the Title field and click **OK** to save the new name. In Figure 43, we named our new column **TCP Delta**.

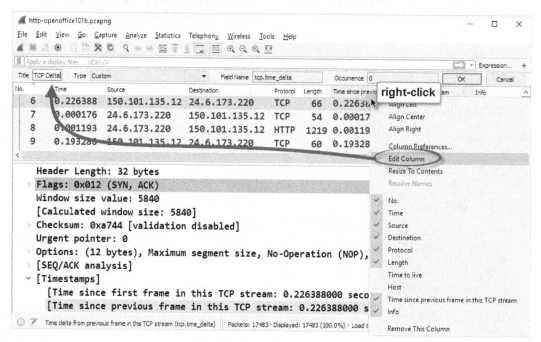

*Figure 43. Right-click on a column heading and choose **Edit Column** to change the column name. [http-openoffice101b.pcapng]*

Let's examine the difference between the **Time** column value and this new **TCP Delta** column in a new trace file.

In Figure 44, we opened *http-pcaprnet101.pcapng*, clicked on, and dragged the new **TCP Delta** column to the right of the existing **Time** column. We sorted on the **Time** column from high to low to see the difference in time values between the **Time** column and **TCP Delta** column.

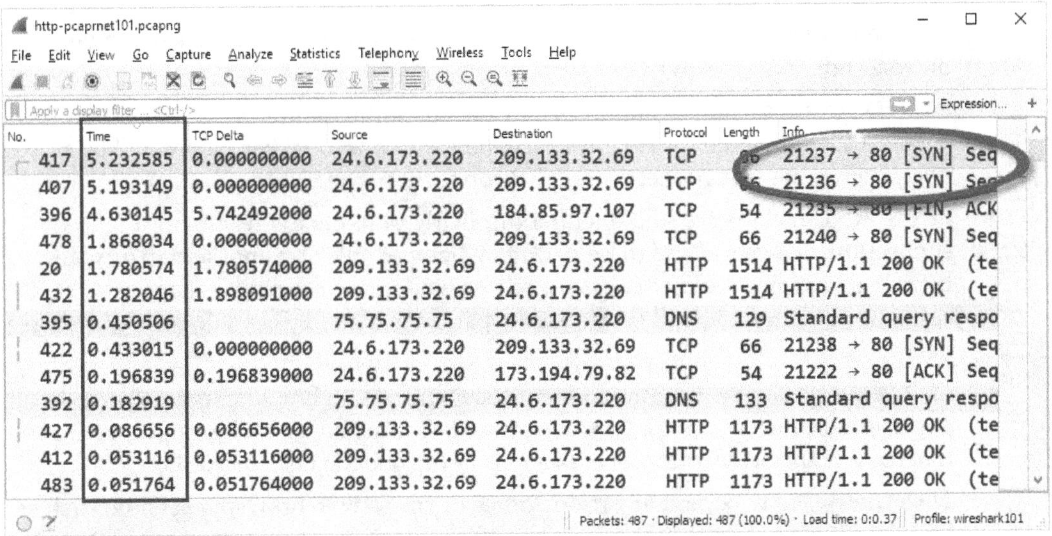

Figure 44. SYN packets show up as high latency in this trace file, but these are false positives [http-pcaprnet101.pcapng]

Before we sort on the **TCP Delta** column to find delays inside individual TCP conversations, let's examine why some delays can be considered normal.

Don't Get Fooled – Some Delays are Normal

Some delays are not noticed by the end user (such as the loading of an .ico file, the icon on the browser tab). Other delays are just considered "normal" and acceptable. Do not spend your time troubleshooting delays before these types of packets.

- **.ico file requests** are eventually launched by the browser to put an icon on your browser tab.

- **SYN packets** are sent to establish a new connection with a TCP peer. You may begin capturing and then ask a user to connect to a web server. There will be a delay before the first packet of the TCP connection (the SYN packet).

- **FIN or RST packets** are sent to either implicitly or explicitly terminate a connection. Browsers send these packets when you click on another tab or when there has been no recent activity to a site or when the browsing session is configured to automatically close after a page has loaded. Users do not notice these delays.

- **GET requests** can be generated when a user clicks on a link to request the next page. Other times, some GET requests may be launched by background processes that have no priority whatsoever (such as in the .ico file GET requests).

- **DNS queries** may be sent at various times during a web browsing session, such as when a page that has numerous hyperlinks loads at the client.

- **TLSv1 encrypted alerts** are often seen just before a connection close process (TCP Resets). Although encrypted, the alert is likely a TLS Close request.

In Figure 44, the largest delays precede SYN packets and FIN packets. Don't spend time troubleshooting these delays as they are likely caused by waiting for a user to request a file or the eventual timeout process of a connection.

In Figure 45, we are still working in *http-pcaprnet101.pcapng*. Previously, we sorted based on the **Time** column. Now, when we sort the **TCP Delta** column from high to low we notice the 18 second delay before the three background graphics are requested. That common delay is typical of a background process. The FIN/ACK packets are never a concern as they happen transparently in the background to time out a TCP connection.

The OK responses in frame 20 and 432[22], however, are a very real concern. This is high server latency. In this trace file, there are delays of 1.898091 seconds and 1.780574 seconds that are worth looking into. We don't expect such large delays before the server sends the required web page element. The server is either overloaded, it doesn't hold the information locally, or perhaps the requested element is located in a database that needs to be queried before responding.

---

[22] If packets 432 and 20 appear as [TCP segment of a reassembled PDU], you need to change your TCP preference settings to disable *Allow subdissector to reassemble TCP streams*. Select **Edit | Preferences ⟩ Protocols | TCP** to set this.

In this situation, the latter is the case. When you load the *pcapr.net* web site and type in a protocol or application name, that value is used to search a database for entries that match your query.

Also see *Use Filters to Spot Communication Delays* on page 186.

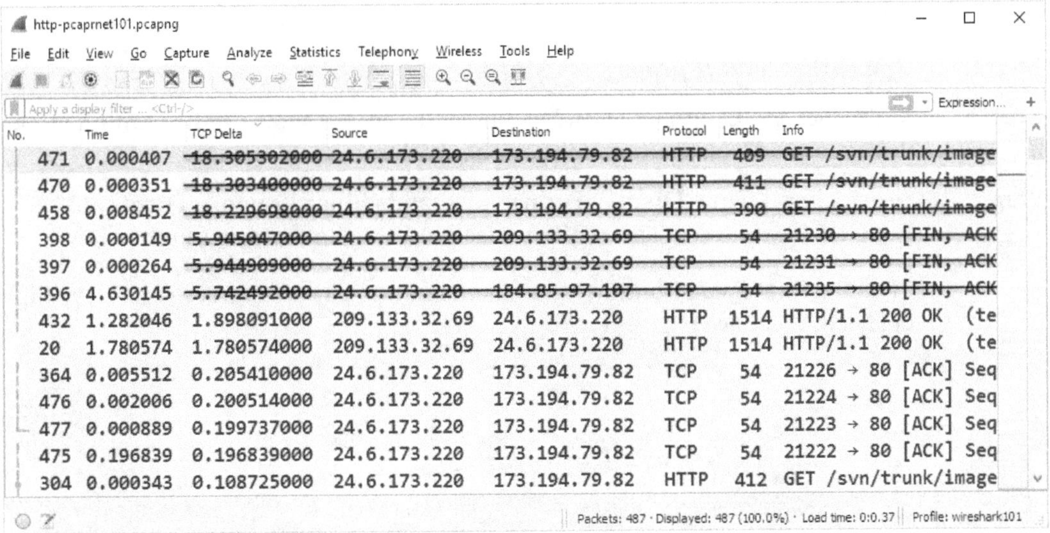

*Figure 45. Sort your **TCP Delta** column from high to low when looking for delays in individual TCP conversations – do not get distracted by "normal" delays (crossed out in the image above). [http-pcaprnet101.pcapng]*

！TIP

When you approach a complaint that the network is slow, always look at the latency times to see if that is part of the problem. If an application runs over TCP, we can detect path and server latency by looking for delays during the TCP handshake (path latency) and the delay between an ACK from the server (acknowledging a request from a client) and the actual data that follows.

🖥 Lab 8: Spot Path and Server Latency Problems

Let's practice using these two columns to detect latency. In this lab you will set the **Time** column to *Seconds Since Previous Displayed Packet* and add the **TCP Delta** column.

You may have some of these columns set already if you followed along with the previous section.

Step 1:   Open *http-slow101.pcapng*.

Step 2:   Right-click the **Length** column heading and unselect the **Length** column to hide it. This provides more room for your new column.

Step 3:   Select **View | Time Display Format | Seconds Since Previous Displayed Packet**. Click on your **Time** column heading twice to sort from high to low.

Click the **First Packet** button 👆 on the main toolbar. We can see some very high delays in this trace file.

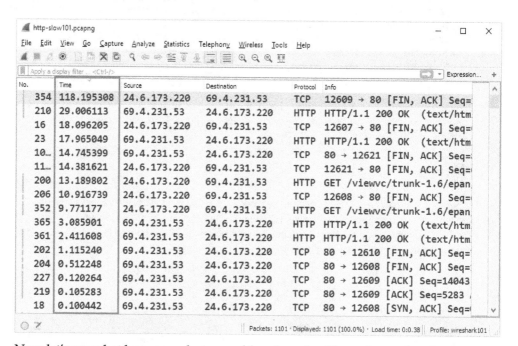

Now let's see what happens when we add and work with a column that depicts TCP conversation timestamps.

Step 4:   Click on the **No.** (Number) column heading to return the trace file to its default sort order. Scroll up or click the **Go to First Packet** button on the main toolbar to go to **frame 1**.

Step 5:   Right-click the **TCP header** in the Packet Details pane of frame 1 and select **Expand Subtrees**. Scroll down and right-click on the **Time since previous**

frame in this TCP stream and select **Apply as Column**. You now have a new column in the Packet List pane, as shown below.

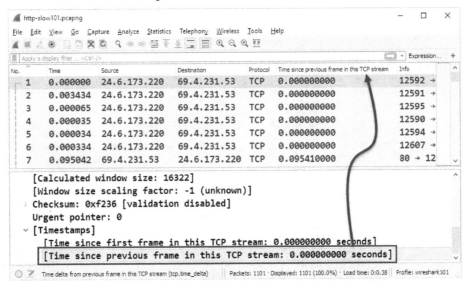

Step 6: Right-click on the new column and select **Edit Column**. Type **TCP Delta** in the Title area and click **OK**.

As we sort on the **TCP Delta** column, keep in mind the types of traffic that can contain "normal delays" as listed in *Don't Get Fooled – Some Delays are Normal* on page 94.

Step 7:   Click on your new **TCP Delta** column heading and drag the column to the right of the existing **Time** column. Click twice on your new **TCP Delta** column heading to sort from high to low. Since there are multiple TCP conversations intertwined in this trace file, this **TCP Delta** column gives an accurate display of latency times in the trace file.

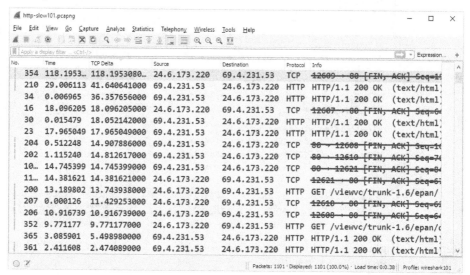

Do you see anything in common with the top delays in the traffic? There are several very large delays before the HTTP server said "OK." You can probably imagine that the user would complain about terrible performance when browsing to this web site.

Step 8: | **LAB CLEAN-UP** | Click once on the **No.** (Number) column heading to sort from low to high. This is the original sorting order of trace files.

Right-click on the **TCP Delta** column heading and unselect that column from the list to hide it. If you want to view this column again later, you can right-click on any column heading and select it from the column list.

Look at the TCP delta times in your web browsing sessions, network logins, or email traffic. Get a feel for the round trip latency times from your client to numerous hosts.

Chapter 1 Challenge

Open *challenge101-1.pcapng* and use the techniques covered in this chapter to answer these Challenge questions. The answer key is located in Appendix A.

This trace file includes an HTTP communication running over a non-standard port. If you are using an earlier version of Wireshark (Wireshark v1.x), you must force Wireshark to dissect this traffic as HTTP.

Question 1-1.   In which frame number does the client request the default web page ("/")?

Question 1-2.   What response code does the server send in frame 14? (This will be in frame 17 if you have the TCP reassembly feature enabled – see Lab 5.)

Question 1-3.   What is the largest TCP delta value seen in this trace file?

Question 1-4.   How many SYN packets arrived after at least a 1 second delay?

[This page intentionally blank.]

Chapter 2 Skills: Determine the Best Capture Method and Apply Capture Filters

Approach networking protocols like you would human conversations. Think of how people talk to each other, how they act when they want something, how they show gratitude when they get it. Look for those types of themes in the packets and network traffic will become easier to understand and communication nuances will be easier to remember. The time investment is worth it. When you understand packets, you understand everything in networking.

Betty DuBois
Chief Detective of *Network Detectives* and Wireshark University Certified Instructor

Quick Reference: Capture Options

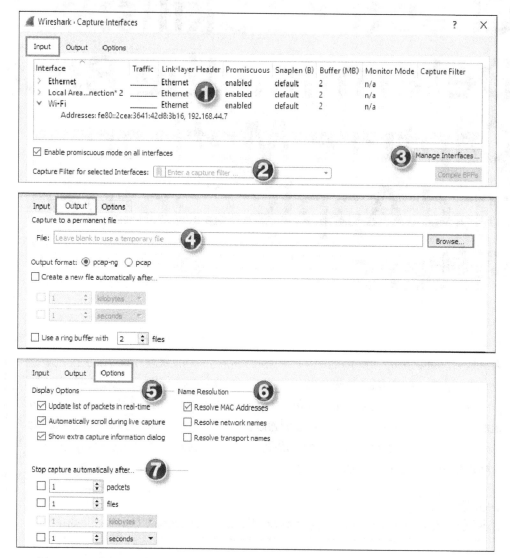

(1)   **Interface List** — Select one or more interfaces (multi-adapter capture)

(2)   **Capture Filter** — Displays applied capture filter

(3)   **Manage Interfaces** — Click here to add new local/remote interfaces

(4)   **Capture to Permanent File(s)** — Save to multiple files, define when the next file should be created, and set a ring buffer

(5)   **Display Options** — Set auto-scroll and view packets while capturing

(6)   **Name Resolution** — Enable/disable name resolution for MAC addresses, IP addresses, and ports (transport names)

(7)   **Stop Capture** — Set an auto-stop condition based on number of packets, number of files created, quantity of data captured, or elapsed time

2.1. Identify the Best Capture Location to Troubleshoot Slow Browsing or File Downloads

The first step in analyzing network performance problems is to capture traffic in the right spot. Place Wireshark in the wrong spot and you may spend too much time dealing with unrelated traffic or following "false positives."

The Ideal Starting Point

Begin by capturing traffic at or near the host that is experiencing a performance problem, as depicted in Figure 46. This allows you to see traffic from that host's perspective. You can detect the round trip latency times, packet loss, error responses, and other problems that the host is experiencing. If a user complains about slow email downloads, you want to see the performance problems from their perspective. If you capture somewhere in the middle of the network, your packet capture tool may be upstream from the point where performance issues are injected into the communications.

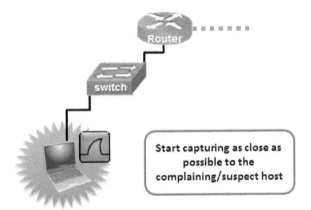

Figure 46. You can see the concerns from this host's perspective when you start capturing as close to this host as possible.

Move if Necessary

After getting a general idea of what is happening from the complaining host's perspective, you may have to move your packet capture tool to another location to get a different perspective. For example, if packet loss seems to be the cause of poor performance, you'll want to move Wireshark (or set up a second Wireshark system) on the other side of the switches or routers to determine where the packets are being dumped. Most packet loss occurs at interconnecting devices, so that's where you would focus.

 TIP

Start capturing at the client system to get that client's perspective. Watch for high round trip times to a target, indications of packet loss, problems with buffer sizes (zero window condition—as discussed in *Receive Buffer Congestion Indications* on page 255), and suspicious or unnecessary background traffic. Many times you won't have to go any further than the client's perspective.

2.2.   Capture Traffic on Your Ethernet Network

There are lots of ways to capture traffic on your Ethernet network. Knowing your options will help ensure you use the most efficient method to capture traffic. You have three options for capturing close to the complaining host. Options 1 through 3 are displayed in Figure 47.

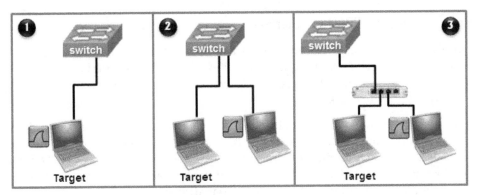

Figure 47. You have three basic options for capturing traffic on an Ethernet network.

Option 1: Capture directly on the complaining host

This may be a great option if you are allowed to install packet capture software on that host. You don't have to install Wireshark. Consider using a simple packet capture utility such as tcpdump.

Option 2: Span the host's switch port

If the switch above the user supports port spanning and you have rights to configure that switch, consider setting up that switch to copy all traffic to or from the user's switch port down your Wireshark port. One concern to note, however, is that switches will not forward link-layer error packets so you may not see all the traffic related to poor performance.

Option 3: Set up a Test Access Port (TAP)

Taps[23] are full-duplex devices that are installed in the path between the host of interest and the switch. By default, taps forward all network traffic, including link-layer errors. Although taps can be expensive, they can be a life-saver if you want to listen to all traffic to or from a host.

TIP

Prepare and practice your capture process well in advance. You don't want to run around looking for the switch port spanning configuration information while people are screaming about network problems. If you are going to use a tap to listen to traffic to/from a server, consider keeping the tap in place, always ready when you need it.

---

[23]   The term "tap" is used as a general term for the acronym TAP.

2.3. Capture Traffic on Your Wireless Network

Wireshark can help you understand how wireless networks (WLANs) work and also help you find the cause of lousy performance on your home or work network. You have a few options for capturing on the WLAN side. First, determine what your native WLAN adapter can see while running Wireshark.

What can Your Native WLAN Adapter See?

Click the **Close File** button ✖ to return to the Start Page. Examine the sparklines to determine if your wireless adapter is listed and if it sees traffic through Wireshark. If the sparkline is flat, but you know there is WLAN traffic, your native adapter probably isn't going to work with Wireshark.

If you do see some activity on your native adapter's sparkline, double-click that adapter to begin a capture. If your adapter can see WLAN beacons as well as data packets and you see 802.11 headers, your adapter might work as a packet capture interface. However, if the adapter does not add metadata, such as the signal strength at the time of capture, you are missing out on some important data required for analysis[24].

Use an AirPcap Adapter for Full WLAN Visibility

AirPcap adapters are specifically designed to capture all types of WLAN traffic, apply WLAN decryption keys (if supplied), and add metadata about the captured frames.

AirPcap adapters can capture 802.11 control, management, and data frames. In addition, these adapters run in monitor mode (also referred to as RF monitor or RFMON mode), which enables the adapter to capture all traffic without having to associate with a specific Access Point. This means the AirPcap adapter can capture traffic on any 802.11 network, not just the one to which the local host typically associates itself.

AirPcap adapters can be configured to affix either a PPI (Per-Packet Information) or RadioTap header to each WLAN frame. These headers contain some great information, such as the frequency on which the frame arrived, the signal strength and noise level at the moment and location of capture, and more. Figure 48 depicts a trace file (*wlan-ipadstartstop101.pcapng*) captured with an AirPcap adapter. The Packet Details pane displays the additional information contained in the RadioTap header.

If you need to capture WLAN traffic, the AirPcap adapters are an excellent option. For more information on AirPcap adapters, visit *www.riverbed.com*.

Use the Npcap Driver for WLAN/Loopback Visibility

The Npcap Project developed a new packet sniffing library for Windows systems. Although Npcap is based on the WinPcap/Libpcap libraries, Npcap offers the following advantages:

---

[24] The signal strength information is not contained in a field of the 802.11 header, so this information must be added by the adapter or a special driver.

- NDIS 6 support which is faster than the old deprecated NDIS 5 API (which Microsoft may kill off at some point).

- Monitor Mode for capture on wireless networks.

- Security through the use of the User Account Control (UAC) dialog.

- WinPcap compatibility for programs that require the WinPcap libraries.

- Loopback packet capture by creating an adapter named Npcap Loopback Adapter.

- Monitor Mode for capture on wireless networks.

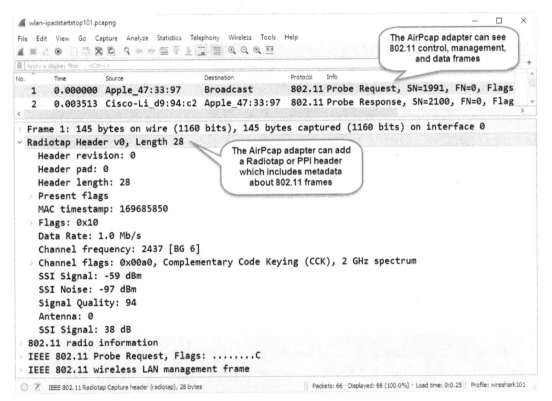

Figure 48. The AirPcap adapter enables you to see control, management, and data frames. In addition, the adapter prepends a Radiotap or PPI header with 802.11 metadata to the frames. [wlan-ipadstartstop101.pcapng]

When troubleshooting or securing WLAN networks, begin as close as possible to the complaining/suspect host (just like you did when capturing on a wired network).

TIP

Try capturing on your native adapter to determine its capabilities. You need to see true 802.11 headers as well as management, data, and control frames. AirPcap adapters are a worthwhile investment if you are going to be analyzing wireless network traffic.

2.4. Identify Active Interfaces

If Wireshark can't see an interface, you can't capture traffic. If you have more than one interface, you need to determine which one to use. Mastering the interface options is required to be successful as an analyst.

Determine Which Adapter Sees Traffic

Click the Capture Options button ⚙ and examine the sparkline activity to quickly determine which interface is seeing traffic and to which network each interface is connected.

Click the ▷ in front of an adapter to view addresses associated with that adapter.

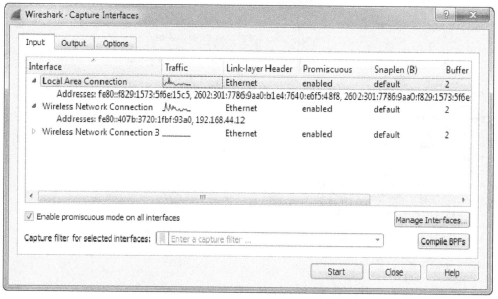

Figure 49. We can easily tell which interface is able to capture traffic by looking at the sparkline activity.

Consider Using Multi-Adapter Capture

In the Capture Options window, you can use Ctrl+click (or Command+Click on a Mac) to select multiple interfaces upon which to capture. This is useful if you want to capture on the wired and wireless network simultaneously. For example, if you are trying to troubleshoot a WLAN client on the network, you can capture on the client's WLAN adapter and the wired network simultaneously, as shown in Figure 50.

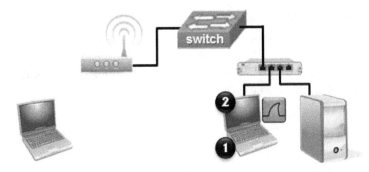

Figure 50. You can simultaneously capture a client's traffic as it travels through to wireless and wired networks.

2.5. Deal with TONS of Traffic

Inside a busy enterprise, the traffic can overload Wireshark[25] leaving you with an incomplete trace file that makes your analysis thoroughly inaccurate. Learn to deal with high rates of traffic to ensure you can track down problems on any size network.

In Chapter 8 we will look at command-line capture techniques using Tshark and Dumpcap.

Why are You Seeing So Much Traffic?

If a user is complaining about slow web browsing, begin capturing traffic and then ask the user to browse to some web sites. Keep capturing until your user has demonstrated the slow browsing problem. You will have captured traffic that will help you determine if the performance problem is linked to the client, server, or path.

When you capture close to the client, you should see much less traffic than if you'd tapped into the middle of the enterprise. It is likely that Wireshark can keep up with traffic rates to and from the client.

If you are dealing with a security issue (perhaps you think a host contains malware), you may want to capture all traffic to or from this host for quite a while. During this capture process, don't let a user access the keyboard of this machine. You don't want to capture user behavior.

You can get severe back pains from sleeping on the office floor or quickly fill up a hard drive if you don't set this up as an unattended capture process.

This is the Best Reason to Use Capture Filters

Dealing with too much data is one of the best reasons to use capture filters. By reducing the number of packets Wireshark must capture, you reduce the load on Wireshark while reducing the amount of traffic you must wade through. Keep in mind, however, that an overly restrictive capture filter may cause you to miss key packets. Look at capturing to file sets as a safe option.

Capture to a File Set

Wireshark can capture traffic to file sets. File sets are individually linked files that can be examined using Wireshark's **File | File Set | List Files** feature.

Click the **Capture Options** button ⊛ , select on the interface(s) on which to capture, and click the **Output** tab. Enter the path and file name for the file set, as shown in Figure 51. Check **Create a new file automatically after...** to define the criteria to create the next file.

In our example, Wireshark will create a set of 100 MB-sized files in *.pcapng* format. We didn't set a stop criteria so we'll need to manually stop the capture process at some point.

---

25   Since Dumpcap is the tool that is capturing traffic for Wireshark, it is actually Dumpcap that can be overwhelmed if traffic is arriving faster to Dumpcap than Wireshark is picking it up from Dumpcap.

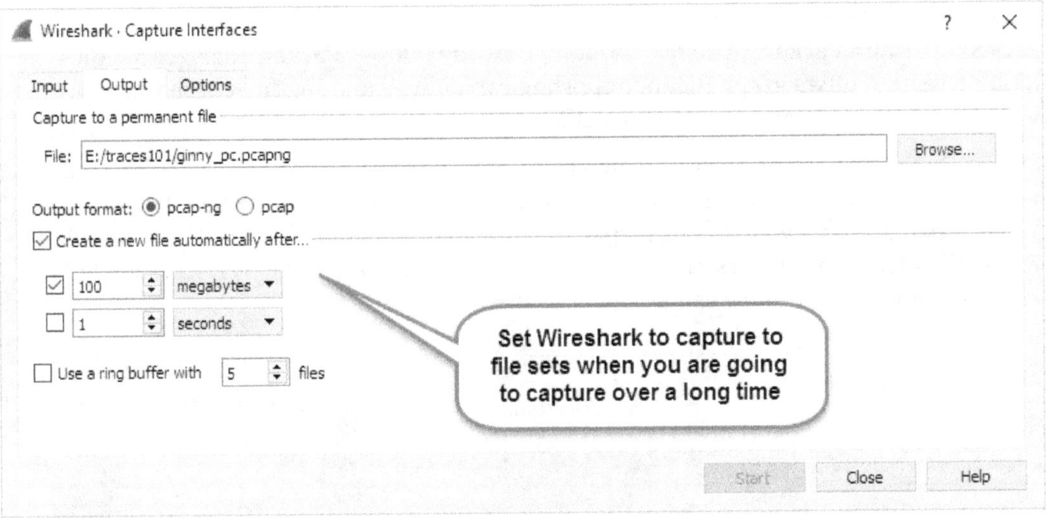

Figure 51. We set up Wireshark to capture to a set of 100 MB-sized files.

In the example shown in Figure 51, since we suspect malware is running on a host, we will let Wireshark capture the traffic to and from this host for the next 12 hours to see if there is a phone home process running in the background. You may need to capture for longer or shorter times, depending on what you see in the trace file(s).

When Wireshark saves to these file sets, the files will be named *ginny_pc* followed by a file number and date/time stamp. For example, if we captured three files, they would be named something like:

- *ginny_pc_00001_20170115180713.pcapng*
- *ginny_pc_00002_20170115184116.pcapng*
- *ginny_pc_00003_20170115190252.pcapng*

Open and Move around in File Sets

To work with file sets, use **File | Open** and select any of the files in your file set. For example, open any one of the book trace files that begin with "*split250.*" Each of these files is part of a file set. After opening the first file from this set, use **File | File Set | List Files** to see all the files in your file set.

Click on each file to quickly move from one file to another. See also *Use Special Capture Techniques to Spot Sporadic Problems* on page 116.

Consider a Different Solution—SteelCentral™ Packet Analyzer

It was evident back in 2007 that trace files were getting larger and larger as network speeds increased and file sizes expanded to include multimedia elements. Wireshark suddenly became a cumbersome tool to use on these files.

In 2009, Loris Degioanni, creator of WinPcap, began work on a product that is now known as SteelCentral™ Packet Analyzer (formerly Cascade Pilot)[26]. Packet Analyzer handles large trace files, offers graphing and reporting capabilities missing in Wireshark, and integrates tightly so you can export specific packets for closer inspection.

One of Packet Analyzer's most welcome features is the ability to handle larger trace files. For example, in a recent test, it took 1 minute and 52 seconds to open a 1.3 GB file in Wireshark. Each time we added a display filter, column, or coloring rule, Wireshark had to reload the file. Wireshark essentially became unusable. In Packet Analyzer, we loaded the IP conversations view of the same file in less than 3 seconds.

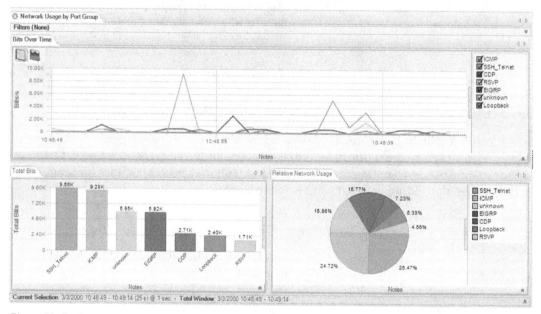

Figure 52. Packet Analyzer offers a graphical view of the traffic and is a great item to have in your network analysis toolkit.

TIP

Try to keep your file size below 100 MB. Larger file sizes will cause Wireshark to become sluggish when you add columns, apply filters, or build graphs. Wireshark is not very good at handling huge trace files. Packet Analyzer was created to work with the larger trace files and to integrate seamlessly with Wireshark. If you must capture and work with very large trace files (well over 100 MB), look into Packet Analyzer as a solution.

---

[26]   I was fortunate to sit with Loris during the initial design phase of this product before it even had an interface. The underlying architecture was sleek and sophisticated. Watching the product take shape and discussing potential features was a fabulous experience.

🖵 Lab 9: Capture to File Sets

In this lab you will get a chance to practice capturing to file sets using an auto-stop condition.

Step 1:   Click on the **Capture Options** button 🔘 on the main toolbar.

Step 2:   Select the adapter you are currently using to connect to the Internet.

Step 3:   Click the **Output** tab. Click the **Browse** button to navigate to and select the directory in which you want to save your trace files. Enter *captureset101.pcapng* in the File area.

Step 4:   Check the **Create a new file automatically after** check box. Set the next file to be created after **10 seconds**.

Your Output settings should be similar to those shown below.

Step 5:   Click the **Options** tab. Under **Stop capture automatically after,** click the check box for **files** and enter **4** to indicate that you want Wireshark to stop capture after 4 files have been created.

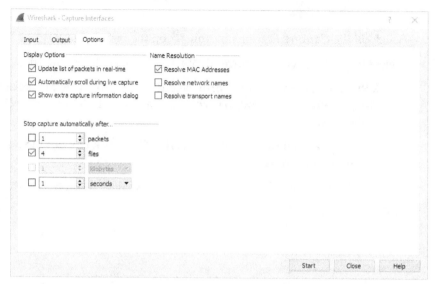

Step 6:   Click **Start**. (If the Start button is not active, click the **Input** tab and ensure an adapter has been selected.)

Step 7:   Open your browser and visit **www.openoffice.org**. Browse around the web site for at least 40 seconds.

Toggle back to Wireshark and look at the Title Bar. You should see your file name stem (*captureset101*) followed by a file number (*_00004* shown below) and the date and timestamp.

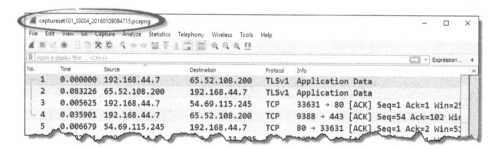

Step 8:   Select **File | File Set | List Files**. Wireshark displays all four files of your file
            set. Click one of the listed files to quickly open it.

Wireshark · 4 Files in Set			? ✕
Filename	Created	Modified	Size
captureset101_00001_20160109094645.pcapng	2016-01-09 09:46:45	2016-01-09 09:46:55	5216 bytes
captureset101_00002_20160109094655.pcapng	2016-01-09 09:46:55	2016-01-09 09:47:05	299 kB
captureset101_00003_20160109094705.pcapng	2016-01-09 09:47:05	2016-01-09 09:47:15	171 kB
captureset101_00004_20160109094715.pcapng	2016-01-09 09:47:15	2016-01-09 09:47:15	260 bytes

Step 9:   **LAB CLEAN-UP** Close your File List window. Note that Wireshark retains many
            of your capture options. You will need to check the capture option settings
            when you prepare for the next capture process.

TIP

When you are dealing with a lot of traffic, consider saving to file sets. Wireshark will load the files faster if they
are under 100 MB. You will find yourself using file sets more often as you need to capture larger amounts of
traffic.

2.6. Use Special Capture Techniques to Spot Sporadic Problems

Sporadic, roaming problems often plague analysts. Using a few key Wireshark functions you can be ready to catch these annoyingly elusive events.

If you have a sporadic problem, one that seems to appear on and off through a network, you will need to be a bit more creative with your capture process. In this case, you should capture traffic continuously until the problem occurs again.

Use File Sets and the Ring Buffer

In this situation, set up Wireshark to capture traffic to file sets, but use the ring buffer option. In Figure 53, we defined a new file name (*roamingprob.pcapng*) and indicated that we want to keep a total of 5 files (ring buffer setting of 5).

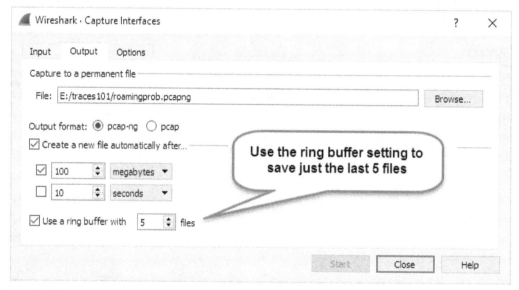

Figure 53. We are going to examine the last 500 MB of traffic leading up to the problem point in time.

When Wireshark finishes capturing the fifth 100 MB file, it will delete the first 100 MB file and create a sixth 100MB file. Let Wireshark run continuously. The file set feature won't fill up the hard drive and you will have the last 500 MB leading up to the problem.

Stop When Complaints Arise

When the user complains about performance, stop the capture process manually and look at the most recent file to see what happened.

Wireshark will keep numbering the files so you know how many 100 MB files have been created and deleted (if older than the last five files).

For example, we may see file names such as:

- *roamingprob_00007_20170127203453.pcapng*
  (created at 8:34:53PM on January 27th, 2017)
- *roamingprob_00008_20170127023321.pcapng*
  (created at 2:33:21AM on January 27th, 2017)
- *roamingprob_00009_20170127091141.pcapng*
  (created at 9:11:41AM on January 27th, 2017)
- *roamingprob_00010_20170127094214.pcapng*
  (created at 9:42:14AM on January 27th, 2017)
- *roamingprob_00011_20170127100107.pcapng*
  (created at 10:01:07AM on January 27th, 2017)

This is a great way to let Wireshark automatically capture traffic for later review.

TIP

Practice this skill by configuring Wireshark to capture to file sets with a ring buffer as you are going about your daily work. As Wireshark runs in the background, you are ready to capture the traffic leading up to any type of problem that arises. For example, if you suddenly notice a web site loads more slowly than usual, you can toggle to Wireshark and stop the capture to see what recently happened.

🖳 Lab 10: Use a Ring Buffer to Conserve Drive Space

In this lab exercise, we will set up a ring buffer to ensure we see the most recent traffic. We will create a problem and manually stop the capture to analyze the issue.

Step 1:   Click on the **Capture Options** button ⊙ on the main toolbar.

Step 2:   Select the adapter you are currently using to connect to the Internet.

Step 3:   Click the **Output** tab. Check the **Capture to a permanent file** check box and then click the **Browse** button to navigate to and select the directory in which you want to save your trace files. Enter *stopproblem101.pcapng* in the File area. Click **Save**.

Step 4:   Check the **Create a new file automatically after** check box. Set the next file to be created after **10 seconds**.

Step 5:   Select the **Ring Buffer** option to **3** to limit the number of files to retain.

Step 6:   Click **Start**.

Step 7:   Open your browser and visit **www.wireshark.org**. Spend at least 30 seconds browsing around the site.

Step 8:   Now browse to **www.chappellu.com/nothere.html**. This should generate a 404 error because the file does not exist.

Step 9:   Quickly toggle back to Wireshark and click the **Stop Capture** button ■.

Step 10:   Look in the Title Bar. You can see how many file numbers have been assigned to this point. When you select **File | File Set | List Files**, you only see three files because your ring buffer was set up to save only the last three files.

Step 11:   Click the **Last Packet** button 　 and scroll backwards through the trace file from the end towards the start to locate the 404 error message from the server, as shown below.

In Lab 18, you will use a display filter to quickly locate 404 error responses.

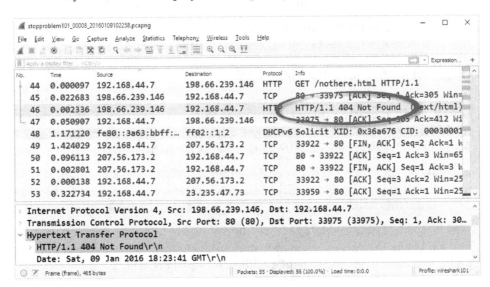

Step 12:   **LAB CLEAN-UP** Note that Wireshark retains many of your capture options. You will need to check the capture option settings when you prepare for the next capture process.

Using a ring buffer and manual stop process allows you to detect what happened up to and at the time performance went awry.

2.7. Reduce the Amount of Traffic You have to Work With

Rather than prepare for a week of sifting through packets, consider reducing the work load significantly by capturing at the proper location and filtering during the capture process.

If you must capture traffic inside the enterprise or on a server that is very busy, you may find that Wireshark cannot keep up with the traffic rate.

Detect When Wireshark Can't Keep Up

Wireshark launches *Dumpcap.exe* to capture traffic. Wireshark pulls the traffic from Dumpcap. If Dumpcap cannot keep up with the traffic during a capture process (most likely because Wireshark is not pulling the traffic from Dumpcap fast enough), the phrase "Dropped: x" will appear on Wireshark's Status Bar in the center column.

Most likely, your trace file will contain numerous *ACKed Lost Segment* indications. You cannot work with a faulty trace file. Your assumptions and analysis would be as incomplete as the data from which you worked. Such a trace file is unusable.

This is a perfect time to apply capture filters.[27] Figure 54 shows that capture filters are applied before the packets are sent to the capture engine. By applying capture filters at this point, you have a better chance of avoiding dropped packets.

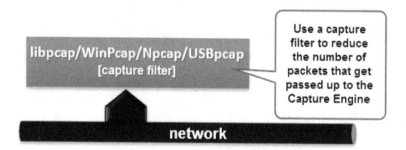

Figure 54. Capture filters reduce the load on the Capture Engine.

---

[27]   I generally tell folks to avoid capture filters whenever possible. This is because you can't get those packets back after you filter them out. An ideal time to use capture filters is when Dumpcap can't keep up with the traffic. So let's lighten up the load heading to the Capture Engine.

Detect when a Spanned Switch Can't Keep Up

Packet drops can also occur when you are spanning ports on a very busy switch. Consider what would happen if you spanned a physical switch port that connects to a very busy network. You connect to the network on a 1 Gb link (which is actually 2 Gb because of full-duplex operations). If this network is very busy and you span several switch ports down your lowly 1 Gb downlink, that switch is likely going to drop some packets. This situation is called oversubscription.

In this case, Wireshark won't note **Dropped: x** in the Status Bar. Instead, you may see numerous *ACKed Lost Segment* and *Previous Segment Not Captured* indications. Wireshark doesn't indicate that it has dropped any packets, because it hasn't—the switch didn't forward the packets to Wireshark.

This switch span capture configuration is not going to work. You'll need to change where and how you capture traffic. A full-duplex tap is a great solution in this case, as shown in Figure 55. Intelligent taps can even offer some capture filtering capability at the tap.

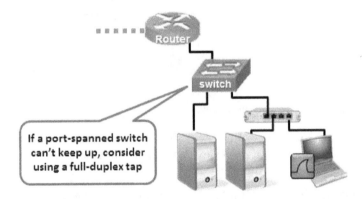

Figure 55. Place the tap between the server and the switch.

You also might consider capturing to file sets with a maximum file size of 100 MB. Wireshark really doesn't like working with huge trace files. We covered using file sets in *Use Special Capture Techniques to Spot Sporadic Problems* on page 116.

Apply a Capture Filter in the Capture Options Window

To apply a capture filter, click the **Capture Options** button ⊙. Select your desired adapter(s) and type your capture filter directly into the **Capture Filter for selected Interfaces** area as shown in Figure 56.

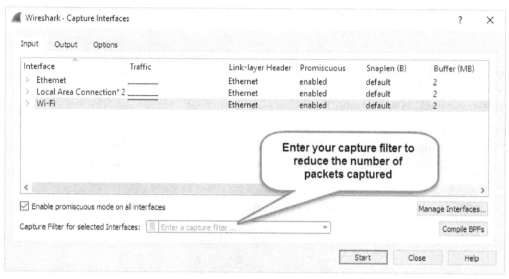

Figure 56. Select an interface before entering a capture filter.

If you know the syntax of your capture filter, simply type it in the Capture Filter area. Remember — Wireshark uses BPF (Berkeley Packet Filtering) syntax. This is the format supported by Dumpcap for capture filters.

Wireshark color codes the background as you type to alert you to capture filter errors. A red background indicates the filter syntax is invalid. Most likely, the capture filter contains a typo or perhaps you used display filter syntax. A green background means that the filter syntax is valid.

Wireshark offers a predefined set of capture filters. To view the saved capture filter list, click the Capture Filter Bookmark ▦ arrow to the left of the Capture Filter area or select **Capture | Capture Filters** from the main menu.

Figure 57 shows the list of predefined capture filters.

For more information on capture filtering techniques, see *Capture Traffic based on Addresses (MAC/IP)* on page 124.

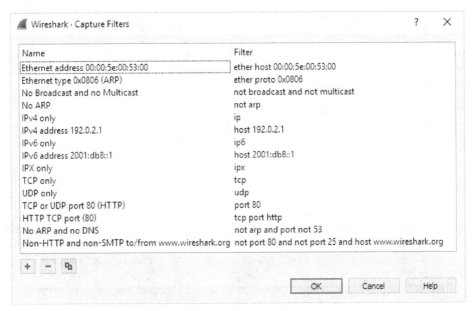

Figure 57. Wireshark provides a predefined set of capture filters.

For additional information on capture filters, visit *wiki.wireshark.org/CaptureFilters.*

2.8. Capture Traffic based on Addresses (MAC/IP)

Capturing traffic to and from a particular IP address (or range of IP addresses) or a MAC address is a key skill that you will use when focusing on a particular problem, studying an application's behavior, or investigating a potentially breached host.

Capture filters use the BPF syntax and are actually applied by WinPcap or libpcap. Display filters, which you will examine later in this book, use a proprietary Wireshark format. Display filters are not limited by the capabilities of dumpcap and the BPF syntax.

TIP

Before you get too excited with all the options for using capture filters, let me make a recommendation. Use capture filters sparingly and display filters liberally. If you filter something out using capture filters, you can never get those packets back. For example, if you applied a capture filter for traffic to and from port 80 and found that the browsing session targeted a strange IP address for the web server, it would be nice to see the DNS process that took place beforehand. Too late. You filtered those packets out. If you'd captured without a capture filter, you would be able to work with display filters to focus on those port 80 packets and then look at the DNS traffic.

Capture Traffic to or from a Specific IP Address

If you are capturing in a location where you see many hosts communicating, you might consider using a capture filter for the IP address of the hosts whose traffic you are analyzing. The following provides examples of IP address capture filters.

`host 10.3.1.1`	Capture traffic *to/from* 10.3.1.1
`host 2406:da00:ff00::6b16:f02d`	Capture traffic *to/from* the IPv6 address 2406:da00:ff00::6b16:f02d
`not host 10.3.1.1`	Capture all traffic *except* traffic *to/from* 10.3.1.1
`src host 10.3.1.1`	Capture traffic *from* 10.3.1.1
`dst host 10.3.1.1`	Capture traffic *to* 10.3.1.1
`host 10.3.1.1 or host 10.3.1.2`	Capture traffic *to/from* 10.3.1.1 and any host it is communicating with and traffic *to/from* 10.3.1.2 and any host it is communicating with
`host www.espn.com`	Capture traffic *to/from* any IP address that resolves to *www.espn.com* (this will only work if the host name can be resolved by Wireshark prior to capture)

Capture Traffic to or from a Range of IP Addresses

When you want to capture traffic to or from a group of addresses, you can use CIDR (Classless Interdomain Routing) format or use the `mask` parameter.

`net 10.3.0.0/16`	Capture traffic *to/from* any host on network 10.3.0.0
`net 10.3.0.0` `mask 255.255.0.0`[28]	Same result as previous filter
`ip6 net 2406:da00:ff00::/64`	Capture traffic *to/from* any host on network 2406:da00:ff00:0000 (IPv6)
`not dst net 10.3.0.0/16`	Capture all traffic *except* traffic to an IP address starting with 10.3
`dst net 10.3.0.0/16`	Capture traffic *to* any IP address starting with 10.3
`src net 10.3.0.0/16`	Capture traffic *from* any IP address starting with 10.3

Capture Traffic to Broadcast or Multicast Addresses

You can learn a lot about hosts on the network by just listening to broadcast and multicast traffic.

`ip broadcast`	Capture traffic to 255.255.255.255
`ip multicast`	Capture traffic to 224.0.0.0 through 239.255.255.255 (also catches traffic to 255.255.255.255 unless you add `and not ip broadcast`)
`dst host ff02::1`	Capture traffic to the IPv6 multicast address for all hosts
`dst host ff02::2`	Capture traffic to the IPv6 multicast address for all routers

If you are just interested in all IP or IPv6 traffic, use the capture filters `ip` or `ip6`, respectively.

Refer to *Capture Traffic for a Specific Application* on page 131 for more capture filter examples.

Capture filters can be used during command-line capture as well. For more information, refer to *Use Capture Filters during Command-Line Capture* on page 316. Also refer to *wiki.wireshark.org/CaptureFilters*.

---

28   This would all be on one line in Wireshark — the line wraps in the book due to space issues.

TIP

Wireshark includes a default set of capture filters. Select Capture | Filters on the main menu to view the predefined capture filters. You'll find some good examples of common capture filters used with Wireshark. You can also add your own capture filters to this list.

Capture Traffic based on a MAC Address

When you want to capture IPv4 or IPv6 traffic to or from a host, create a capture filter based on the host's MAC address.

Since MAC headers are stripped off and applied by routers along a path, ensure you are on the same network segment as the target host.

`ether host 00:08:15:00:08:15`	Capture traffic to or from 00:08:15:00:08:15
`ether src 02:0A:42:23:41:AC`	Capture traffic *from* 02:0A:42:23:41:AC
`ether dst 02:0A:42:23:41:AC`	Capture traffic *to* 02:0A:42:23:41:AC
`not ether host 00:08:15:00:08:15`	Capture traffic to or from any MAC address *except* for traffic to or from 00:08:15:00:08:15

In Lab 12, you will create a NotMyMAC capture filter to listen in on the traffic to or from other hosts on the network while not capturing your own traffic.

📷 Lab 11: Capture Only Traffic to or from Your IP Address

In this lab you will determine your current IP address and apply a capture filter for that traffic.

Step 1:   Click the **Capture Options** button ⚙ on the main toolbar.

Step 2:   Expand the interface on which you typically connect to the Internet. Wireshark displays your IP address(es) for the interfaces listed. You could also use either *ipconfig* or *ifconfig* to copy your IP address and paste in to your filter if desired.

You will use this address information to create your capture filter.

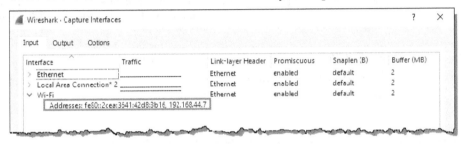

Step 3:   Select the interface you want to use for this capture process. If an interface is not selected before creating your capture filter, Wireshark will color the capture filter area background red.

In the capture filter area, enter **host x.x.x.x** (replacing x.x.x.x with your IP address) to filter on your IPv4 traffic. If you are going to capture on your IPv6 address, enter **host xxxx:xxxx:xxxx:xxxx:xxxx:xxxx:xxxx:xxxx**.

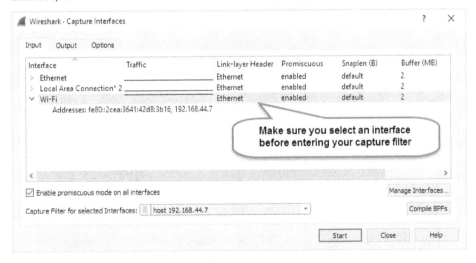

Step 4: Click the **Output** tab and make sure you are not configured to capture to a file or file set. Ensure your ring buffer option is not selected as well.

Click the **Options** tab and ensure you do not have an autostop condition defined.

Click **Start** to begin the capture process.

Step 5: Now open your command prompt and type `ping www.chappellu.com`.

Step 6: Toggle back to Wireshark and click the **Stop Capture** button ▪. Examine your trace file. All the traffic shown should be to or from your IP address. You should see the ICMP Echo packets used for the ping process. You may also see background processes that communicate on the network to and from your machine.

Step 7: **LAB CLEAN-UP** Note that Wireshark retains many of your capture options. You will need to check the capture option settings when you prepare for the next capture process.

Consider following the same steps to build a filter to or from your MAC address (create a "MyMAC" filter). In the next lab, we will create a filter for everyone else's traffic (based on a MAC address filter) and we will save our new capture filter.

▢ Lab 12: Capture Only Traffic to or from Everyone Else's MAC Address

In this lab you will determine your current MAC address and apply a capture filter that filters out your traffic—you are interested in everyone else's traffic only[29].

Step 1:   Run either *ipconfig/all* or *ifconfig/all* at the command prompt to determine the MAC address of your active interface[30].

Step 2:   Click on the **Capture Options** button ⊙ on the main toolbar.

Step 3:   Select the desired interface.

Step 4:   In the Capture Filter area, enter `not ether host xx.xx.xx.xx.xx.xx` using your Ethernet address. If you expand the Capture Interfaces window you will see your Capture Filter listed on the row of the interface selected.

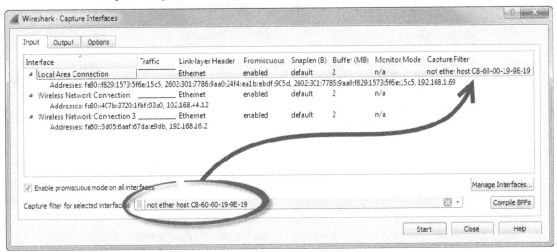

Step 5:   To save this new capture filter, click the **Capture Filter Bookmark** button 🔖 and select **Save this filter**. Enter **NotMyMAC** in the Name area. The Filter value should already be set.

---

[29]   If you have a dual-stack host, it is much more effective to make a single filter based on your MAC address than to make a more complex filter based on your IPv4 and IPv6 addresses.

[30]   On a Windows host select **Start** and select the **Command Prompt** from the program list or type `cmd` in the file search area. On a MAC OS X host, open **Applications | Utilities | Terminal**. There are various terminal applications available on Linux hosts—look for *terminal* or *Xterm*, for example.

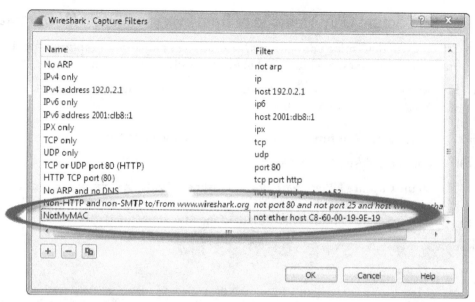

Step 6: Click **OK** to close the Capture Filters window.

Step 7: Check your other capture settings under the **Output** tab and **Options** tab. We won't set up multiple file capture, ring buffer use, or auto-stop in this lab so leave those options unchecked.

Step 8: Click **Start** to begin the capture process. Now browse to various sites, log in to your server, or send email.

Step 9: Toggle back to Wireshark and click the **Stop Capture** button ■.

Step 10: Scroll through your trace file to examine the traffic captured during your communications processes. No traffic to or from your host will be captured. You will likely see some background broadcast and multicast traffic, but none of those packets will be sent from your host since you filtered your traffic out of the trace file during the capture process.

Step 11: **LAB CLEAN-UP** Note that Wireshark retains many of your capture options. You will need to check the capture option settings when you prepare for the next capture process.

There's no reason to capture your own traffic when you are analyzing someone else's communications. Running your NotMyMAC filter will ensure your traffic is not caught during the capture process.

2.9. Capture Traffic for a Specific Application

You will often want to look at traffic from a single application or even sets of applications. Get the unrelated packets out of the way by applying a capture filter based on the TCP or UDP port used by your target application(s).

The capture filter syntax (Berkeley Packet Filtering format) does not recognize application names. You need to define an application based on the port in use.

It's all About the Port Numbers

Here is a quick list of some of the most popular application capture filters. For more information on capture filters, refer to *wiki.wireshark.org/CaptureFilters*.

`port 53`	Capture UDP/TCP traffic to or from port 53 (typically DNS traffic)
`not port 53`	Capture all UDP/TCP traffic *except* traffic to or from port 53
`port 80`	Capture UDP/TCP traffic to or from port 80 (typically HTTP traffic)
`udp port 67`	Capture UDP traffic to or from port 67 (typically DHCP traffic)
`tcp dst port 21`	Capture TCP traffic to port 21 (typically the FTP command channel)
`portrange 1-80`	Capture UDP/TCP traffic to or from ports from 1 through 80
`tcp portrange 1-80`	Capture TCP traffic to or from ports from 1 through 80

Combine Port-based Capture Filters

When you want to capture traffic to or from various non-contiguous port numbers, combine them with a logical operator, as shown below.

`port 20 or port 21`	Capture all UDP/TCP traffic *to or from* port 20 or port 21 (typically FTP data and command ports)
`host 10.3.1.1 and port 80`	Capture UDP/TCP traffic *to or from* port 80 that is being sent *to or from* 10.3.1.1
`host 10.3.1.1 and not port 80`	Capture UDP/TCP traffic *to or from* 10.3.1.1 *except* traffic to or from port 80
`udp src port 68 and udp dst port 67`	Capture all UDP traffic from port 68 to port 67 (typically traffic sent from a DHCP client to a DHCP server)
`udp src port 67 and udp dst port 68`	Capture all UDP traffic from port 67 to port 68 (typically traffic sent from a DHCP server to a DHCP client)

Try to avoid capture filters whenever possible. I cannot stress this enough! It is much better to have too much traffic to wade through than to find out you're missing a piece of the picture. Once you capture this large amount of traffic, use display filters (which offer many more filtering options) to focus on specific traffic.

TIP

If you need to make capture filters that look for a specific ASCII string in a TCP frame, use Wireshark's *String-Matching Capture Filter Generator* (*http://www.wireshark.org/tools/string-cf.html*). For example, if you only want to capture HTTP GET requests, simply enter in the string **GET** and set the TCP offset to 0 (where HTTP request methods, or commands, reside).

2.10. Capture Specific ICMP Traffic

Internet Control Messaging Protocol (ICMP) is a protocol you should watch for when performance or security issues plague a network.

The table below shows the structure of numerous ICMP capture filters. In this case we must use an offset to indicate the field location in an ICMP packet. Offset 0 is the ICMP Type field and offset 1 is the location of the ICMP Code field.

`icmp`	Capture all ICMP packets.
`icmp[0]=8`	Capture all ICMP Type 8 (Echo Request) packets.
`icmp[0]=17`	Capture all ICMP Type 17 (Address Mask Request) packets.
`icmp[0]=8 or icmp[0]=0`	Capture all ICMP Type 8 (Echo Request) packets or ICMP Type 0 (Echo Reply) packets.
`icmp[0]=3 and not icmp[1]=4`	Capture all ICMP Type 3 (Destination Unreachable) packets except for ICMP Type 3/Code 4 (Fragmentation Needed and Don't Fragment was Set) packets.

Although we could have listed `not icmp` as a possible capture filter above, you likely would never want to use that filter since ICMP provides so much information about network activity and configurations.

Lab 13: Create, Save and Apply a DNS Capture Filter

In this exercise you will use several skills learned in this chapter. You will configure Wireshark to capture only DNS traffic and save that traffic to a file called *mydns101.pcapng*.

Step 1:   Click the **Capture Options** button ⊚ on the main toolbar.

Step 2:   Select the adapter you are currently using to connect to the Internet.

Step 3:   In the Capture Filter area, enter **port 53**, as shown below. The background turns from white to red to green as you type in the filter.

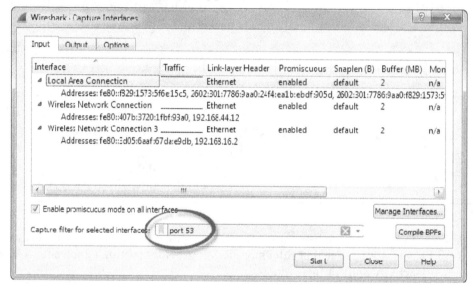

Step 4:   To save this new capture filter, click the **Capture Filter Bookmark** button and select **Save this filter**. Enter **DNS** in the Name area. The Filter value should already be set. Click **OK**.

Step 5:   In the Capture Interfaces window, click the **Output** tab. Click the **Browse** button to navigate to and select the directory in which you want to save your trace files. Enter *mydns101.pcapng* in the Name area. Click **Save**. Your directory and file name should appear in the File section in the Capture Interfaces Output area.

Step 6: Check the box in front of **Create a new file automatically after** and check both boxes for file size and time definitions. Define the next file to be created after **1 megabyte** and **10 seconds**. Whichever condition is met first causes the creation of the next file. Do not set a Ring Buffer value or auto-stop condition (under the Options tab). You will manually stop the capture process.

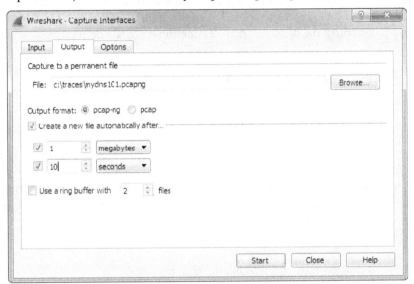

Step 7: Click **Start** to begin the capture process.

Launch a browser and browse to at least 5 different sites on the Internet. For example, you could visit two news sites, a bank site, Amazon and *www.wireshark.org*. Try to visit sites that you have not browsed to recently to ensure DNS information is not loaded from your cache.

Step 8: Toggle back to Wireshark and click the **Stop Capture** button ▮.

Step 9: Scroll through your trace file(s) to examine the DNS traffic generated during your browsing process. You may be surprised to see how many DNS queries are generated when you browse these sites.

Step 10: **LAB CLEAN-UP** Note that Wireshark retains many of your capture options. You will need to check the capture option settings when you prepare for the next capture process.

Consider saving any capture filter that you might use more than once. This will save you time if you need to repeatedly use a complex capture filter.

Chapter 2 Challenge

This challenge requires access to the Internet. You will capture traffic to a web site and analyze your findings. The answer key is located in Appendix A.

First, configure Wireshark to capture only traffic to and from your MAC address and TCP port 80, and save the traffic to a file named *mybrowse.pcapng*. Then ping and browse to *www.chappellU.com*. Stop the capture and examine the trace file contents.

Question 2-1.   Did you capture any ICMP traffic?

Question 2-2.   What protocols are listed for your browsing session to *www.chappellU.com*?

Now configure Wireshark to capture all your ICMP traffic, and save your traffic to a file called *myicmp.pcapng*. Again, ping and browse to *www.chappellU.com*. Stop the capture and examine the trace file contents.

Question 2-3.   How many ICMP packets did you capture?

Question 2-4.   What ICMP Type and Code numbers are listed in your trace file?

Chapter 3 Skills: Apply Display Filters to Focus on Specific Traffic

Wireshark is an extraordinary tool for network analysis and discovery. It's obviously critical for debugging low-level network problems, but I find it's often the best way to debug higher level applications too. Web traffic is one such example. Sure, I could read the web server logs, but those often omit critical details. Network traffic, on the other hand, doesn't lie. It shows me exactly what is going on.

Wireshark may appear complex and intimidating when you first start it up, but with a little guidance and practice you'll find that it's easier than you think.

Gordon "Fyodor" Lyon
Founder of the Open Source *Nmap Security Scanner Project*

Quick Reference: Display Filter Area

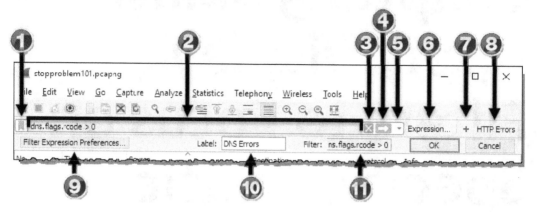

(1)   Bookmark (view, save, manage, and recall display filters)
(2)   Display Filter Area (includes auto-complete and error detection)
(3)   Clears the display filter area so no display filter is applied to the trace file
(4)   Applies the currently shown display filter during a live capture or to an opened trace file
(5)   Display filter drop-down history list
(6)   Expressions to walk you through creating display filters
(7)   Saves the display filter as a Filter Expression button
(8)   Filter Expression button area (blank by default)
(9)   Filter Expression Preferences (edit, activate/deactivate, reorder, or delete Filter Expression buttons) – only visible when saving a Filter Expression button
(10)   Filter Expression Button Label (define button label) – only visible when saving a Filter Expression button
(11)   Filter Expression Button Syntax (define button filter syntax) – only visible when saving a Filter Expression button

3.1. Use Proper Display Filter Syntax

Becoming a master of display filters is absolutely essential to the network analyst. This is the skill you will use to find the needle in the haystack. Learn to build, edit, and save key display filters to save yourself many hours of frustration wading through "packet muck."

Whereas capture filters use the BPF syntax, display filters use a Wireshark proprietary format. Except for a few instances, Wireshark capture filters and display filters look very different.

The Syntax of the Simplest Display Filters

The simplest display filters are based on a protocol, application, field name, or characteristic. Display filters are case sensitive. Most of these simple display filters use lower case[31] characters.

Display Filter Type	Example	Description
Protocol	`arp`	Displays all ARP traffic including gratuitous ARPs, ARP requests, and ARP replies
Protocol	`ip`	Displays all traffic that contains an IPv4 header.
Protocol	`ipv6`	Displays all IPv6 traffic including IPv4 packets that have IPv6 headers embedded in them, such as 6to4, Teredo, and ISATAP traffic
Protocol	`tcp`	Displays all TCP-based communications
Application	`bootp`	Displays all DHCP traffic (which is based on BOOTP). See *Determine Why Your dhcp Display Filter Doesn't Work* on page 159
Application	`dns`	Displays all DNS traffic including TCP-based zone transfers and the standard UDP-based DNS requests and responses
Application	`tftp`	Displays all TFTP (Trivial File Transfer Protocol) traffic

---

[31] Watch out for VoIP display filters—for some reason there are several VoIP-related display filters that use upper case and lower case characters.

Application	`http`[32]	Displays all HTTP commands, responses and data transfer packets, but does not display the TCP handshake packets, TCP ACK packets or TCP connection teardown packets
Application	`icmp`	Displays all ICMP traffic
Field existence	`bootp.option.hostname`	Displays all DHCP traffic that contains a host name (DHCP is based on BOOTP)
Field existence	`http.host`	Displays all HTTP packets that have the HTTP host name field. This packet is sent by the clients when they send a request to a web server
Field existence	`ftp.request.command`	Displays all FTP traffic that contains a command, such as the USER, PASS, or RETR commands
Characteristic	`tcp.analysis.flags`	Displays all packets that have any of the TCP analysis flags associated with them — this includes indications of packet loss, retransmissions, or zero window conditions
Characteristic	`tcp.analysis.zero_window`	Displays packets that are flagged to indicate the sender has run out of receive buffer space

TIP

The most common mistake made when entering a display filter is using capture filter syntax. Capture filters use the BPF format whereas display filters use a proprietary format. There are a few times when the same filter works as both a capture and display filter. For example, `ip` and `icmp` can be used both as capture filters and display filters.

---

[32] Watch out when using display filters based on a TCP-based application name. Running a filter for "http" will not show you the entire picture of a browsing session. For more information, see *Be Cautious Using a TCP-based Application Name Filter* on page 142.

In Figure 58, we filtered on the DNS traffic in a web browsing session. This is a great filter when you want to know the interdependencies between web sites. Using this filter, we can see that browsing to *www.wireshark.org* causes a storm of DNS queries to resolve the IP addresses associated with the links on the page.

The Status Bar indicates that there are 208 DNS packets in this trace file.

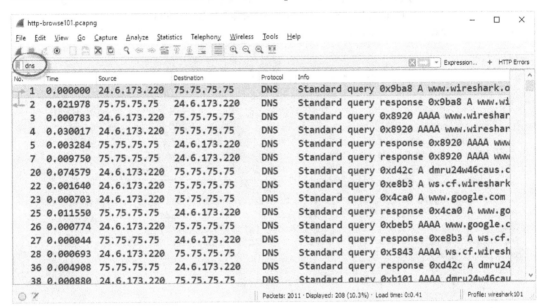

Figure 58. *We filtered on all the DNS traffic to see what host names were resolved. [http-browse101.pcapng]*

Use the Display Filter Error Detection Mechanism

Remember that display filters are case sensitive. If you type DNS instead of dns, Wireshark will show a red background in the display filter area to indicate this filter will not work. A yellow background is a warning that your filter may not work as desired. A green background indicates your filter is properly formed, but be careful. Wireshark does not do a logic test.

We will look into display filter problems in *Determine Why Your dhcp Display Filter Doesn't Work* on page 159 and *Why didn't my ip.addr != filter work?* on page 174.

Learn the Field Names

Many of the display filters you will apply are based on field names (such as `http.host`). To learn a field name, select the field in the Packet Display list and look at the Status Bar, as shown in Figure 59. In this example, we clicked on frame 10 in the Packet List pane and then expanded the HTTP header in the Packet Details pane. When we clicked on the Request Method line in the HTTP section of the packet, the Status Bar indicated this field is called `http.request.method`.

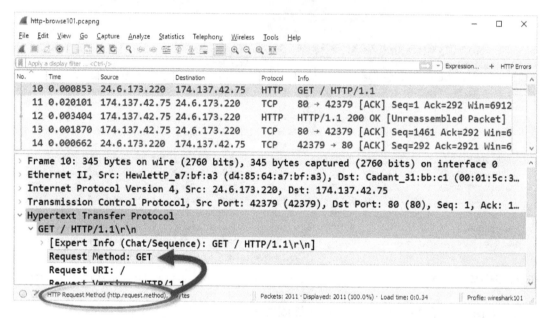

Figure 59. Click on a field and look at the Status Bar to learn the field name. You may need to expand this column on the Status Bar to see the entire field name. [http-browse101.pcapng]

In Figure 60, we typed `http.request.method` in the display filter area to display all packets that contain this field[33]. Notice that the Status Bar indicates that this trace file, *http-browse101.pcapng*, contains 2,011 packets and only 103 packets match our filter.

This is a great filter to determine what elements are requested by an HTTP client. Web servers do not send HTTP request methods, they send HTTP response codes. In Lab 18 you will build a filter for the HTTP 404 response code.

---

[33]   You will learn to use the right-click **Prepare a Filter** and **Apply as Filter** features to create a filter based on a field name and value in *Quickly Filter on a Field in a Packet* on page 151.

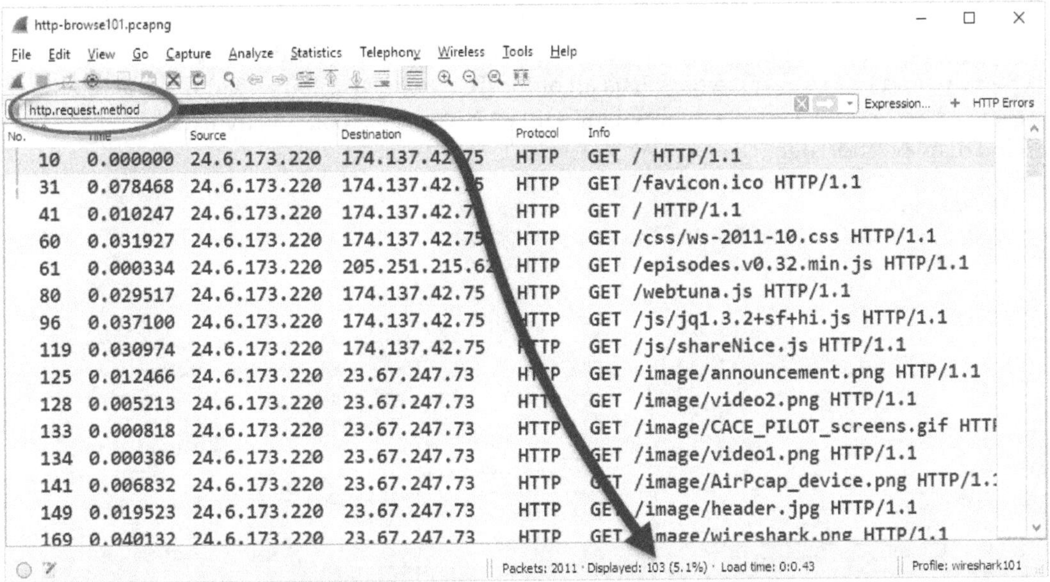

Figure 60. Look at the Status Bar to determine how many packets matched your filter. You may need to expand the Packets section of the Status Bar to see the Displayed information. [http-browse101.pcapng]

Use Auto-Complete to Build Display Filters

As you type **http.request.method** in the filter area, Wireshark opens a window to "walk you through" the filter options. When you type **http.** (including the dot), you see a list of all possible display filters that begin with this string. Continue typing **http.request.** and you will see filters that begin with this phrase, as shown in Figure 61.

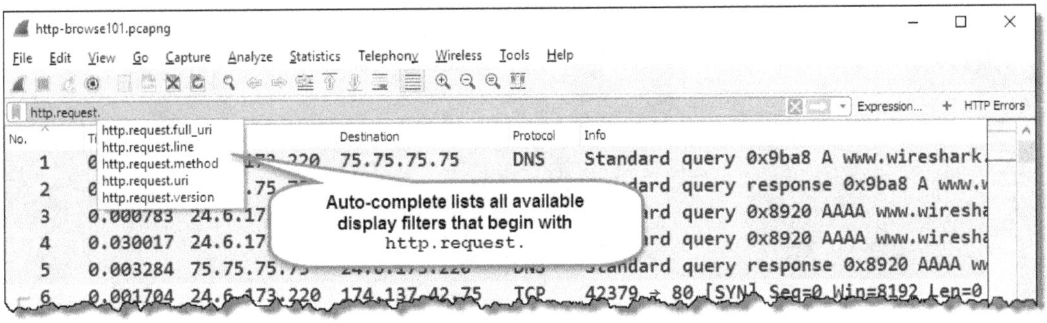

Figure 61. The auto-complete feature can help you build your display filter. [http-browse101.pcapng]

You can use this auto-complete feature to discover available display filters. For example, if you type **tcp.** (again including the dot), Wireshark lists all TCP filters available. If you type **tcp.analysis.,** Wireshark lists all of the TCP analysis filters dealing with TCP problems and performance, as shown in Figure 62. You can click on any listed filter to use it in the display filter area.

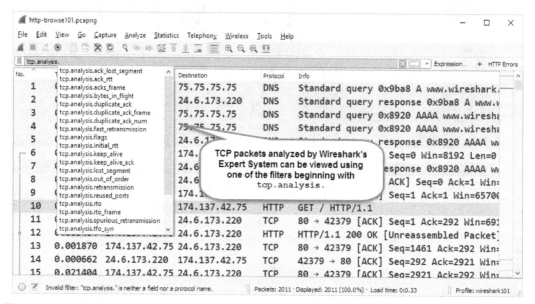

Figure 62. Type **tcp.analysis.** *to determine what TCP analysis flag filters are available.*
[http-browse101.pcapng]

Display Filter Comparison Operators

You can expand your filter to look for a particular value in a field. Wireshark supports numerous comparison operators for this purpose. The following table lists Wireshark's seven comparison operators.

Operation	English	Example	Description
==	eq	`ip.src == 10.2.2.2`	Display all IPv4 traffic from 10.2.2.2
!=	ne	`tcp.srcport != 80`	Display all TCP traffic from any port *except* port 80[34]
>	gt	`frame.time_relative > 1`	Display packets that arrived more than 1 second after the previous packet in the trace file
<	lt	`tcp.window_size < 1460`	Display when the TCP receive window size is less than 1460 bytes
>=	ge	`dns.count.answers >= 10`	Display DNS response packets that contain at least 10 answers
<=	le	`ip.ttl <= 10`	Display any packets that have 10 or less in the IP Time to Live field
	contains	`http contains "GET"`	Display all the HTTP client GET requests sent to HTTP servers

Use comparison operators when filtering for TCP-based applications. For example, if you want to see your HTTP traffic that runs over port 80, use `tcp.port==80`.

TIP

You do not need a space on either side of an operator. The filter `ip.src==10.2.2.2` works the same as `ip.src == 10.2.2.2`.

---

[34]   Be careful using the `!=` operator. Refer to *Why didn't my `ip.addr` != filter work?* on page 163 for more details on issues with this operator.

Use Expressions to Build Display Filters

If you absolutely have no idea how to filter on something, click the **Expression** button on the display filter toolbar. In the Filter Expression window, you can type the name of the application or protocol in which you are interested to jump to that point in the Field Name list. In Figure 63, we typed "SMB" in the Search area and expanded the SMB – SMB (Server Message Block Protocol) listing to view the available fields.

The Relation option can be used to either create a field existence filter (field is present) or to add a comparison operator. You may find predefined values for the field you select. Unfortunately, not all fields are broken out as thoroughly as the smb.nt_status field.

We selected smb.nt_status as the field, > as the relation and STATUS_SUCCESS as the predefined value. Wireshark displays the value 0x0 which is the value seen in the NT Status field in responses indicating success. Since we selected the > operator, we are looking for responses that are not successful (when the value is greater than 0x0 in the NT Status field). Wireshark placed smb.nt_status > 0x0 in the display filter area. We clicked the **OK** and then the display filter **Apply** button the place the filter on the traffic. LCLC NOTE that != is broken in Display Filter Expressions area.

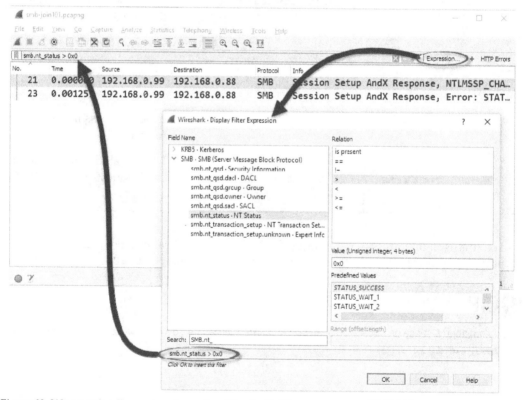

Figure 63. We are using Expressions to create a filter for SMB error responses (SMB NT status values greater than 0x0, STATUS_SUCCESS). [smb-join101.pcapng]

▣ Lab 14: Use Auto-Complete to Find Traffic to a Specific HTTP Server

In this lab we use Wireshark's auto-complete feature to filter on specific HTTP communications. Ultimately, we are interested in client requests to a particular server. This trace file, *http-sfgate101.pcapng*, was captured as someone browsed a web site and then filled in a feedback form on that site asking about iPad support.

Step 1:   Open ***http-sfgate101.pcapng***. Look through the trace file to get a feel for the traffic. You should see lots of DNS and HTTP traffic in this trace file. The target site, SF Gate, is an online paper focused on events in San Francisco, California. The online paper is owned by the Hearst Corporation—you will see numerous references to "Hearst" in the trace file[35].

Step 2:   We will use the auto-complete feature to begin this display filter. In the display filter area, type **http.** (including the dot). A drop-down menu appears listing all the filters available that begin with the **http.** pattern.

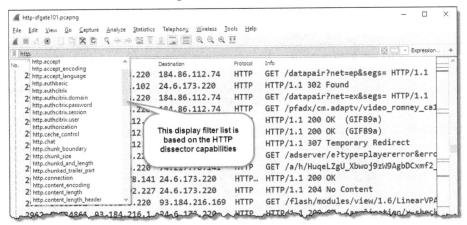

Step 3:   Let's use this list to find out what HTTP hosts were accessed in this trace file. Scroll down the list to find and click **http.host**. Click the **Apply** button ⏵ or press **Enter**. The Status Bar should indicate that 464 packets matched your filter. Each of those packets contains an HTTP Host field.

---

35   Yes—that is the same "Hearst" as Patty Hearst, the famous Symbionese Liberation Army (SLA) bank robber/millionaire socialite. The Hearst Corporation was founded by Patty Hearst's grandfather, William Randolph Hearst.

Step 4:   You certainly do not want to scroll through 464 packets to look into the HTTP Host field of each packet. Let's add a column for this field so we can easily see which hosts were contacted.

This **Host** column may already exist since you created this column in Lab 4. If your **Host** column is hidden, right-click on any column heading and enable the **Host** column entry.

If your **Host** column was not saved, click on any packet displayed, expand the **Hypertext Transfer Protocol** section in the Packet Details pane (use right-click and select **Expand Subtrees** to fully expand the HTTP section of the packet).

Right-click on the **Host** field and select **Apply as Column**.

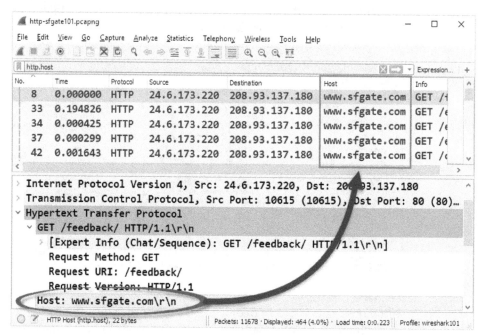

Step 5:   Scroll through the trace file to see the numerous hosts that the client requested files from during this web browsing session. Consider using this **Host** column when you are analyzing web browsing sessions.

Now let's find out what the client sent to a particular server. As mentioned earlier in this lab, SF Gate is owned by the Hearst Corporation.

Type in the display filter area to expand your display filter to `http.host contains "hearst"`.

Only 10 packets should match your filter now. In the image below, we can see why packet 159 is displayed. The word "hearst" appears in the http.host field.

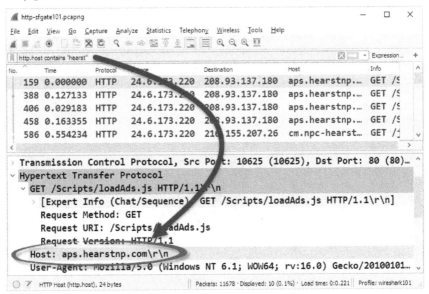

Step 6:   It's time to look specifically for a POST command.

First, examine the HTTP section of any packet in the Packet Details pane. Make sure the HTTP section is fully expanded. Click on the **Request Method** field in one of these HTTP packets (just a few lines above the Host field). Notice the name of the field in the Status Bar area—**http.request.method**. We are looking for a POST request method in this field. We know the field name and now we know the value we want to find.

In the display filter area, replace your current filter with **http.request.method=="POST"** and click the **Apply** button 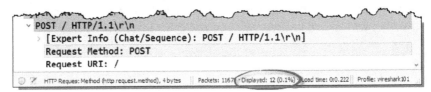 or press Enter [36].

Twelve packets should match your new filter.

---

[36] We could have also used **http.request.method contains "POST"**.

Step 7:   Scroll through the 12 packets to look for a reference to *extras.sfgate.com* in your **Host** column. That's the server on which the user posted the message about iPad support.

You should be looking at frame 10,022. Look through the Packet Bytes pane to read the message that was posted. You should see the name of the submitter too—Scooter. You could also see this information at the end of the HTTP section in the Packet Details pane (see the **HTML Form URL Encoded** section).

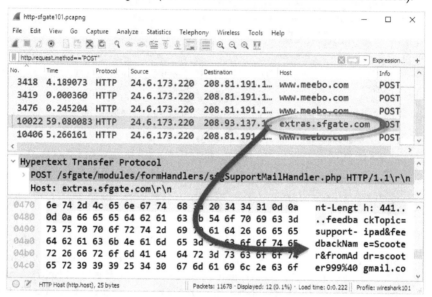

Step 8:   **LAB CLEAN-UP** Right-click on your new **Host** column and unselect that column from the list to hide it. If you want to view this column again later, you can right-click on any column heading and select it from the column list.

Click the **Clear** button ⊠ to remove your display filter.

Practice with Wireshark's display filters to extract just the traffic of interest. Keep reading through this chapter to learn various tips and tricks for display filtering.

3.2.   Edit and Use the Default Display Filters

You don't need to start from scratch. Wireshark includes many default display filters that you can use as a reference to make new display filters. Add to these default display filters to create a more efficient analysis system.

Click the Bookmark button ▌ in the display filter area to view saved predefined or custom filters as shown in Figure 64.

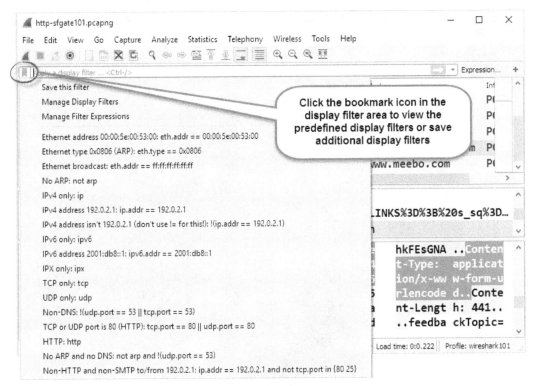

Figure 64. Consider removing any predefined display filters that you will not use. [http-sfgate101.pcapng]

Be careful before using a default display filter. The Ethernet and IP host filters have values that likely do not match your network. You must edit these filters or use these filters as a "seed" to create your own set of Ethernet or IP address filters. You will use this technique in Lab 15.

To quickly apply more complex filters to your traffic, you can easily add to this list of saved display filters.

TIP

Display filters are saved in a file called *dfilters*. It is just a text file and you can use any text editor to edit the file (to add filters, delete filters, or rearrange filters, for example). To find out where your *dfilters* file is, first look at the name of the profile in which you are working. The current profile name is shown on the right side of the Status Bar. If this area indicates you are in your "Default" profile, select **Help | About Wireshark | Folders** and double-click the Personal Configuration folder hyperlink. The *dfilters* file is in this directory.

If you are using a different profile, follow the same steps to open your Personal Configuration folder, but look for a *profiles* subdirectory. There will be a subdirectory under *profiles* that is named after each available profile. Look inside the appropriate profile directory to find the *dfilters* file.

Lab 15: Use a Default Filter as a "Seed" for a New Filter

You can use the default display filters as a template to create and save new custom display filters. This method helps you remember the display filter syntax and ensures that the syntax is correct. We will create a display filter for all traffic to or from your IP address.

Step 1:   To obtain your IP address, either click the **Capture Options** button ⊛ and expand the interface information or use the command-line tools *ipconfig* or *ifconfig*.

Step 2:   Click the display filter **Bookmark** button ▌ (to the left of the display filter area) and select **Manage Display Filters**.

Step 3:   Select the **IPv4 address 192.0.2.1** display filter and click the **Copy** button ▐▌. This creates a new copy of that default display filter and places it at the bottom of the display filter list.

Step 4:   Change the new filter name to "**My IP Address**" and replace 192.0.2.1 with your IP address in the Filter area. We used the IP address 10.1.0.1 in our example below.

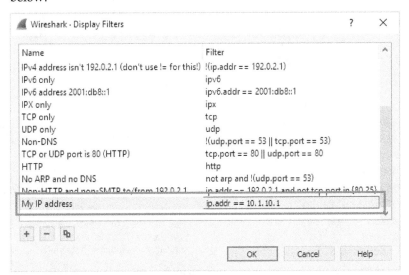

Step 5:   Click **OK** to save your new display filter and close the Display Filter window. When you want to use this filter, you can now click the Bookmark button and select it off the saved display filter list.

Spend some time creating a set of filters based on your Wireshark system's IP address and MAC address (an Ethernet address filter). You might want to delete default filters that you do not need, for example, if you plan to type the display filter for TCP only traffic (tcp), you can delete this filter. If you never plan on using one of the display filters (IPX only, perhaps), delete it. Keep your filter list as clean as possible.

3.3. Filter Properly on HTTP Traffic

Being able to properly filter on browsing sessions is important when you are troubleshooting your own web browsing session or helping determine why the company web site loads slowly. Don't make the most common mistake of all—using an application name in your filter.

There are two methods used to filter on HTTP traffic.

> http
> tcp.port==xx (where xx denotes the HTTP port in use)

The second filter method is a better option when analyzing traffic. Let's examine why by comparing the use of each filter on a trace file of a web browsing session.

Test an Application Filter Based on a TCP Port Number

First let's open *http-wiresharkdownload101.pcapng*. This trace file contains a connection to *www.wireshark.org* and a request to download a copy of Wireshark. We applied the tcp.port==80 display filter and find that, indeed, all of the packets match our filter, as shown in Figure 65. That's good because that's all we have in the trace file.

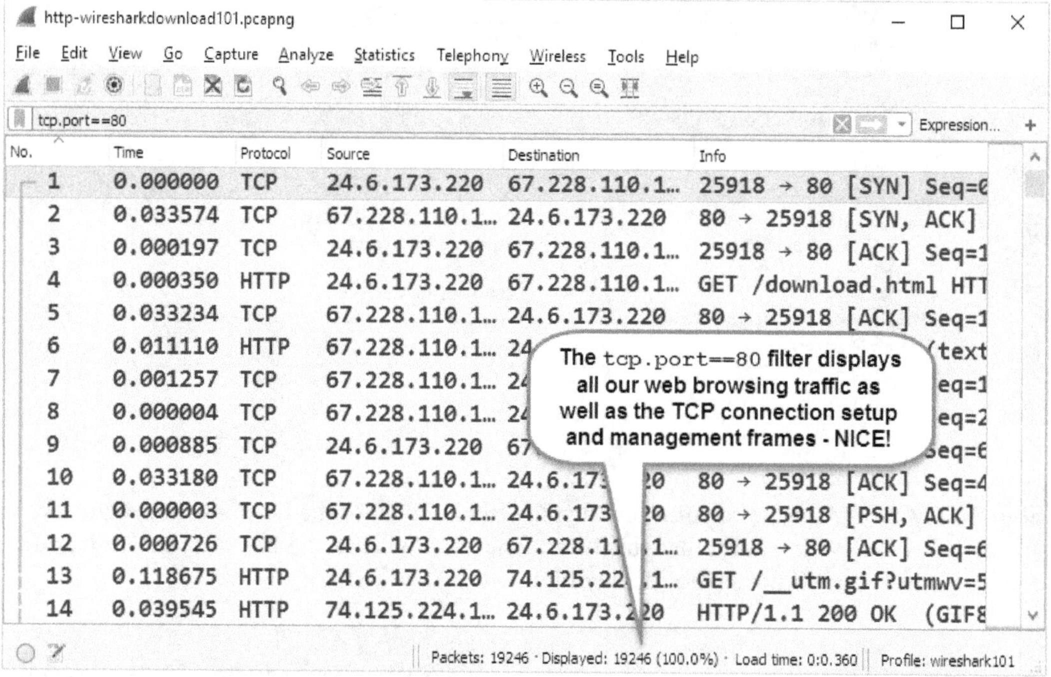

Figure 65. Our port number-based filter displays all the packets in this wireshark.org browsing session. [http-wiresharkdownload101.pcapng]

Look closely at the **Protocol** column of packet 20 in Figure 65 (also shown below).

| 20 | 0.056291 | 67.228.110.1… | 24.6.173.220 | TCP | 80 → 25919 [ACK] Seq=1 … |

Notice that Wireshark indicates this is a TCP packet, not an HTTP packet. Wireshark doesn't see any HTTP commands or responses in the packet so the HTTP dissector wasn't applied to the packet. It's just a TCP packet (TCP ACKs, FINs, RSTs, and the three-way TCP handshake are simply listed as TCP).

If you want to see the TCP connection establishment, maintenance and teardown packets, this is the filter to use (and you always want to see those TCP packets, by the way).

Be Cautious Using a TCP-based Application Name Filter

Now let's see what happened when we placed the `http` filter on the traffic. In Figure 66, you can see that Wireshark displays 85 packets. Those are the packets that contain HTTP in the **Protocol** column.

Note: If you see only 12 frames, your TCP preference is set to reassemble TCP streams. Review Lab 5 to properly configure Wireshark for this lab.

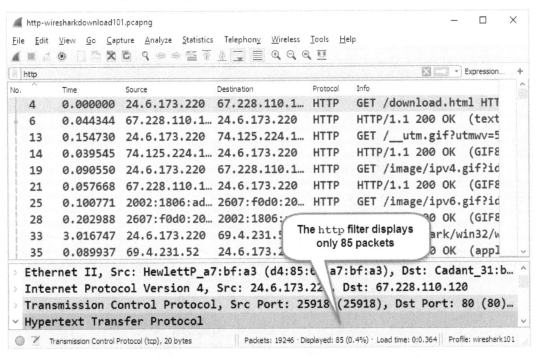

Figure 66. The `http` filter does not show the TCP handshake, ACKs, or connection teardown process. [http-wiresharkdownload101.pcapng]

This is an incomplete picture of the web browsing session and we wouldn't be able to detect TCP errors using this http filter. It is always better to use a port number filter on applications that use TCP.

TIP

Unfortunately, Wireshark's default filter for HTTP traffic is simply http. Consider editing this default filter to look for HTTP traffic based on a port number.

📖 Lab 16: Filter on HTTP Traffic the Right Way

This is a quick lab. We will just compare the results from applying two different display filters to the traffic. We will use `http` and then we will replace it with the proper filter for this web browsing traffic.

Step 1:   Open *http-disney101.pcapng*. If you still have a filter applied from following along with the earlier section, simply click the **Clear** button ❌ to remove it.

Step 2:   Apply an **http** filter. How many frames matched your filter? You should see 4,093 frames. If 205 frames are displayed, your TCP preference is set to reassemble TCP streams. Follow the instructions in Lab 5 to disable this TCP preference setting.

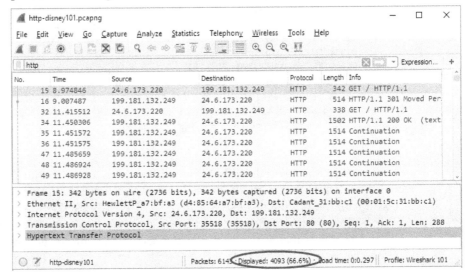

Step 3:   Replace your filter with **tcp.port==80** and click the **Apply** button 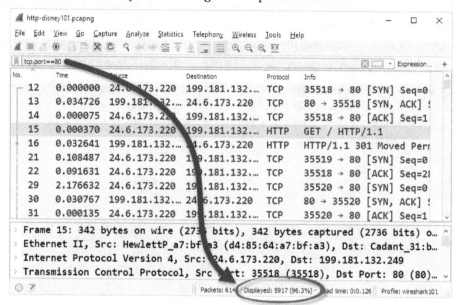 or press **Enter**. How many packets matched your filter now? (5,917 packets?) That's much better—you are seeing the full picture now.

Scroll through the trace file with this new filter in place. Notice the **Protocol** column indicates that many of the packets are TCP, not HTTP. Wireshark classifies all the TCP handshake packets and TCP ACK packets as simply "TCP." We want to see these packets because we want to analyze the entire web browsing session, including the connection establishment process and acknowledgments.

Step 4:   **LAB CLEAN-UP** Click the **Clear** button ⊠ to remove your display filter before continuing.

Always try to build application display filters based on port numbers. Although Wireshark's display filtering mechanism understands various application names, you won't get a complete picture if you use application names in your filters.

3.4. Determine Why Your `dhcp` Display Filter Doesn't Work

This catches everyone who doesn't have grey hair. We are so accustomed to talking about DHCP on an IPv4 network without acknowledging that DHCP is based on BOOTP. You only have to learn this frustrating rule once, thank goodness.

If you type just dhcp as your display filter, the display filter area turns red indicating a syntax problem, as shown in Figure 67. (Color images are only available in ebook format.)

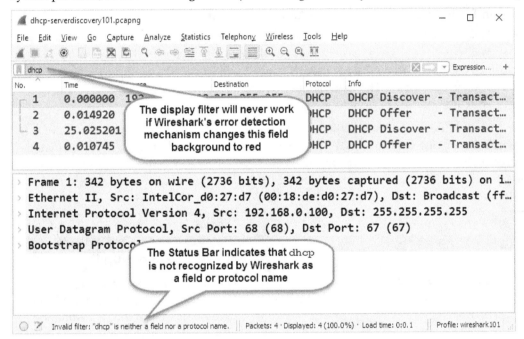

Figure 67. Since DHCP over IPv4 is based on BOOTP, you must use `bootp` as your filter – dhcp won't work. [dhcp-serverdiscovery101.pcapng]

Although the **Protocol** column indicates the packets are DHCP, this filter will not work because DHCP is based on BOOTP (Bootstrap Protocol).

The correct display filter syntax is **bootp**.

If you want to display DHCPv6 traffic, however, you can use dhcpv6 (DHCPv6 is not based on BOOTP).

3.5. Apply Display Filters based on an IP Address, Range of Addresses, or Subnet

Instead of applying a capture filter (and possibly missing related traffic because it was tossed aside during the capture process), use display filters to focus on someone's traffic. These IP address display filters are probably the most widely used filters. There are many options available when you want to see traffic to or from a specific IP address, range of addresses, or subnet.

Filter on Traffic to or from a Single IP Address or Host

We will use the field names `ip.src`, `ip.dst`, `ip.host`, and `ip.addr` for IPv4 traffic and `ipv6.src`, `ipv6.dst`, `ipv6.host`, and `ipv6.addr` for IPv6 traffic. Note that when you click on an IP address in the Packet Details pane, it will be called `ip.src`, `ip.dst`, `ipv6.src`, or `ipv6.dst`. The field names `ip.host` and `ipv6.host` and `ip.addr` and `ipv6.addr` do not exist in packets.

The `ip.host` and `ipv6 host` filters looks for any IPv4 or IPv6 addresses that resolve to a specific host name in either the IPv4/IPv6 source address field or IPv4/IPv6 destination address field. The `ip.addr==[address]` and `ipv6.addr==[address]` filters looks for specific IPv4/IPv6 addresses in either the IPv4/IPv6 source address field or IPv4/IPv6 destination address field.

`ip.addr==10.3.1.1`	Display frames that have 10.3.1.1 in the IP source address field or the IP destination address field
`!ip.addr==10.3.1.1`	Display all frames *except* frames that have 10.3.1.1 in the IP source address field or 10.3.1.1 in the IP destination address field
`ipv6.addr==2406:da00:ff00::6b16:f02d`	Display all frames to or from 2406:da00:ff00::6b16:f02d
`ip.src==10.3.1.1`	Display traffic *from* 10.3.1.1
`ip.dst==10.3.1.1`	Display traffic *to* 10.3.1.1
`ip.host==www.wireshark.org`[37]	Display traffic to or from the IP address that resolves to *www.wireshark.org*

---

[37] You must enable Wireshark's **Resolve network (IP) addresses** setting (**Edit | Preferences | Name Resolution**) in order to use this display filter.

Filter on Traffic to or from a Range of Addresses

You can use the `ip.addr` or `ipv6.addr` filters with the > or < comparison operators and the logical operator && (and) to look for packets that contain an address within a range.

`ip.addr > 10.3.0.1 &&` `ip.addr < 10.3.0.5`	Display traffic to or from 10.3.0.2, 10.3.0.3 or 10.3.0.4

`(ip.addr >= 10.3.0.1 &&`
`ip.addr <= 10.3.0.6) &&`
`!ip.addr==10.3.0.3`
	Display traffic to or from 10.3.0.1, 10.3.0.2, 10.3.0.4, 10.3.0.5 or 10.3.0.6 — the IP address 10.3.0.3 is excluded from the range specified

`ipv6.addr >= fe80:: &&` `ipv6.addr < fec0::`	Display traffic to or from IPv6 addresses beginning with 0xfe80 through 0xfec0.

Filter on Traffic to or from an IP Subnet

You can define a subnet in CIDR (Classless Interdomain Routing) format with the `ip.addr` field name. This format uses the IP address followed by a slash and a suffix that indicates the number of bits that define the network portion of the IP address.

`ip.addr==10.3.0.0/16`	Display traffic that contains an IP address starting with 10.3 in the source IP address field or destination IP address field
`ip.addr==10.3.0.0/16 &&` `!ip.addr==10.3.1.1`	Display traffic that contains an IP address starting with 10.3 in the source IP address field or destination IP address field *except* 10.3.1.1
`!ip.addr==10.3.0.0/16 &&` `!ip.addr==10.2.0.0/16`	Display all traffic except traffic that contains an IP address starting with 10.3 or 10.2 in the source IP address field or destination IP address field

📖 Lab 17: Filter on Traffic to or from Online Backup Subnets

In this lab, we will apply a subnet display filter to examine traffic to or from a backup server for Memeo which offers an online backup product. This traffic runs in the background, constantly checking in with the server.

Step 1:   Open *mybackground101.pcapng*.

Step 2:   Apply a display filter for DNS traffic. Note the IP addresses supplied for the *api.memeo.info*, *api.memeo.com*, and *memeo.info* hosts. They all begin with 216.115.74. We will build a subnet filter based on these starting bytes. We scrolled to the right in the image below to see more of the **Info** column.

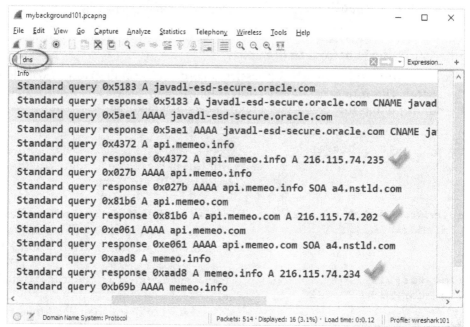

Step 3:   Apply a display filter for `ip.addr==216.115.74.0/24` to view all traffic to or from any of the hosts on this subnet. There should be 51 packets that match your display filter.

Step 4:   **LAB CLEAN-UP** Click the **Clear** button ❌ to remove your display filter before continuing.

If you want to filter the traffic to or from the Memeo subnets *out* of view, apply the same filter, but precede it with the not ("!") operator)— `!ip.addr==216.115.74.0/24`.

3.6. Quickly Filter on a Field in a Packet

When you're looking for all traffic that contains a particular characteristic, you can go the long way or take the short path. Unless you are training for a marathon, take the short path. Although you can type display filters and click the **Apply** button 🔲 or press **Enter**, using the right-click method is a faster way to build and apply display filters.

You can right-click on any field or characteristic in a packet and select either **Apply as Filter** (which creates and applies the filter right away) or **Prepare a Filter** (which puts the new filter in the display filter area, but does not automatically apply it to the trace file).

Work Quickly – Use Right-Click | Apply as Filter

For example, in Figure 68 we opened *http-espn101.pcapng*. In the Packet Details pane of frame 8, we expanded the HTTP section and right-clicked on the **Request URI** line that indicates the user wants to download the main page of a web site (/). We selected **Apply as Filter | Selected**.

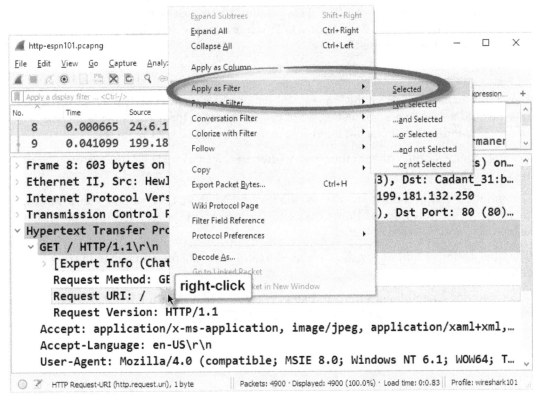

Figure 68. Use the right-click method to quickly apply a filter based on content in a field or on a packet characteristic. [http-espn101.pcapng]

Wireshark creates the proper display filter (`http.request.uri=="/"`) and applies it to the trace file. We now have two packets displayed. It appears this user is requesting the main page from two different IP addresses, as shown in Figure 69.

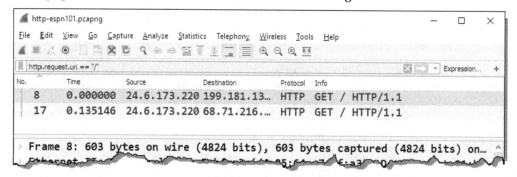

Figure 69. Two packets matched our filter for `http.request.uri=="/"`. [http-espn101.pcapng]

If you want to exclude these types of HTTP requests from view, simply add an exclamation point or the word *not* before the filter. This is called an *exclusion filter*. You can also create this exclusion filter by right-clicking on a GET request for the default page and selecting **Apply as Filter | Not Selected**[38].

Using this exclusion filter on the *http-espn101.pcapng* trace file would display 4,898 packets, but it would not be a very interesting set of packets to wade through. Consider expanding this filter to indicate that you are interested in the other HTTP GET requests.

Leaving your exclusion filter in the display filter area, locate an HTTP GET request packet (packet 70, for example).

Expand the HTTP section so you can see the Request Method: GET request line. Right-click this line and select **Apply as Filter**. This time you are going to add on to the existing filter using the **...and Selected** option.

The filter options beginning with ... are used to add on to the filter shown in the display filter area.

After selecting **... and Selected**, your display filter should look as follows. Now 146 packets match your filter. You are looking at all the HTTP GET requests *except* for the default page requests (/).

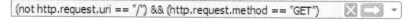

---

[38] You do not need to clear the previous filter because the new filter will replace the existing one.

Be Creative with Right-Click | Prepare a Filter

Use **Prepare a filter** when you want to change the filter or check the syntax before it is applied. For example, perhaps you want to know if anyone has made a request for a .jpg file. Right-click the Request URI line in packet 70 of *http-espn101.pcapng* and select **Prepare a Filter | Selected**.

Wireshark places `http.request.uri=="/prod/scripts/mbox.js"` in the display filter area, but it does not apply the filter to the traffic. Change the display filter to `http.request.uri contains "jpg"` and click the **Apply** button ▭ or press **Enter**. Twenty-two packets should match your new filter, as shown in Figure 70.

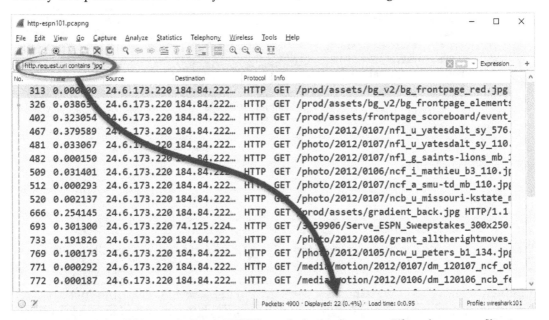

*Figure 70. After right-clicking on the Request URI line and selecting **Prepare a Filter**, change your filter to look for frames that contain "jpg" in this field. [http-espn101.pcapng]*

Right-Click Again to use the "..." Filter Enhancements

When you performed the right-click **Apply as Filter** and **Prepare a Filter** operations, you saw four other filter options that begin with "...", as shown in Figure 71. In this example, we still have our `http.request.uri contains "jpg "` filter and we also want to look for *go.espn.com* in the Referer[39] line.

---

[39]   This is not a typo. The HTTP specifications spell Referer this way (with a missing "r").

Any filter option that begins with "…" will be appended to the existing display filter.

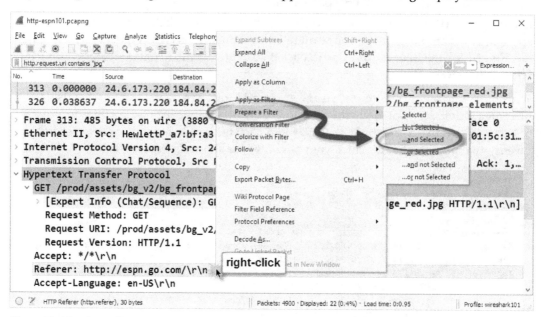

Figure 71. Use the … filter options to expand an existing display filter. [http-espn101.pcapng]

Your new filter would look like this:

The following table demonstrates how the add-on filters can be used if we already have a `tcp.port==80` filter in place.

Right-click on...	Choose	Filter Created (description)
Request Method: GET	Selected	`http.request.method == "GET"` This will replace the current display filter and display all HTTP packets that contain the GET request method.
Request Method: GET	Not Selected	`!(http.request.method == "GET")` This will replace the current display filter and display any packets *except* HTTP packets that contain the HTTP GET request method.

Request Method: GET	... and Selected	`(tcp.port==80) && (http.request.method == "GET")`
		This will display packets to or from port 80 that contain the HTTP GET request method.
Request Method: GET	... or Selected	`(tcp.port==80) || (http.request.method == "GET")`
		This will display packets to or from port 80 as well as any HTTP packets that contain the GET request method. For example, if your HTTP traffic uses port 81, you will still see all the HTTP GET requests from that traffic.
Request Method: GET	... and not Selected	`(tcp.port==80) && !(http.request.method == "GET")`
		This will display all traffic to or from port 80, but not any HTTP packets on that port that contain the GET request method.
IP Source Address 10.2.2.2	... or not Selected	`(tcp.port==80) || !(ip.src==10.2.2.2)`
		This will display packets to or from port 80 or any traffic that is not from 10.2.2.2

TIP

Watch out for the **...or not Selected option**. Many times people use this by mistake when they want to add on to an exclusion filter (something that hides specific traffic types).

For example, if you don't want to see ARP traffic or DNS traffic, using the **...or not Selected** option would create `!arp || !dns`. This filter would not do anything. DNS packets would be shown because they are not ARP packets (matching the first side of the *or* operator) and ARP packets would be shown because they are not DNS packets (matching the second side of the *or* operator).

If you are trying to filter packets out of view, most likely you want the **...and not Selected** option.

🖥 Lab 18: Filter on DNS Name Errors or HTTP 404 Responses

In this lab we will look for specific DNS or HTTP error responses using the right-click method. This is a great filter that you may want to save.

Step 1:   Open *http-errors101.pcapng*. Scroll through and look at the **Info** column of the Packet List pane to see the problems in this web browsing session. If you applied a filter while following along in the earlier section, clear it now.

Step 2:   Click on **frame 18**. This is a DNS Name Error response. Expand the DNS subtrees so you can see the fields inside the Flags section, as shown below. Right-click on the **Reply code: No such name (3)** field and select **Prepare a Filter | Selected**. The first part of your filter appears in the filter area.

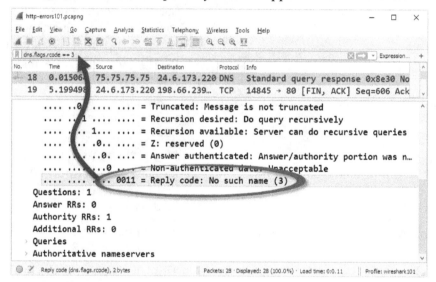

Step 3:   Click on **frame 9**. This is an HTTP 404 Response. We will add on to our existing filter and view it before applying it.

In frame 9, expand the **HTTP section of the packet**. Right-click on the **Status Code: 404** line, select **Prepare a Filter | ...or Selected**. Your display filter area should show the following:

`(dns.flags.rcode==3) || (http.response.code==404).`

Step 4:   Click the **Apply** button 🔜 or press **Enter**. Three frames should match your filter.

Step 5:   **LAB CLEAN-UP** Click the **Clear** button ✖ to remove the filter. If you need to use this filter again soon, click the arrow to the right of the filter area. We set Wireshark to remember the last 30 display filters in Lab 5.

This is a great filter, but it can be improved by looking for all DNS or HTTP error reply codes (`dns.flags.rcode != 0 or http.response.code > 399`). Note that the display filter area turns yellow because of the "`!=`", but this filter will actually work fine.

3.7. Filter on a Single TCP or UDP Conversation

When you want to analyze communication between a client application and a server process, you are looking for a "conversation." That conversation is based on the IP addresses and port numbers of the client application and the server process. Often your trace file will contain hundreds of conversations. Knowing how to quickly locate and filter on the conversation you are interested in will move your analysis process forward quickly.

The following lists four ways to extract a single TCP or UDP conversation from a trace file:

- Extract a UDP/TCP conversation by right-clicking a UDP or TCP packet in the Packet List pane and selecting **Conversation Filter | [TCP|UDP]**.

- Extract a UDP/TCP conversation by right-clicking a UDP or TCP packet in the Packet List pane and selecting **Follow | [TCP|UDP] Stream**.

- Extract a conversation from Wireshark **Statistics | Conversations.**

- Extract a UDP/TCP conversation based on the stream index number (in the UDP or TCP header).

Use Right-Click to Filter on a Conversation

When you browse through packets and you want to quickly filter on a TCP conversation, right-click on any packet in the Packet List pane and select **Conversation Filter | TCP**, as shown in Figure 72.

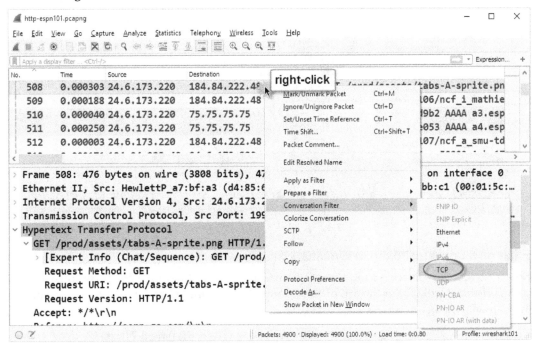

Figure 72. Right-click on a packet to filter on a specific conversation. [http-espn101.pcapng]

We right-clicked on **packet 508** in *http-espn101.pcapng* and selected **Conversation Filter |
TCP**. Wireshark created and applied the following display filter to the traffic:

> (ip.addr eq 24.6.173.220 and ip.addr eq 184.84.222.48)
>   and (tcp.port eq 19953 and tcp.port eq 80)

You can use the same method to filter on a conversation based on IP addresses, Ethernet
addresses, or UDP address/port number combinations.

Use Right-Click to Follow a Stream

To view the application commands and data exchanged in a conversation as well as apply a
conversation filter, right-click on any packet in the Packet List pane and select **Follow |
[TCP|UDP] Stream**, as shown in Figure 73. If you select **Follow | UDP Stream** or **Follow
| TCP Stream**, the display filter will be based on the UDP or TCP Stream Index field value.

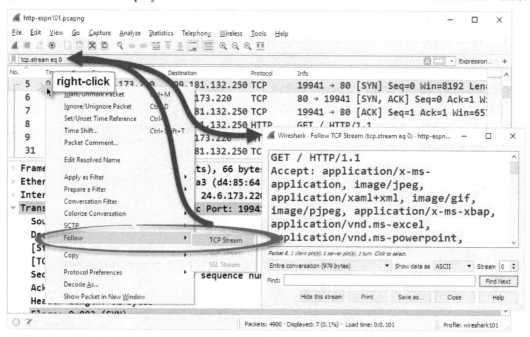

*Figure 73. Right-click on a TCP or UDP packet in the Packet List pane and select **Follow | [TCP|UDP]
Stream**. This creates a conversation filter based on the selected packet while displaying the conversation in a
separate window.*

Filter on a Conversation from Wireshark Statistics

Select **Statistics | Conversations** to view, sort, and quickly filter on a conversation. Click
one of the protocol tabs at the top of the Conversations window to select the conversation
type in which you are interested.

Right-click on a conversation line to select **Apply as Filter**, **Prepare a Filter**, **Find**, or
Colorize.

When you select **Apply as Filter** or **Prepare a Filter**, some interesting options appear. In Figure 74, we selected **Statistics | Conversations** and sorted on the **Packets** column. Next, we right-clicked on the top conversation and saw the option to apply or prepare a filter using the standard options (**Selected**, **Not Selected**, etc.). We can also choose to define the direction or inclusion of "Any" in the filter.

Under the **UDP** and **TCP** tabs, the term "A" refers to both columns labeled with "A" – the **Address A** column and the **Port A** column (`ip.addr==24.6.173.220 && tcp.port==19996`).

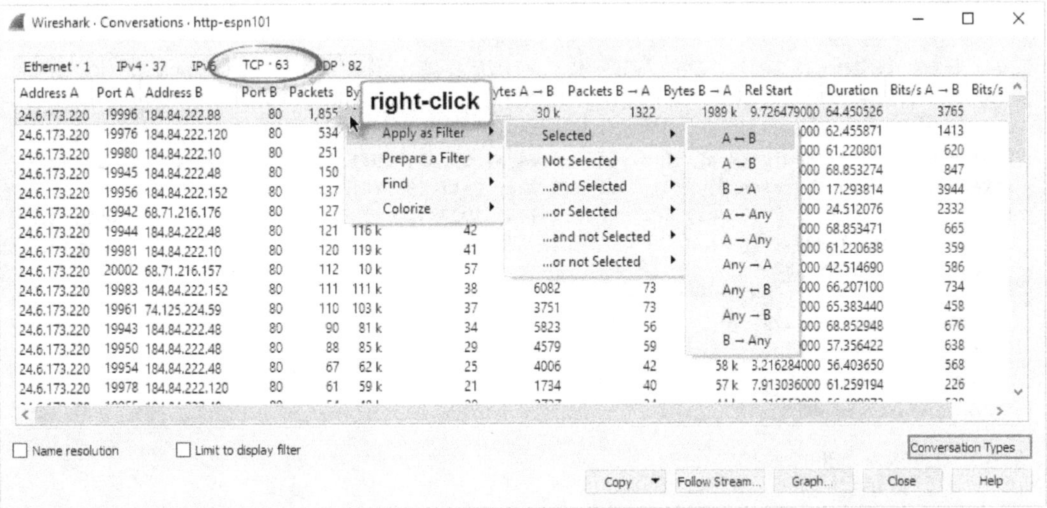

Figure 74. Right-click on a row and select **Apply as Filter** to view special options for conversation filtering. [http-espn101.pcapng]

!TIP

You can perform the same basic steps from the **Statistics | Endpoints** window, although you will not have the "A" and "B" designations available.

Filter on a TCP or UDP Conversation Based on the Stream Index Field

In TCP or UDP headers, you can also right-click on the Stream Index field to create a conversation filter. In Figure 75, we expanded a TCP header, right-clicked on the Stream Index field, and selected **Apply as Filter**, which created a `tcp.stream==2` conversation filter.

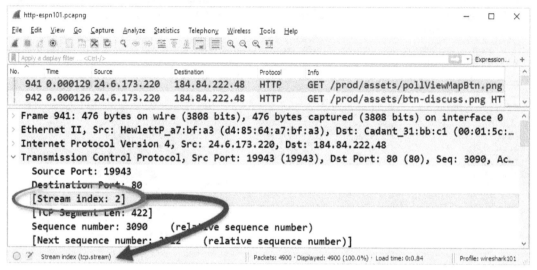

Figure 75. Wireshark gives each TCP and UDP conversation a unique Stream index number. [http-espn101.pcapng]

TIP

This stream index number can be a great help when you are working with a trace file that has many intertwined conversations. Right-click on this field and select **Apply as Column**. Use the values in your **TCP Stream index** column to easily identify separate conversations.

💻 Lab 19: Detect Background File Transfers on Startup

There may be a number of background processes that run when you start up your machine. Some of these may update your virus detection mechanism, your operating system, or applications. In this lab, you will detect and filter on the most active conversation of a host (24.6.169.43) that is just starting up.

Step 1: Open *gen-startupchatty101.pcapng*.

Step 2: Select **Statistics | Conversations | TCP** and sort the **Bytes** column from high to low to locate the most active TCP conversation based on byte count.

Step 3: Right-click on the most active conversation and select **Apply as Filter | Selected | A ⬅➡ B**. The Status Bar should indicate 2,886 packets matched your filter. The TCP peer in this conversation is 50.17.223.168.

We can see this is a Transport Layer Security (TLS) conversation.

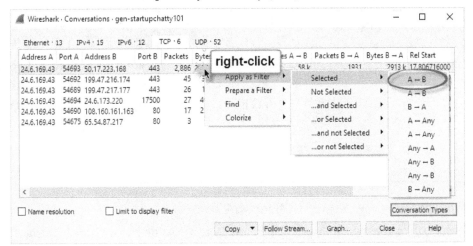

Step 4: Frame 311 is the first packet in this conversation. Click the **Clear** button ⊠ to remove your filter and look for a name resolution process before frame 311. Based on frames 309 and 310, this appears to be a Dropbox server. The client must be checking in and downloading a file from their Dropbox folder.

Step 5: **LAB CLEAN-UP** Click the **Clear** button ⊠ to remove any unwanted display filters.

You can use the right-click method to quickly apply filters directly from many Wireshark statistics windows, including the Conversations, Endpoints, and Protocol Hierarchy windows.

3.8. Expand Display Filters with Multiple Include and Exclude Conditions

There will be many times when you want to filter on the values in more than one field. For example, you might be interested in seeing all packets that contain the command GET in the HTTP Request Method field and ".exe" in the HTTP Request URI field. You should combine these two conditions using a logical operator.

Use Logical Operators

Wireshark understands four logical operators. The next table provides examples of how Wireshark logical operators can be used to expand your display filters by adding conditions.

Operator	English	Example	Description
&&	and	`ip.src==10.2.2.2 && tcp.port==80`	View all IPv4 traffic from 10.2.2.2 that is to or from port 80
||	or	`tcp.port==80 || tcp.port==443`	View all TCP traffic to or from ports 80 or 443
!	not	`!arp`	View all traffic *except* ARP traffic
!=	ne	`tcp.flags.syn != 1`	View TCP frames that do not have the TCP SYN flag (synchronize sequence numbers) set to 1

Why didn't my `ip.addr != ` filter work?

People often get stuck on the != operator. Here are some tips on how Wireshark interprets this operator.

Incorrect: `ip.addr != 10.2.2.2`

Display packets that do not have 10.2.2.2 in the IP source address field *or* IP destination address field. If an address other than 10.2.2.2 is contained in the source *or* destination IP address fields, the packet will be displayed. This uses an implied *or* and will not filter out any packets.

Correct: `!ip.addr == 10.2.2.2`

Display packets that do not have 10.2.2.2 in the IP source address field and also does not have 10.2.2.2 in the destination address field. This is the proper filter syntax when excluding traffic to or from a specific IP address.

Why didn't my `!tcp.flags.syn==1` filter work?

Just when you begin to embrace the process of splitting up the "`!`" from the "`=`"… something isn't quite right. If you were trying to display all TCP packets that did not have the SYN bit set to 1, this filter will not work.

Incorrect: `!tcp.flags.syn==1`

This filter is interpreted as "display all packets that do not have a TCP SYN bit set to 1." Other protocol packets, such as UDP and ARP packets will match this filter, after all, they don't have a TCP SYN bit set to 1.

Correct: `tcp.flags.syn != 1`

This filter will only display TCP packets that contain a SYN set to 0.

On a Boolean field, such as the SYN bit field, it is much more efficient to simply filter on the bit set to a 0 if that is what you are interested in. For example, just use `tcp.flags.syn==0` in this case.

TIP

Don't be afraid to use the `!` = operator when you know there is only one field that matches your filter field name. Sometimes this is the best filter operator to use. If you aren't sure if only one field matches the filter field name, you can find the field in the Expressions dialog (click on the Expressions button) and look for "or." For example, ip.addr is listed as "Source or Destination address."

3.9.   Use Parentheses to Change Filter Meaning

Be aware how parentheses can change the meaning of your filters when you create and add conditions to your filter.

For example, consider the following display filters:

```
(tcp.port==80 && ip.src==10.2.2.2) || tcp.flags.syn==1

tcp.port==80 && (ip.src==10.2.2.2 || tcp.flags.syn==1)
```

Placement of parentheses changes the meaning of these two filters.

In the first example above, port 80 traffic from 10.2.2.2 will be displayed. In addition, all TCP packets that have the SYN bit set (regardless of port numbers or IP addresses) will be displayed.

In the second example above, port 80 traffic will be displayed as long as the traffic is either (a) from 10.2.2.2, or (b) the traffic has the TCP SYN bit set.

TIP

Always use parentheses when you mix "and" with "or" in your filters. If you don't, Wireshark will turn the display filter background area yellow to warn you that you may not get the results you expected.

🖥 Lab 20: Locate TCP Connection Attempts to a Client

Client processes send TCP connection requests to server processes. There are very few reasons to allow incoming TCP connections to user machines on your network (as they typically won't be running server processes). In this lab we will create a display filter that detects incoming TCP connection attempts to anyone on a particular subnet. We will focus on subnet 24.6.0.0/16.

Step 1:   Open *general101b.pcapng*.

Step 2:   We first want to detect TCP connection attempts based on the TCP flags area. The first frame in this trace file is a TCP connection request as noted by the [SYN] in the **Info** column. The response indicates [SYN, ACK] in the **Info** column.

In the Packet List pane, expand the **TCP header** of frame 1 and right-click on the **Flags** line. Select **Prepare a Filter | Selected**. This `tcp.flags==0x0002` filter will display the first packet (SYN) of the TCP handshake.

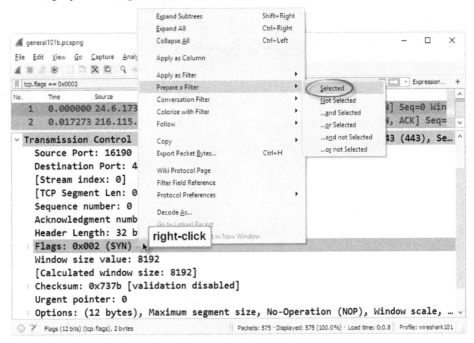

If we had created a filter for just the TCP SYN bit set to 1
(`tcp.flags.syn==1`), we would see the first two packets of each handshake (the SYN and SYN/ACK packets).

Step 3:   Click the **Apply** button ⟶ or press **Enter** to see what this filter does.
            Unfortunately, this filter alone won't help us. We want to see if anyone tries to
            make a TCP connection to any of our clients on this network. Add **&&**
            ip.dst==24.6.0.0/16 to your filter and click the **Apply** button ⟶ or press
            Enter again. Only 5 packets should match your new filter.

            Our results in this lab indicate that 121.125.72.180 and 24.6.169.43 are trying to
            make a connection to 24.6.173.220. Since our 24.6.173.220 client doesn't run
            server software, this is questionable traffic.

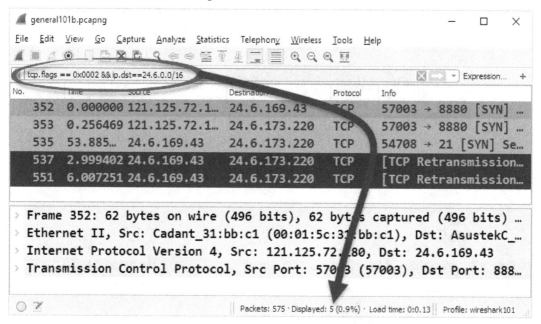

Step 4:   **LAB CLEAN-UP** Click the **Clear** button ☒ to remove your display filter before
            continuing.

Run this same filter on *mybackground101.pcapng* to spot another suspicious incoming
connection attempt. We found this incoming connection attempt in *Analyze Sample
Background Traffic* on page 47.

3.10. Determine Why Your Display Filter Area is Yellow

As you become more adventurous putting together display filters, you will likely hit a point when Wireshark colors the display filter area yellow or even red. Wireshark performs error detection on every display filter and, based on the error detection results, colors your display filter area background red (error), green (ok), or yellow (what the heck?).

Red Background: Syntax Check Failed

When the display filter area is red, the filter will not work at all. When you click the **Apply** button or press **Enter**, Wireshark will generate a message such as *"ip.addr=10.2.2.2" isn't a valid display filter: "=" was unexpected in this context. See the help for a description of the display filter syntax.*

Green Background: Syntax Check Passed

When the display filter background is green, the filter will work based on the syntax checks. Wireshark does not do a "logic check," however. Consider the filter `http && udp`. Normal HTTP communications run over TCP, not UDP. No packets should match this filter. Although the filter is illogical, it can be processed because it passes the syntax check.

Yellow Background: Syntax Check Passed with a Warning (! =)

When the display filter background is yellow, the filter has passed the syntax check, but may not give you the results you expect. This color is automatically triggered when Wireshark sees " ! =" in a filter. Remember to avoid this filter when you specify a field name that may match two actual fields in a packet. For example, `ip.addr` indicates you are looking at both the source and destination IPv4 address fields. Another example would be `tcp.port` which would look at both the source and destination port number fields.

If you use a field name that refers to a single-occurrence field, go ahead and use the " ! =" syntax. For example, `ip.src != 10.2.3.1` would work perfectly even though Wireshark colored the display filter background yellow. There is only one field that could match this filter.

TIP

The two most common causes of a red background are (1) a typo in the filter and (2) using capture filter syntax instead of display filter syntax. No matter what you try to do, a filter with a red background will not run on Wireshark.

3.11. Filter on a Keyword in a Trace File

There will be times when you are looking for a particular word, such as "admin" in a trace file. You may want to look through entire frames or in particular fields. You may even want to search for a text string in upper case, lower case, or mixed case. All of these are possible.

Use `contains` in a Simple Keyword Filter through an Entire Frame

You can use `frame contains "string"` to look for a keyword throughout a frame. For example, `frame contains "admin"` would look for the string *admin* (all in lower case) through the entire frame, from the Ethernet header through the Ethernet trailer.

This is really a simple and lazy filter. It might yield too many false positives. For example, if you use this filter when you are only interested in finding out if someone tried to log in to the admin FTP account, you might also see people browsing to *www.admin.com* and file requests for *adminhandbook.pdf*.

Use `contains` in a Simple Keyword Filter based on a Field

Consider building your filter to look just at the field of interest to reduce false positives. For example, if you look inside an FTP packet that contains a user name (packet 6 in *ftp-clientside101.pcapng*) and expand the FTP portion fully in the Packet Details pane, you'll see the FTP user's name is in the `ftp.request.arg` field as noted on the Status Bar in Figure 76. You can simply type the filter `ftp.request.arg contains "anonymous"` to look for "anonymous" in the FTP request argument field. You should find one packet that matches this filter in *ftp-clientside101.pcapng*.

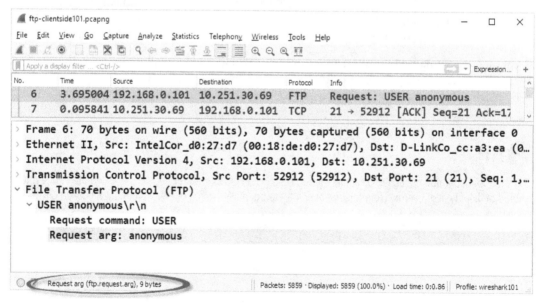

Figure 76. Click on a field and look at the Status Bar to find out the field name to use in your filters. [ftp-clientside101.pcapng]

Use `matches` and `(?i)` in a Keyword Filter for Upper Case or Lower Case Strings

If you are looking for "Anonymous" with an initial upper case *or* lower case letter, you can expand your last display filter with a logical operator. The filter `ftp.request.arg contains "Anonymous" or ftp.request.arg contains "anonymous"` would work.

Wireshark supports Perl-Compatible Regular Expressions (PCRE) in display filters. Regular expressions are special text strings used to define a search pattern. If you want to filter for an entire string in upper case or lower case, consider using Regular Expressions (regex) and the `matches` operator.

For example, to look for "anonymous" in any variation of upper case or lower case letters in the FTP argument field, use `ftp.request.arg matches "(?i)anonymous"`. The `matches` operator indicates that you are using Regular Expressions and the `(?i)` indicates that the search is case insensitive.

What if you are looking anywhere in a frame for a string that contains an upper case or lower case character at a specific location in a string? For example, consider the following strings:

- buildingAeng
- buildingaeng

We know "building" and "eng" are always in lower case, but the character between those strings can be either upper case or lower case.

In Wireshark, we can use `frame matches "building[Aa]eng"`. That means we are looking for an "A" or "a" between the lower case strings. If you are also interested in upper case or lower case B in that location, expand your display filter to `frame matches "building[AaBb]eng"`.

Use `matches` for a Multiple-Word Search

There is also a simple way to specify alternate search words with regex. Combine the words in parentheses and separate them with " | ". For example, if we are interested in finding the words *cat* or *dog* in upper case or lower case anywhere in a trace file, we can use the filter `frame matches "(?i)(cat|dog)"`.

TIP

Take the time to learn regex. Visit Jan Goyvaerts' *www.regular-expressions.info* web site. If you plan on adding more complex regex filters to Wireshark, consider purchasing Regex Buddy and Regex Magic – both products were created by Jan Goyvaerts and are fabulous tools for building, testing, and deciphering regex-based display filters. Regex is used in Wireshark, as well as Nmap, Snort, Splunk, and many other popular tools.

▣ Lab 21: Filter to Locate a Set of Key Words in a Trace File

In this lab we will use the `matches` operator to find the keywords *sombrero* or *football* in upper case or lower case anywhere in a trace file.

Step 1:　Open *http-pictures101.pcapng*.

Step 2:　Let's begin with a simple keyword filter for *sombrero*. In the display filter area, type `frame contains "sombrero"`. One packet should match this filter.

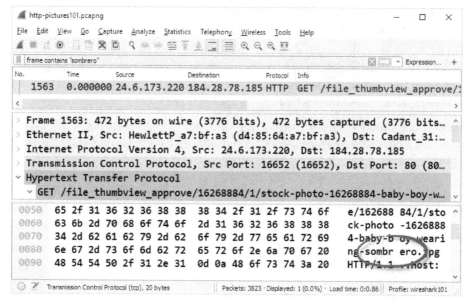

Step 3:　Now enhance your key word filter using the `matches` operator. Replace your previous filter with `frame matches "(?i)(sombrero|football)"`. Note that the monospace font makes it appear as if there is a space before the ")" and after the "(" and on either side of the "|." There are no spaces anywhere inside the quotes. Three packets should match this filter.

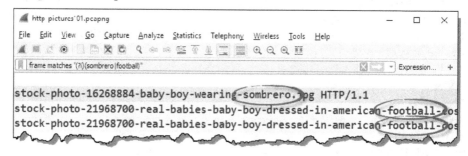

Step 4:   **LAB CLEAN-UP** Click the **Clear** button ⊠ to remove your filter before continuing.

Filtering on key words is simple using the matches operator and regular expressions. This is a useful skill when looking for passwords or user account names or known-to-be-malicious patterns in your trace files.

3.12. Use Wildcards in Your Display Filters

Sometimes you may need to look for variations in a string. In this case, you need to use a wildcard in your display filter. This is where a solid understanding of regular expressions really comes in handy.

Use Regex with "."

In Wireshark, you can use regex with the `matches` operator to represent a string with variables. In regex, the "." represents any character except line break and carriage return. When you are looking for the literal ".", you must escape it with a backslash ("\").

The display filter `ftp.request.arg matches "me.r"` uses "." as a wildcard.

This filter will look at the string after an FTP command (`ftp.request.arg`) for the letters "me" followed by any character (except a line break or a carriage return) and then an "r". Try running this on *ftp-crack101.pcapng*. This filter will display two packets that contain the string *symmetry* after the PASS command, as shown in Figure 77.

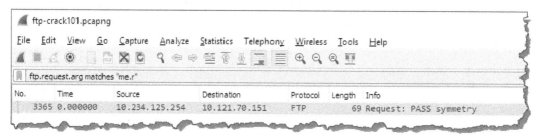

*Figure 77. Use the **matches** operator with repeating wildcards to find passwords in use. [ftp-crack101.pcapng]*

Now change the filter to allow two wildcards in between your characters. The filter `ftp.request.arg matches "me..r"` will find the string *homework* in the argument field.

Setting a Variable Length Repeating Wildcard Character Search

You can also specify that the wildcard should be repeated numerous times. The display filter would be `ftp.request.arg matches "me.{1,3}r"`. This filter will look for the "." (any character) once, twice, and three times in between me and r. In *ftp-crack101.pcapng*, this filter displays packets that contain *mercury, symmetry,* and *homework* in the FTP argument field. You can also add `(?i)` in front of **me** to add case insensitivity.

TIP

Once you create some great keyword filters, consider how you might combine them into a single filter and save that one filter as a button, as explained in *Turn Your Key Display Filters into Buttons* on page 190.

📖 Lab 22: Filter with Wildcards between Words

In this lab we will use the `matches` operator to find the keywords *baby* and *smiling* in a trace file. We will see how the repeating character option settings can affect what matches your filter.

Our display filter `ftp.request.arg matches "me.{1,3}r"` would look for the "." up to three times between the "me" and "r" as mentioned in this section.

This time we will look for the keywords *baby* and *smiling* with up to 3 characters separating the words.

Step 1:   Open *http-pictures101.pcapng*.

Step 2:   Type the filter **http.request.uri matches "baby.{1,3}smiling"**. Two packets should match this filter.

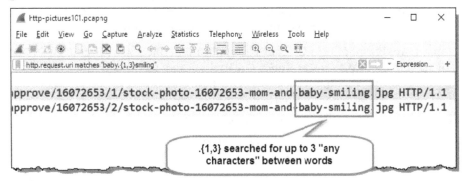

Step 3:   Now change **{1,3}** to **{1,20}** and apply this new filter. Three packets should now match this filter because the file *stock-video-10195917-baby-on-belly-smiling.jpg* has the two words within 20 characters.

Step 4:   **LAB CLEAN-UP** Click the **Clear** button ❎ to remove your display filter before continuing.

This is another great type of filter to master. Many times, when looking for security breaches, we try to locate strings within a certain distance from each other.

3.13. Use Filters to Spot Communication Delays

When someone complains of slow network performance, look for delays between packets as a sign that a network path, client, or server is slow. Create a filter to look for these delays to spot these problems faster.

There are two time measurements that can be used to filter on delays in a trace file – basic delta time and TCP delta time.

Filter on Large Delta Times (`frame.time_delta`)

The `frame.time_delta` field is located in the Frame section of each packet. You can create a filter for large values in this field. To set a filter for delays over 1 second, use `frame.time_delta > 1`. Keep in mind, however, that this filter looks at all the packets in the trace file to display the time from the end of one packet to the end of the next packet. Conversations can be intermingled, however, and delays in a UDP or TCP conversation can go unnoticed because of intervening packets from other conversations.

If you are troubleshooting a UDP-based application, filter on a specific UDP stream of interest then use **File | Export Specified Packets** and save a new trace file. Apply your `frame.time_delta` filter to the new trace file.

Filter on Large TCP Delta Times (`tcp.time_delta`)

The `tcp.time_delta` value can only be used after you enable Wireshark's *Calculate conversation timestamps* TCP preference.

In Lab 5, you checked to ensure the *Calculate conversation timestamps* TCP preference setting was enabled. When this setting is enabled, a [Timestamp] section is added to the end of each expanded TCP header in the Packet Details pane.

In Figure 78, we applied a filter for TCP delta delays over 1 second with `tcp.time_delta > 1`. There are four packets that arrived over 1 second after the previous packet in their TCP stream.

Consider clicking the **Add Filter Expression** button ⊞ on the display filter toolbar to make this a Filter Expression button. See *Turn Your Key Display Filters into Buttons* on page 190.

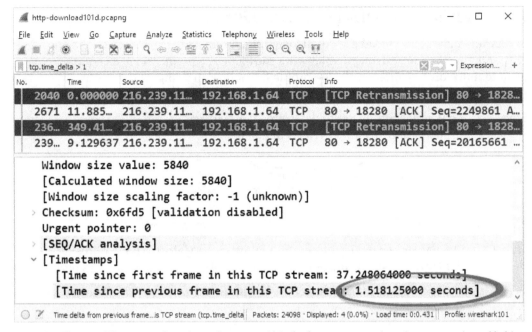

*Figure 78. The new [Timestamps] section only appears if **Calculate conversation timestamps** is enabled in your TCP preferences. Now you can filter on the TCP delta value. [http-download101d.pcapng]*

▢ Lab 23: Import Display Filters into a Profile

In this lab you will download a set of display filters from *www.wiresharkbook.com* and import them into your existing display filter file (*dfilters*). Use this same technique if you want to move display filters from one profile to another on a single host or other Wireshark systems.

Step 1:   Look in the **Status Bar** to determine your current profile. You should be using the *wireshark101* profile created in Lab 6.

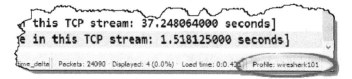

Step 2:   Open your personal configuration folder using **Help | About Wireshark | Folders | Personal configuration** and double-click on the folder hyperlink.

Navigate to the *profiles* directory and locate the *wireshark101* directory, as shown below.

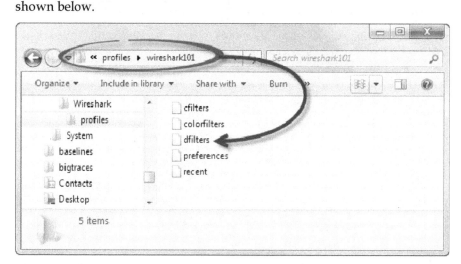

Step 3:   You created a **My IP Address** filter in Lab 15, therefore you should already have a *dfilters* file. If you don't have that file, return to Lab 15.

Open the *dfilters* file with a text editor.

Step 4: Now extract the *dfilters_sample.txt* file from the *wireshark101filespart2.zip* file that you downloaded from *www.wiresharkbook.com*. If you haven't downloaded these files yet, see the instructions on page iv. This file contains 6 display filters (and one heading line) that we will add to your existing *dfilters* file.

```
dfilters_sample.txt  Notepad
File  Edit  Format  View  Help
"Wireshark 101 Book Sample Display Filters (www.wiresharkbook.co
"      TCP Delta Time > 1 Second" tcp.time_delta > 1
"      DNS or HTTP Errors" (dns.flags.rcode != 0) || http.respo
"      HTTP GET/POST" http.request.method == "GET" or http.reque
"      Packets with Comments" pkt_comment
"      File Not Found (STATUS_OBJECT_NAME_NOT_FOUND)" smb.nt_sta
"      SMB2 Login-Administrator Account" ntlmssp.auth.username
```

Step 5: Open *dfilters_sample.txt* and copy the contents to your buffer.

Step 6: Toggle to the *dfilters* file in your *Wireshark101* directory and paste the contents onto the end of the display filters listed. **Make sure you add a blank line at the end of the *dfilters* file or your last filter will not be displayed.** Close and save your edited *dfilters* file.

Step 7: Return to Wireshark. The *dfilters* file is loaded when you load your profile. Change to the *Default* profile and return to the *wireshark101* profile.

Step 8: Click on the **Display filter** bookmark 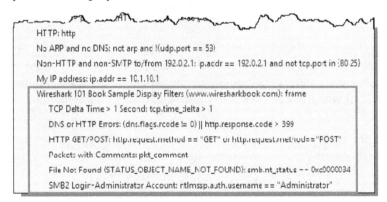 on the filter toolbar. You should see your new display filters at the bottom of the list[40].

```
HTTP: http
No ARP and no DNS: not arp and !(udp.port == 53)
Non-HTTP and non-SMTP to/from 192.0.2.1: ip.addr == 192.0.2.1 and not tcp.port in {80 25}
My IP address: ip.addr == 10.1.10.1
Wireshark 101 Book Sample Display Filters (www.wiresharkbook.com): frame
     TCP Delta Time > 1 Second: tcp.time_delta > 1
     DNS or HTTP Errors: (dns.flags.rcode != 0) || http.response.code > 399
     HTTP GET/POST: http.request.method == "GET" or http.request.method=="POST"
     Packets with Comments: pkt_comment
     File Not Found (STATUS_OBJECT_NAME_NOT_FOUND): smb.nt_status == 0xc0000034
     SMB2 Login-Administrator Account: ntlmssp.auth.username == "Administrator"
```

It is easy to share filters because filters are simple text files (*cfilters* for capture filters and *dfilters* for display filters). If you are working on a team, consider creating a master set of filters that are created and shared by the team.

---

[40] The new display filter title "Wireshark 101 Book Sample Display Filters" uses the filter string `frame`. It will not filter anything out of view if someone clicks on it by mistake.

3.14. Turn Your Key Display Filters into Buttons

You want your analysis processes to be as efficient as possible. In order to do this, make your most popular display filters into buttons in the display filter area. This way you can quickly open a trace file and click a button to filter on key packet characteristics.

Create a Filter Expression Button

It is very easy to turn a display filter into a button. Simply type your display filter in the display filter area and click the **Add a Display Filter** button ⊞ at the end of the display filter toolbar.

Provide a label name for your filter as shown in Figure 79 and click the **OK** button.

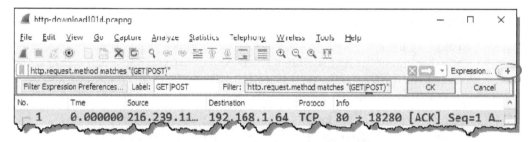

*Figure 79. Click the **Add a Display Filter** button and simply name your Filter Expression button.*

There are no limits to the number of Filter Expression buttons you can create. If you run out of room for your buttons, Wireshark displays "»", which you can click on to see more buttons.

In Figure 80, we created five Filter Expression buttons to use when analyzing HTTP traffic. Not all of the Filter Expression buttons can fit in the display filter area because we reduced the size of our Wireshark window. Wireshark places two Filter Expression buttons in the display filter area, but we must click » to view and select one of the remaining three Filter Expression buttons.

If we keep adding to the Filter Expression buttons list, eventually, Wireshark will place a down arrow at the bottom of the list so we can scroll further in the list.

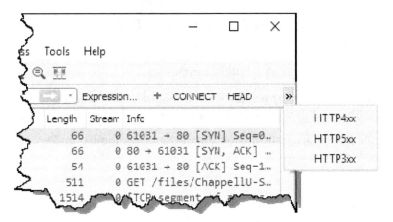

Figure 80. Click » *to view Filter Expression buttons that won't fit in the display filter area.*

Edit, Reorder, Delete, and Disable Filter Expression Buttons

There are three ways to access the Filter Expression management window.

1. Select **Edit | Preferences | Filter Expressions**.

2. Click the **Add Filter Expression** button ⊞ that resides at the end of the display filter toolbar and then click the **Filter Expression Preferences** button.

3. Click the **Bookmark** button ▌ on the display filter toolbar and select **Manage Filter Expressions**, as shown in Figure 81.

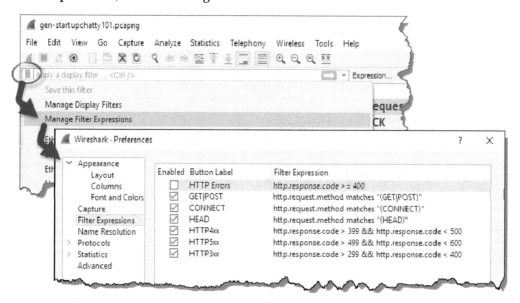

Figure 81. You must access Wireshark's Preferences window to edit, reorder, delete, or disable *Filter Expression* buttons.

Edit the Filter Expression Area in Your *preferences* File

Filter Expression buttons are saved in the *preferences* file of the profile in which you are currently working. Your current profile is shown in the right-hand column of the Status Bar. To find your profile's *preferences* file, select **Help | About Wireshark | Folders** and double-click the **Personal Configuration** folder hyperlink. The *preferences* file for the *Default* profile is in this directory. The *preferences* files for any other profiles are in a subdirectory under the *profiles* directory.

The *preferences* file is just a text file. Don't be afraid to edit the file directly with a text editor. Filter Expression button settings are maintained under the Filter Expressions heading.

The following is a sample of the Filter Expression area in the *preferences* file. These settings are used to create the active Filter Expression buttons seen in Figure 81.

```
####### Filter Expressions ########
gui.filter_expressions.label: GET|POST
gui.filter_expressions.enabled: TRUE
gui.filter_expressions.expr: http.request.method matches
"(GET|POST)"
gui.filter_expressions.label: CONNECT
gui.filter_expressions.enabled: TRUE
gui.filter_expressions.expr: http.request.uri contains "CONNECT"
gui.filter_expressions.label: HEAD
gui.filter_expressions.enabled: TRUE
gui.filter_expressions.expr: http.request.uri contains "HEAD"
gui.filter_expressions.label: HTTP4xx
gui.filter_expressions.enabled: TRUE
gui.filter_expressions.expr: http.response.code > 399 &&
http.response.code < 500
gui.filter_expressions.label: HTTP5xx
gui.filter_expressions.enabled: TRUE
gui.filter_expressions.expr: http.response.code > 499
gui.filter_expressions.label: HTTP3xx
gui.filter_expressions.enabled: TRUE
gui.filter_expressions.expr: http.response.code > 299 &&
http.response.code < 400
```

🛑**TIP**

When you create some wonderful Filter Expression buttons, share them with your team. Simply copy the Filter Expressions section from your *preferences* file out to a text file. Send the text file to your team members and instruct them to copy the desired button settings into the *preferences* file of their desired profile. Each Filter Expression button requires three lines of information (label, enabled and expr). If they are copying just one button, remind them to copy all three lines.

▢ Lab 24: Create and Import HTTP Filter Expression Buttons

We will begin by creating a single Filter Expression button and then we'll import a set of Filter Expression buttons. At the time this book was written, there wasn't an easy way to turn all your display filters into Filter Expression buttons. That would be a great feature and maybe we'll see that someday and we can replace this lab with another lab about conquering world hunger with customized profiles. Until then, follow along with this lab to import the Filter Expression buttons show in Figure 81 into your *wireshark101* profile.

Step 1:   Open *http-download-a.pcapng*.

Step 2:   Type `http.request.method matches "(GET|POST)"` in the filter area.

Click the **Add Filter Expression** button ⊞ that resides at the end of the display filter toolbar.

Enter **GET|POST** in the label field and click **OK**.

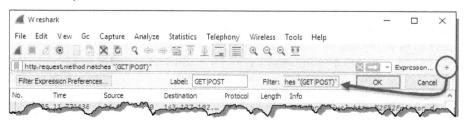

The new GET | POST Filter Expression button is displayed on the display filter toolbar.

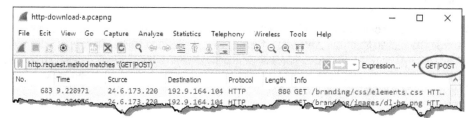

Step 3:   Click the **GET|POST** button to view the packets that match this filter. This is a great button to quickly view requests or information sent to a web server.

This is the standard process used to add a single Filter Expression button. Next we will import a set of Filter Expression buttons directly into the *preferences* file for your *Wireshark101* profile.

Step 4:   Use a text editor, such as WordPad, to open your *preferences* file (contained in your *wireshark101* profile directory).

(If you can't remember how to get to this directory, select **Help | About Wireshark | Folders** and double-click on the hyperlink to your **Personal configuration** folder. Look inside the *profiles* folder for your *wireshark101* folder.)

Step 5: Use the Find feature of your text editor to locate the **Filter Expressions** area in your *preferences* file. You will see that you already have a GET|POST Filter Expression button entry as shown in the image below.

```
# TRUE or FALSE (case insensitive)
#gui.packet_list_show_minimap: TRUE

####### Filter Expressions ########
gui.filter_expressions.label: GET|POST
gui.filter_expressions.enabled: FALSE
gui.filter_expressions.expr: http.request.method matches
"(GET|POST)"

####### Capture ########

# Default capture device
```

Step 6: Extract the *filterexpressions101.txt* file from the *wireshark101filespart2.zip* file that you downloaded from *www.wiresharkbook.com*. If you haven't downloaded these files yet, see the instructions on page iv. Copy the contents of this file directly under your new GET|POST entry in the ####### **Filter Expressions** ######## area. Save and close your *preferences* file.

Step 7: You must reload your *wireshark101* profile to see your new Filter Expression buttons. Simply click on the **Profile** area of the Status Bar, select another profile, and then perform the same steps to return to your *wireshark101* profile.

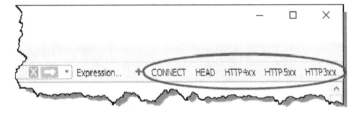

Step 8: **LAB CLEAN-UP** If you do not want these new Filter Expressions buttons to remain visible, click the **Edit Preferences** button on the main toolbar and select **Filter Expressions**. Uncheck the Filter Expressions listed and click **OK**.

Remember that if you have too many buttons to fit in your display filter area, Wireshark displays ». Click on the double arrows to expand your Filter Expression button list.

Chapter 3 Challenge

Open *challenge101-3.pcapng* and use your display filter and coloring rule skills to locate traffic based on addresses, protocols and keywords to answer these Challenge questions. The answer key is located in Appendix A.

You will practice your display filter to locate traffic based on addresses, protocols, and keywords.

Question 3-1.   How many frames travel to or from 80.78.246.209?

Question 3-2.   How many DNS packets are in this trace file?

Question 3-3.   How many frames have the TCP SYN bit set to 1?

Question 3-4.   How many frames contain the string "set-cookie" in upper case or lower case?

Question 3-5.   How many frames contain a TCP delta time greater than 1 second?

Chapter 4 Skills: Color and Export Interesting Packets

Wireshark is one of those tools that every engineer is a bit afraid to use. It's like bringing the big guns on board. Once you get familiar with it and tame the beast, this is the most powerful tool you will have on your networking tool belt.

Lionel Gentil
iTunes Software Reliability Engineer, *Apple, Inc.*

Quick Reference: Coloring Rules Interface

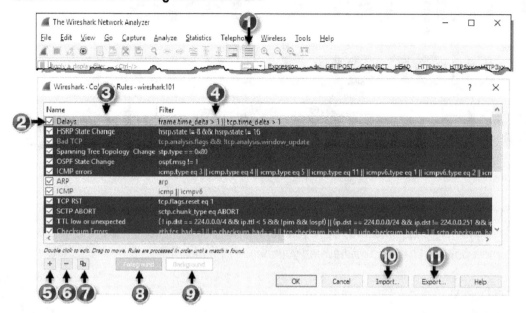

(1)   Enable/disable all coloring rules
(2)   Enable/disable the selected coloring rule
(3)   Coloring rule name (shows current foreground/background color scheme)
(4)   Coloring rule display filter syntax (also shows rule color scheme)
(5)   Add a coloring rule (placed in first position on list by default)
(6)   Delete the selected coloring rule (select **Clear** to reload default coloring rules)
(7)   Copy selected coloring rule
(8)   Set foreground (text) color (launches Select Color window)
(9)   Set background color (launches Select Color window)
(10) Import coloring rules (select a file that contains coloring rules; rules are added to the existing *colorfilters* file)
(11) Export coloring rules (can be exported using any name)

4.1. Identify Applied Coloring Rules

Wireshark automatically colors packets based on a default set of coloring rules. If you become familiar with this default set of colors, you can quickly identify packet types based on their colors instead of spending time digging into the packets.

To quickly determine why a packet is colored a certain way, expand the Frame section of the packet and look at the **Coloring Rule Name** and **Coloring Rule String** lines, as shown in Figure 82.

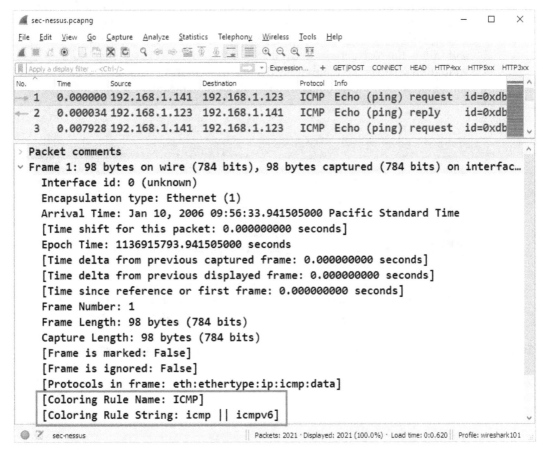

Figure 82. Look inside the Frame section of a packet to find out why a packet is colored a certain way. [sec-nessus101.pcapng]

TIP

Coloring rules are maintained in a text file called *colorfilters*. This file can be edited with a text editor, but since it is loaded when you open a profile, you must switch to another profile and return to the current profile to see the changes.

🖳 Lab 25: Add a Column to Display Coloring Rules in Use

Adding a column to identify coloring rules is a great idea when you are new to Wireshark or you just aren't familiar with the coloring rules set.

Step 1:   Open *http-sfgate101.pcapng*.

Step 2:   Click the **Go To** button 🔛 on the main toolbar, type in **472** and click the **Go to packet** button or press **Enter**.

We see three different coloring rules applied to this area of the trace file. The highlight line for the selected packet allows a bit of the original color to show through. If frame 473 has a black background on your system, return to Lab 5 and follow the instructions to disable your IP, UDP, and TCP checksum validation settings. To completely disable that coloring rule, see the instructions contained in *Disable Individual Coloring Rules* on page 202.

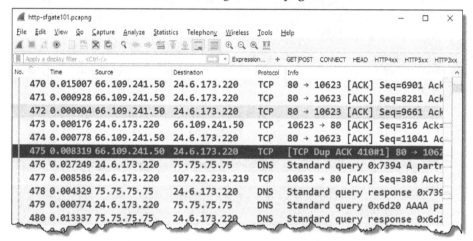

Step 3:   Expand the Frame section in the Packet Details pane for **frame 472**. Frame 472 matches the HTTP coloring rule which uses a green background and black foreground (text).

Step 4:   Right-click on the **Coloring Rule Name** field in the Frame section and select **Apply as Column**. Use this column when you want to quickly list the coloring rule applied to each frame.

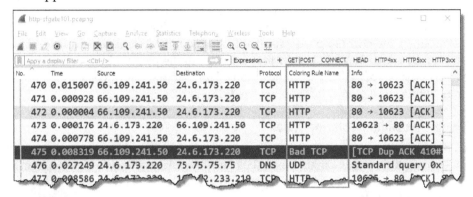

Step 5:   [**LAB CLEAN-UP**] Right-click on the **Coloring Rule Name** column heading and unselect that column from the list to hide it. If you want to view this column again later, you can right-click on any column heading and select it from the column list.

We can see that we have packets that matched the HTTP, Bad TCP, and UDP coloring rules at this point in the trace file. Learning the default set of coloring rules helps you quickly understand communications behaviors.

4.2.   *Turn Off the Checksum Error Coloring Rule*

If you have Ethernet, TCP, UDP, and IP checksum validation preference settings enabled and you are capturing on a host that uses task offload, the Checksum Error coloring rule will create false positive coloring on your trace file. When a system supports task offloading, valid checksums are applied by the network interface card before the frame is sent on the network. Wireshark captures a copy of the packets before that valid checksum is calculated and applied to the frames. Consider disabling the Checksum Errors coloring rule or disabling checksum validation (as we did in Lab 5).

Disable Individual Coloring Rules

To disable one or more coloring rules, open the Coloring Rules window by selecting **View | Coloring Rules** on the main menu. Uncheck the **enable/disable check box** in front of a coloring rule to disable that coloring rule. In Figure 83, we have disabled the Checksum Errors coloring rule.

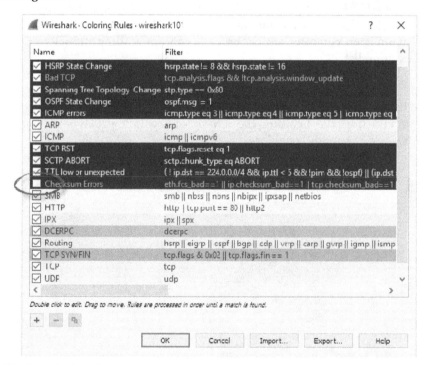

Figure 83. Simple uncheck a coloring rule to disable it.

Disable All Packet Coloring

If you just can't stand working with the coloring rules on, you can toggle all coloring on or off using **View | Colorize Packet List** or click the **Colorize Packet List** button on the main toolbar.

TIP

One of the most irritating coloring rules is the Checksum Errors coloring rule. In earlier versions of Wireshark (prior to version 1.8.x), Ethernet, IP, UDP, and TCP checksum validations were enabled in the respective protocols' preference settings. Since lots of machines use task offloading (with checksum calculations offloaded to the network card), it was common to find all outbound packets from these systems colored with the "Bad Checksum" coloring rule although the adapter applied a perfectly good checksum to the frame before sending it onto the network.

If you updated Wireshark, you may have retained earlier checksum validation settings and you might still see Bad Checksum coloring in your trace file. To remove these inaccurate indications, the best option is to turn off the checksum validation setting for Ethernet, IP, UDP, and TCP using **Edit | Preferences** > **Protocols** and disabling the setting for Ethernet, IP, UDP, and TCP. Otherwise, you can simply disable the Checksum Errors coloring rule, as shown in Figure 83. If you just disable the coloring rule, Wireshark may still indicate that you have checksum errors inside the frame, but the Bad Checksum coloring rule will not be applied to the packets in the Packet List pane.

4.3.   Build a Coloring Rule to Highlight Delays

When users complain about slow network performance, look for delays between packets in their communications. You can easily create a coloring rule to call your attention to these delays in UDP-based or TCP-based communications.

Create a Coloring Rule from Scratch

In *Use Filters to Spot Communication Delays* on page 186, you learned how to filter on delays in a trace file. You can use a similar technique to create a single coloring rule to detect packets that have a high delta time.

Since coloring rule strings use display filter syntax, you can easily turn any of your display filters into coloring rules by copying the display filter into the coloring rule Filter area.

Select **View | Coloring Rules** and click the **Add** button ⊞. Enter the name **T-Delays** in the **Name** field.

In the Filter area, type `frame.time_delta > 1 || tcp.time_delta > 1`, as shown in Figure 84.

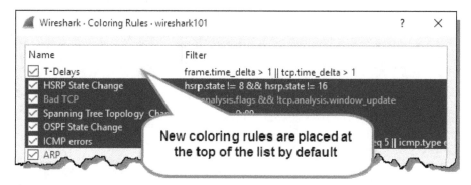

Figure 84. Enter the coloring rule name and filter before setting up the foreground and background colors.

Now it's time to set the foreground (text) and background colors for your coloring rule.

While selecting your new coloring rule, click the Background button. Wireshark offers an array of basic colors and the ability to define and save custom colors. If you want to use a color repeatedly, click the **Add to Custom Colors** button to save it.

Alternately, you can use **Pick Screen Color** to pull a color from your display.

Over the years, I have settled on the color orange as my "butt-ugly color." I'm just not a big fan of the color orange, so I use that background color to alert me to potential problems in the trace file. In Figure 85 I have selected orange from the basic colors set. (This will only be visible to you in the ebook version.)

The intelligent scrollbar works very well with colorized traffic. We will focus on the Intelligent Scrollbar later in this chapter.

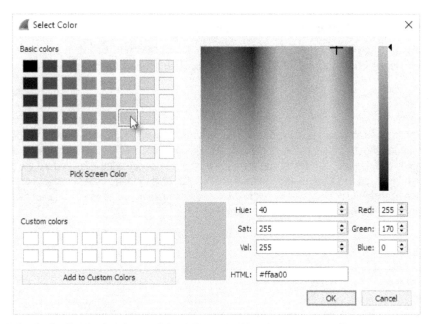

Figure 85. Wireshark offers basic colors and the ability to build and save custom colors.

Wireshark always shows the foreground and background coloring scheme in the Name field so you can ensure it looks just the way you want, as shown in Figure 86 (color is visible in the ebook version).

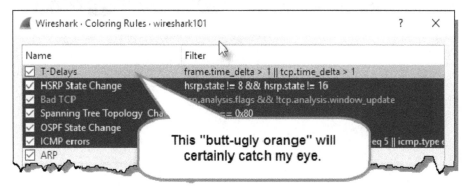

Figure 86. Wireshark applies your foreground and background color scheme to the coloring rules list.

Your new coloring rule will automatically be placed at the top of the Coloring Rules set. Placement of coloring rules is important. Coloring rules are processed in order from top to bottom, and the packet is colored according to the first matching coloring rule.

Use the Right-Click Method to Create a Coloring Rule

The fastest way to create a new coloring rule is to select the field of interest in the Packet Details pane, right-click and select **Colorize with Filter | New Coloring Rule**.

 TIP

Plan your coloring and naming scheme in advance. For example, if a color highlights a performance problem, affix "T-" (for "troubleshooting") to the front of the coloring rule name and make all your troubleshooting coloring rule backgrounds orange. Affix "S-" (for "security") to the front of security coloring rules and set the background color of these rules to red and foreground to white. Affix "N-" (for "notes") to the front of packets of interest to you and set the background color of these rules to dark green and foreground to white. This will help you quickly classify the traffic just based on the color displayed.

The example shown below includes one security coloring rule prefaced with "S-" and two troubleshooting coloring rules prefaced by "T-".

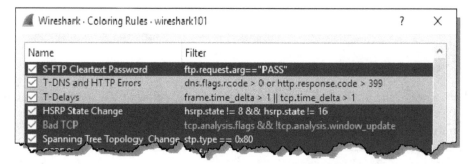

Lab 26: Build a Coloring Rule to Highlight FTP User Names, Passwords, and More

In this lab you will create a coloring rule to call your attention to FTP request arguments, including those associated with USER, PASS, TYPE, SIZE, MDTM, RETR, and CWD commands. We will use *ftp-crack101.pcapng* again.

Step 1:   Open *ftp-crack101.pcapng*. We began capturing in the middle of various FTP communications. In frame 11 we can see "Request: PASS merlin" in the **Info** column of the Packet List pane.

Step 2:   In the Packet Details pane of frame 11, fully expand the **File Transfer Protocol (FTP)** line. There are two sections: Request command and Request arg(ument).

Step 3:   Right-click on the **Request arg** line and select **Colorize with Filter | New Coloring Rule**, as shown below.

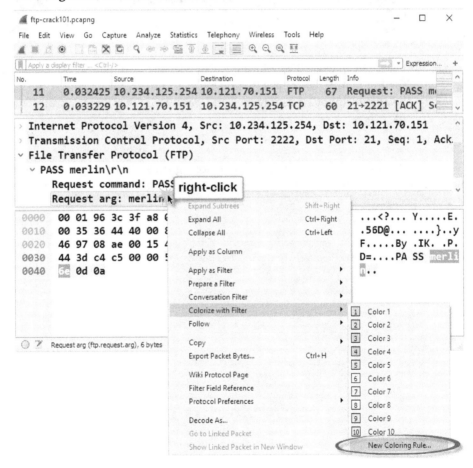

Step 4:   In the Coloring Rules window that appears, name your coloring rule "S-FTP Arguments.[41]" Edit the filter to just `ftp.request.arg`.

Click the **Background** button and select **red** in the **Basic colors** area. Click **OK** to save your background color setting. Click the **Foreground** button and select **white** in the **Basic Colors** area. Click **OK** to save your foreground color setting.

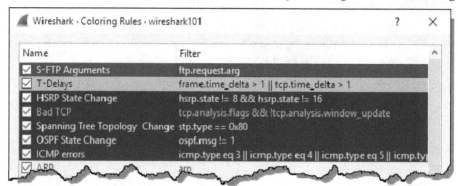

Step 5:   Click **OK** to close the Coloring Rules window and then scroll through this trace file to identify the frames that match your new coloring rule. You should easily be able to spot FTP user names and passwords that were captured in this trace file.

Use the right-click method to quickly make coloring rules. At times you may just right-click and accept the filter string "as is" — other times you might decide to edit the string to be less or more specific.

---

[41]   We are using the "S-" to indicate this is a security concern. This naming convention enables you to create and apply a `frame.coloring_rule.name contains "S-"` to identify all packets that match your security coloring rules.

4.4. Quickly Colorize a Single Conversation

It can be confusing to analyze traffic when your network communications contain numerous intertwined conversations. You can use coloring to visibly separate the conversations in the Packet List pane to differentiate them as you scroll through a trace file.

Right-Click to Temporarily Colorize a Conversation

To temporarily colorize a TCP conversation, right-click on any conversation in the Packet List pane and select **Colorize Conversation | TCP | Color 1**, as shown in Figure 87. Wireshark offers ten temporary colors. Some of the colors are quite similar and may be difficult to distinguish from each other.

Temporary colors are retained until you change to another profile, restart Wireshark, or manually remove them.

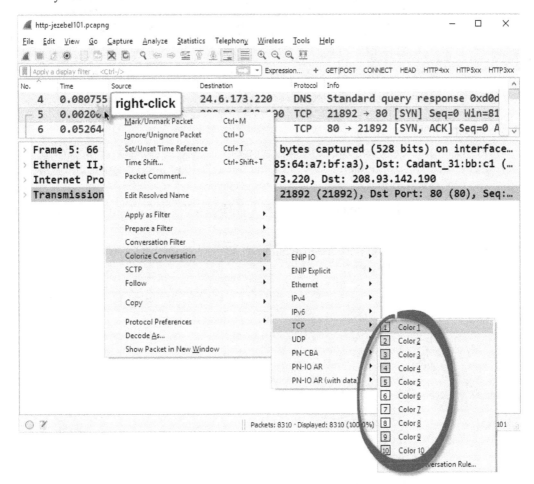

Figure 87. Right-click on a conversation in the Packet List pane, select the type of conversation, and choose a temporary color. [http-jezebel101.pcapng]

In Figure 88, we applied a temporary coloring rule to the TCP conversation that was established to download a site icon file (favicon.ico).

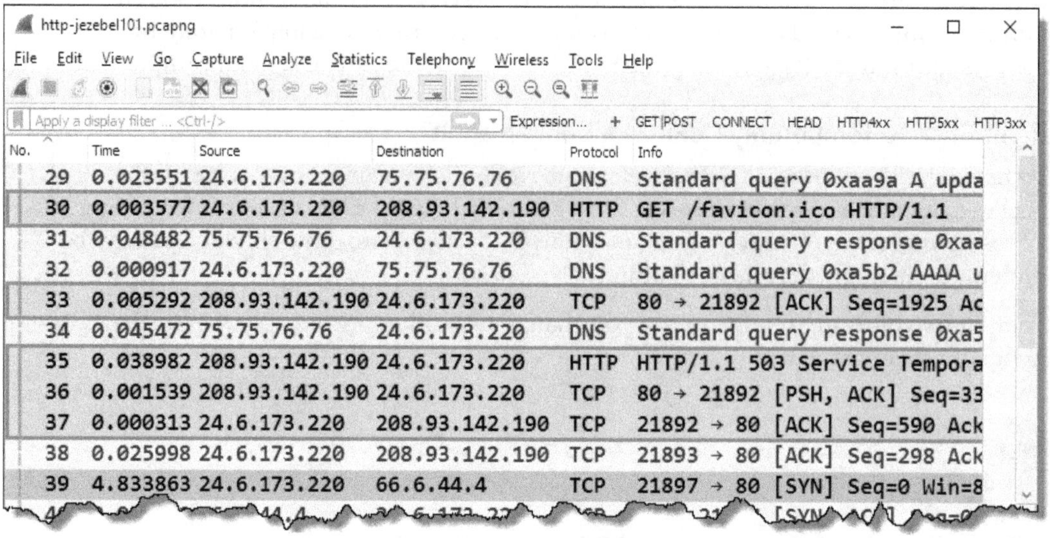

Figure 88. Coloring conversations helps distinguish them in a trace file. [http-jezebel101.pcapng]

Remove Temporary Coloring

Although we refer to these coloring rules as "temporary," if you apply a temporary coloring rule to a conversation and then close the trace file, and open it again, you will notice the color is still in place.

Temporary coloring rules are in effect until you switch profiles, close Wireshark, or remove them.

To remove all your temporary color settings, select **View | Colorize Conversation | Reset Colorization** or use **Ctrl+Space**.

📖 Lab 27: Create Temporary Conversation Coloring Rules

In this lab, you will apply three temporary coloring rules to differentiate TCP conversations. When you scroll through the trace file, you will be able to easily see when an earlier conversation begins to surface.

Step 1:   Open *http-browse101d.pcapng*.

Step 2:   Frame 1 is a TCP handshake packet (SYN). Right-click on **frame 1** in the Packet List pane and select **Colorize Conversation | TCP | Color 1**.

Step 3:   Scroll down until you see the next SYN packet—frame 12. Right-click on **frame 12** in the Packet List pane and select **Colorize Conversation | TCP | Color 4**.

Step 4:   Scroll down until you see the next SYN packet—frame 61. Right-click on **frame 61** in the Packet List pane and select **Colorize Conversation | TCP | Color 8**.

Step 5:   Now scroll through the trace file to see if these three conversations appear later. When you get to frame 138, you will see conversation 3 appearing again.

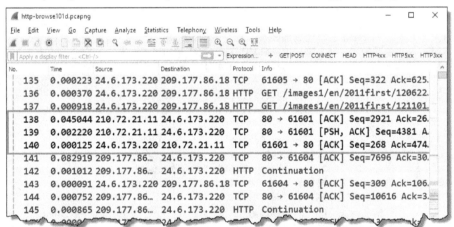

Step 6:   **LAB CLEAN-UP** Select **View | Colorize Conversation | Reset Colorization** to remove your temporary coloring rules.

This temporary coloring is very useful when analyzing applications that require many connections—think Microsoft's SharePoint! It's easy to differentiate the various processes taking place on the network when we colorize different conversations.

4.5.   *Master the Intelligent Scrollbar*

The Intelligent Scrollbar was introduced in Wireshark version 2. This feature essentially gives you a very tall, skinny view of the coloring seen on the Packet List pane so you can quickly locate areas of interest in your trace file.

Note: This is another section of the book that focuses on coloring, which is visible only in the ebook format.

There is limited space on the Intelligent Scrollbar. In most cases the Intelligent Scrollbar will not display the coloring of the entire trace file. You may need to drag the thumb on the scrollbar down to viewing the Intelligent Scrollbar information for other points in the file.

In Figure 89, we have opened *ftp-bounce.pcapng* and moved the thumb of the scrollbar down to a point where we can see a custom coloring rule being applied to packet 31.

We can also see red stripes in the Intelligent Scrollbar. Those represent the TCP Resets seen in the trace file.

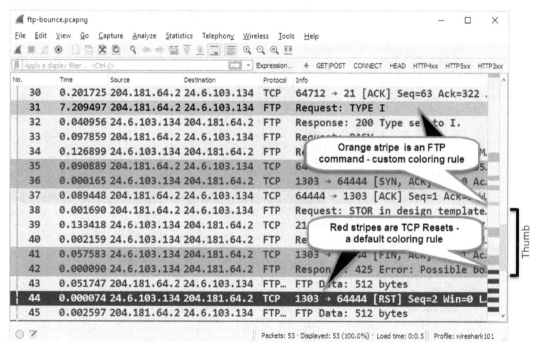

Figure 89. The Intelligent Scrollbar is simply a miniature coloring view of the Packet List pane. [ftp-bounce.pcapng].

Navigate Manually on the Intelligent Scrollbar

Although there is a right-click menu available for the Intelligent Scrollbar (covered next), I have found the fastest way to get to a specific point on the Intelligent Scrollbar is to simply click on the area of interest on the scrollbar. Wireshark jumps to that point in the trace file.

Navigate with the Intelligent Scrollbar Menu

There is a right-click menu available on the Intelligent Scrollbar. One of the options on the right-click menu is **Scroll here**. On a large trace file, the Scroll here feature will get you to the general area of interest, but you can simply click on that point on the Intelligent Scrollbar to jump to that point in the trace file.

Figure 90. The Scroll here feature on the Intelligent Scrollbar can get you to the general location of interest.

Note that turning off your coloring rules individually or with the **Coloring Rules** button ☰ will disable the Intelligent Scrollbar.

The most efficient way to use this new Intelligent Scrollbar is to enhance your coloring rules so the spots of interest stand out on the Intelligent Scrollbar. In Lab 28 you will have a chance to try this out.

📖 Lab 28: Use the Intelligent Scrollbar to Quickly Find Problems

In this lab we will create a new coloring rule to identify TCP retransmissions. TCP retransmissions are a sign of packet loss on a network and are part of Wireshark's TCP analysis flagged packets. We'd like to just look at the Intelligent Scrollbar to know if retransmissions (packet loss indications) are seen.

Step 1:   Open *net-lost-route.pcapng*.

Step 2:   First we will make a new coloring rule to differentiate retransmissions from all other traffic. Select **View | Coloring Rules** to open the coloring rules window.

Step 3:   Click the **Add** button ⊞. Name your new coloring rule **T-Retransmissions**. The filter should be `tcp.analysis.retransmission`.

Step 4:   With your new coloring rule selected, click the Background button and select a **vibrant color** (such as fuchsia or bright pink). Click **OK** to close your Select Color window. Click **OK** again to close your Coloring Rules window.

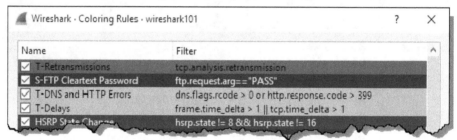

Click the **Reload** button 🔃 on the main toolbar, if your new vibrant coloring does not appear on the Intelligent Scrollbar.

There should be no doubt that there is a packet loss issue in this trace file. By looking at the Intelligent Scrollbar we can see the problem is much worse towards the end of the trace file.

Again, if you are reading the ebook version, you will be able to see the colors in these screenshots. If you are following along with the lab instructions, you can simply see all the colors on your screen, however.

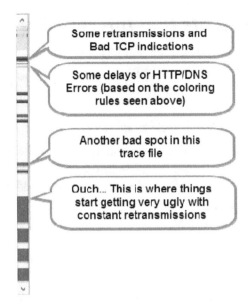

Using our new coloring rule we can easily see where retransmissions really begin to hit a critical level in this trace file. If we further define our coloring rules, we can differentiate between the delays and HTTP/DNS errors (we made both coloring rules butt-ugly orange).

Step 5:   **LAB CLEAN-UP** Select **View | Coloring Rules** and disable **all of your custom coloring rules** at this point. You can enable them again after you finish the labs in this book.

The Intelligent Scrollbar is a great feature. Refining your coloring rules will make it even more useful and help you spot specific issues faster.

4.6.   *Export Packets that Interest You*

When you work with a large trace file that has numerous communication types, consider applying filters based on conversations or protocols and exporting the packets to a new trace file. You will have fewer packets to deal with and your statistics will only apply to the exported packets.

You can easily export displayed packets, marked packets, or a range of packets.

Let's say you opened *net-lost-route.pcapng* and applied a display filter for all HTTP GET or POST traffic (`http.request.method matches "(GET|POST)"`). To export these packets to a new trace file, select **File | Export Specified Packets**, as shown in Figure 91.

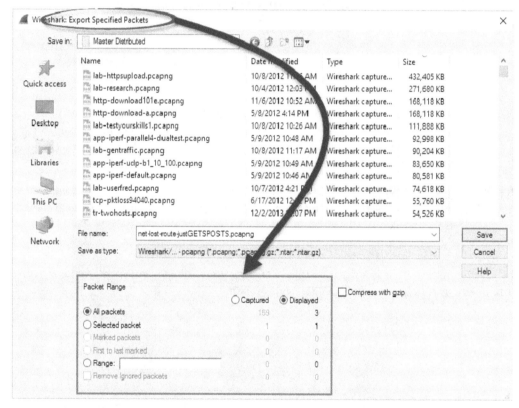

*Figure 91. Use **File | Export Specified Packets** to save the captured packets, displayed packets, marked packets, or a range of packets. [net-lost-route.pcapng]*

If you want to export packets that do not match neatly in a display filter, consider marking the packets before selecting **File | Export Specified Packets**. Right-click on each packet of interest in the Packet List pane and select **Mark/Unmark Packet**. You must mark each packet separately.

By default, marked packets appear with a black background and white foreground. When you select **File | Export Specified Packets**, choose either **Marked packets** or **First to last marked**.

Packet marking is only temporary. When you open the exported packets in your new trace file, the packets will not be marked.

▭ Lab 29: Export a Single TCP Conversation

When you are focused on a specific application or a specific file download, it helps to extract conversations into separate trace files. In this lab, you will create and extract a new trace file after locating traffic from an executable file download process.

Step 1:   Open *http-misctraffic101.pcapng*.

Step 2:   Using your display filtering techniques, filter on a frame that contains ".exe" in the HTTP Request URI field (`http.request.uri contains ".exe"`). Only one frame should match your filter—frame 211, as shown below.

It appears someone is downloading Metasploit, a popular penetration testing program.

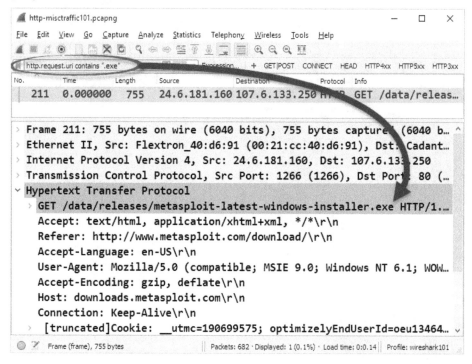

Step 3:   Right-click on **frame 211** in the Packet List pane. Select **Conversation Filter |
TCP** to display this single TCP conversation. The Status Bar should now
indicate that 475 packets match your filter.

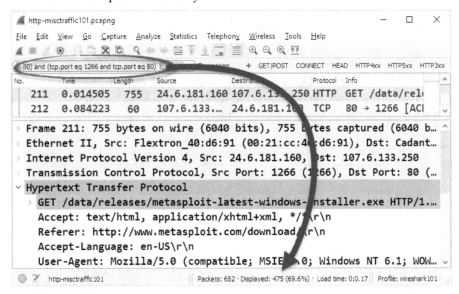

Step 4:   To save this conversation in a separate trace file, select **File | Export Specified
Packets**. Enter the file name *exportexe.pcapng* and ensure the **Displayed** radio
button is selected before clicking **Save**.

Step 5:   **LAB CLEAN-UP** Click the **Clear** button ☒ to remove the conversation display
filter before you continue.

You've now created a new trace file that contains a single conversation from the original
trace file. Working with a single conversation is much easier than wading through
thousands of conversations in a trace file.

4.7. Export Packet Details

If you are going to write a report about network communications or packet contents, it would be nice to show some packets along with your analysis findings. It's easy to export packet details, but be careful you don't get too much information during the process.

Export Packet Dissections

Select **File | Export Packet Dissections** to export packet details, as shown in Figure 92. There are six different export options, but the most commonly used export types are plain text and CSV (comma separated value) formats.

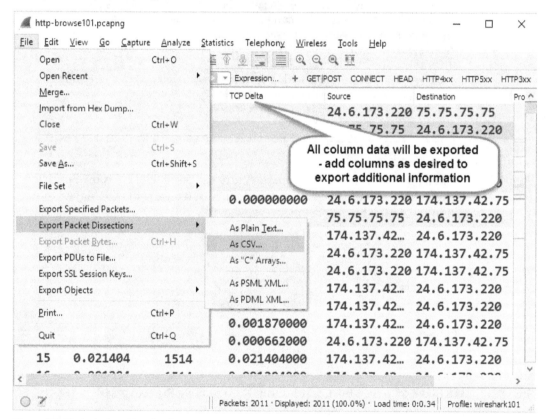

*Figure 92. To include packet details in a report, select **File | Export Packet Dissections**. [http-browse101.pcapng]*

Select the plain text format if you are going to include packet contents or summary information in a report.

Select CSV format to import packet information into another program (such as a spreadsheet program) for further manipulation and analysis.

Define What should be Exported

There are additional options that can be defined. You can choose to export specific packets based on your filters or marked packets. You can also define what packet information should be included in the output process. As shown in Figure 93, you can export the **Packet summary line** (from the Packet List pane, including any columns you've added), **Packet details** (choose **All expanded**, **As displayed** in the Packet Details pane, or **All collapsed**), or the **Packet Bytes** (output with hex and ASCII details).

You can also select to have each packet on a different page. Be careful—you can run through reams of paper this way. Practice exporting packet information to figure out which format would look best in a report.

Figure 93. Decide how much packet detail you need when exporting packet dissections.

Sample Text Output

The output below was created by exporting a single packet in plain text format (.txt) using the packet details as displayed.

Frame 4: 77 bytes on wire (616 bits), 77 bytes captured (616 bits) on interface 0
Ethernet II, Src: HewlettP_a7:bf:a3 (d4:85:64:a7:bf:a3), Dst: Cadant_31:bb:c1
(00:01:5c:31:bb:c1)
Internet Protocol Version 4, Src: 24.6.173.220, Dst: 75.75.75.75
User Datagram Protocol, Src Port: 54997 (54997), Dst Port: 53 (53)
Domain Name System (query)
  [Response In: 7]
  Transaction ID: 0x8920
  Flags: 0x0100 Standard query
  Questions: 1
  Answer RRs: 0
  Authority RRs: 0
  Additional RRs: 0
  Queries

Sample CSV Output

Exporting to CSV format allows you to manipulate the information in another tool, such as Excel. The output below was created by exporting the packet summary line of all the packets of a trace file in comma separated value format (.csv).

```
"No.","Time","Length","TCP Delta","Source","Destination","Time to
live","Host","Protocol","Coloring Rule Name","Info"
"1","0.000000","77","","24.6.173.220","75.75.75.75","128","","DNS","UDP",
"Standard query 0x9ba8 A www.wireshark.org"
"2","0.021978","93","","75.75.75.75","24.6.173.220","59","","DNS","UDP",
"Standard query response 0x9ba8 A www.wireshark.org A 174.137.42.75"
"3","0.000783","77","","24.6.173.220","75.75.75.75","128","","DNS","UDP",
"Standard query 0x8920 AAAA www.wireshark.org"
"4","0.030017","77","","24.6.173.220","75.75.75.75","128","","DNS","UDP",
"Standard query 0x8920 AAAA www.wireshark.org"
"5","0.003284","135","","75.75.75.75","24.6.173.220","59","","DNS","UDP",
"Standard query response 0x8920 AAAA www.wireshark.org SOA
ns1.softlayer.com"
"6","0.001704","66","0.000000000","24.6.173.220","174.137.42.75","128","",
"TCP","HTTP","42379 >  80 [SYN] Seq=0 Win=8192 Len=0 MSS=1460 WS=4
SACK_PERM=1"
"7","0.008046","135","","75.75.75.75","24.6.173.220","59","","DNS","UDP",
"Standard query response 0x8920 AAAA www.wireshark.org SOA
ns1.softlayer.com"
"8","0.013215","66","0.021261000","174.137.42.75","24.6.173.220","54","",
"TCP","HTTP","80  >  42379 [SYN, ACK] Seq=0 Ack=1 Win=5840 Len=0 MSS=1460
SACK_PERM=1 WS=128"
"9","0.000197","54","0.000197000","24.6.173.220","174.137.42.75","128","",
"TCP","HTTP","42379  >  80 [ACK] Seq=1 Ack=1 Win=65700 Len=0"
"10","0.000853","345","0.000853000","24.6.173.220","174.137.42.75","128","w
ww.wireshark.org","HTTP","HTTP","GET / HTTP/1.1 "
"11","0.020101","60","0.020101000","174.137.42.75","24.6.173.220","54","",
"TCP","HTTP","80  >  42379 [ACK] Seq=1 Ack=292 Win=6912 Len=0"
```

TIP

Before you export the Packet Summary information, right-click on any column heading and select **Displayed Columns** to check for hidden columns. Hidden columns will automatically be included in the exported file. You might like this behavior because you can export large amounts of column data without having all the columns visible as you work. Keep in mind, however, that more columns means more work for Wireshark when it opens and displays files, applies display filters, and applies coloring rules. If you don't want these columns exported, you must remove them.

▣ Lab 30: Export a List of HTTP Host Field Values from a Trace File

In this lab, you will alter the Packet List pane to display the HTTP Host field before exporting information to CSV format.

Step 1:   Open *http-au101b.pcapng*.

Step 2:   In Lab 14 you created an HTTP **Host** column. The column may be hidden right now. Right-click on any column heading in the Packet List pane and select **Displayed Column | Host** (which is based on the field http.host).

If you did not retain your HTTP **Host** column in Lab 14, right-click the **Hypertext Transfer Protocol** section in the Packet Details pane of **frame 8** and select **Expand Subtrees**. Right-click on the **Host** field and select **Apply as Column**. You may need to adjust the new **Host** column width to see the full host name.

Step 3:   Enter **http.host** as a display filter and click the **Apply** button ⊐ or press **Enter**. Only packets that contain this field are displayed. Those are the only packets we want to export in this lab.

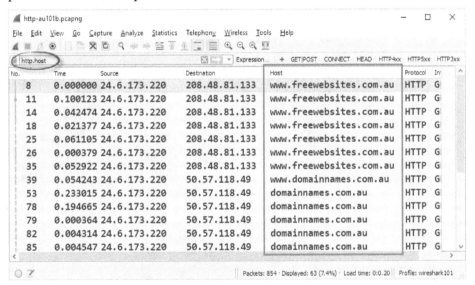

Note that all Packet List pane column information (even information in hidden columns) will be exported. Keep this in mind before adding and hiding lots of columns that you never use. Instead of hiding these columns, consider using **Edit | Preferences | Columns**, selecting the column to delete and clicking the **Delete** button ⊟.

Step 4: Select **File | Export Packet Dissections | As CSV**.

Step 5: Under Packet Range, ensure **All packets** and **Displayed** are selected.

Step 6: Under Packet Format, uncheck **Packet details**. We are only interested in the packet summary line. *Displayed* is already selected in the Export File window.

Enter *hostinformation.csv* in the File Name field and click **Save**.

Step 7: Open your file in a spreadsheet program (such as Excel) and sort on the **Host** column to view a list of all HTTP Host field values seen in the trace file.

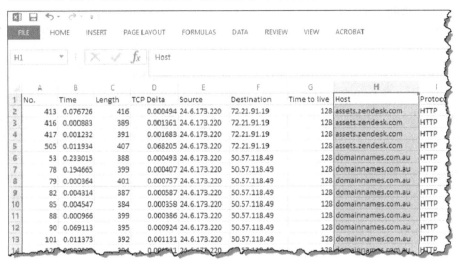

Step 8: Return to Wireshark and click the **Clear** button ☒ to remove your `http.host` filter. Right-click on the **Host** column heading and unselect that column from the list to hide it. If you want to view this column again later, you can right-click on any column heading and select it from the column list.

There are many charts and graphs that cannot be created directly in Wireshark. Exporting the desired fields to a third-party program opens up numerous options for visualizing the traffic.

❶TIP

In Chapter 8, you will learn how to export the HTTP hosts list quickly using the command-line tool Tshark.

Chapter 4 Challenge

Open *challenge101-4.pcapng* and use your packet coloring and export skills in this chapter to answer these Challenge questions. The answer key is located in Appendix A.

Question 4-1.   What coloring rule does frame 170 match?

Question 4-2.   Temporarily color TCP stream 5 with a light blue background and apply a filter on this traffic. How many packets match your filter?

Question 4-3.   Create and apply a coloring rule for TCP delta delays greater than 100 seconds. How many frames match this coloring rule?

Question 4-4.   Export this filtered TCP delta information in CSV format. Using a spreadsheet program, what is the average TCP delta time?

Chapter 5 Skills: Build and Interpret Tables and Graphs

When people ask me why they should use Wireshark, even when they don't have much network protocol knowledge, I tell them to compare Wireshark to an X-ray image. Anyone who sees a pair of scissors on an X-ray image of a person's stomach can tell you what's wrong. There shouldn't be any scissors there.

In Wireshark, there are also things that stand out, like not getting a DNS response or seeing a TCP SYN followed by a TCP RST. By looking more and more at network traces (and reading about the network protocols), you will be able to extract more information from the packets. Just like a doctor who knows what certain tissues should look like, you can extract more information from an X-ray image than the novice eye.

Sake Blok
Wireshark Core Developer
Founder, *SYN-bit*

Quick Reference: IO Graph Interface

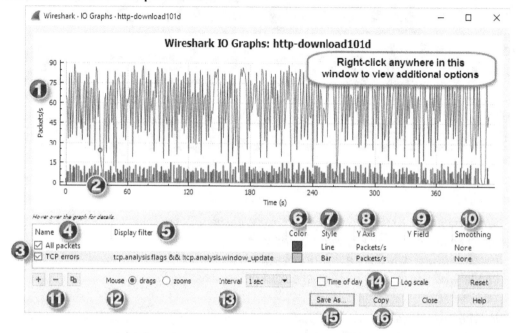

(1) **Graph area (Y axis)** — The Y axis can be set to logarithmic scale[42]

(2) **Graph area (X axis)** — The X axis defaults to seconds; scroll right/left as necessary

(3) **Graph check boxes** — Click these check boxes to enable/disable graph items

(4) **Name of graph item** — This is used as the column heading when you use Copy

(5) **Display Filter area** — Enter a field name or filter to be graphed

(6) **Color** — Select a color for the graph item from a list

(7) **Graph style** — Select what you want your graphed item to look like

(8) **Y Axis** — Change Wireshark's default Y interval setting; access Calc functions (such as SUM, COUNT, AVG, MIN, and MAX) – used with Y Field setting

(9) **Y Field** — Used with the Calc functions

(10) **Smoothing** — Define the Smoothed Moving Average (SMA) values

(11) **Add, Delete, and Copy graph items** — Add as many graph lines as you need!

(12) **Mouse behavior** — Select whether the mouse should drag the graph or zoom in

(13) **Interval** — Change the X axis value

(14) **Log Scale (**Logarithmic scale**)** — Great when plotting disparate number values

(15) **Save As** — Save the graph in PDF, .png, .bmp, .jpg, or .csv format

(16) **Copy** — Buffers the graph item names and plot points to .csv format in memory

---

[42] You will practice logarithmic graphing skills in Lab 36.

5.1. Find Out Who's Talking to Whom on the Network

Whether you are capturing live traffic or are opening a saved trace file, you should always check to see what hosts are communicating on the network.

There are two statistics windows available to determine what hosts are talking on the network: Conversations and Endpoints.

Check Out Network Conversations

We opened the Conversations window in *Filter on a Conversation from Wireshark Statistics* on page 170. In Figure 94 and Figure 95, we opened *http-espn101.pcapng*, selected the **Statistics | Conversations** and expanded the window to see all the columns.

In Figure 94, we selected the **TCP** tab, and sorted the conversations based on the **Bytes** column.

If you have a filter in the display filter area, you can apply that filter to the Conversations window by checking the box in front of **Limit to display filter**. You can also enable the **Name resolution** option, but you must also enable Resolve network (IP) addresses under **Edit | Preferences | Name Resolution**.

Click **Follow Stream** (available under the **TCP** and **UDP** tabs) to reassemble the selected conversation. This often makes it easier to understand communication between hosts.

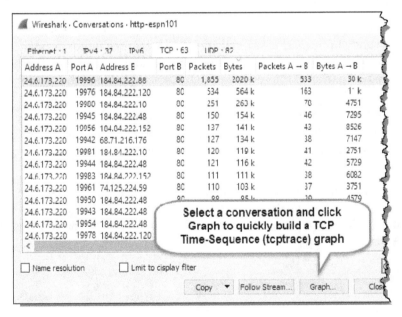

*Figure 94. Select **Statistics | Conversations | TCP** to see which hosts are communicating via TCP.* [http-espn101.pcapng]

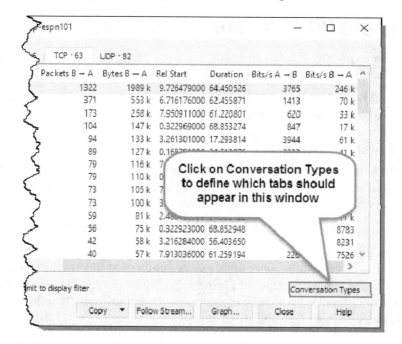

Figure 95. Expand the Conversations window to see the relative start time and duration of the conversations. [http-espn101.pcapng]

If you expand the Conversations window or scroll to the right, you will see the Relative Start (**Rel Start**) and **Duration** columns. The Relative Start time indicates when the conversation started in the trace file. The **Duration** column indicates how much time passed from the first packet of the conversation to the last packet of the conversation.

Quickly Filter on Conversations

To filter on any conversation, right-click on a conversation and select either **Apply as Filter** or **Prepare a Filter**. Unlike standard display filters, when filtering on conversations you can specify the direction you are interested in, as shown in Figure 96.

"A" represents any column that has the "A" designation and "B" represents any column that has the "B" designation. For example, if you click on the **IPv4** tab, you can see Address A and Address B. If you click on the **TCP** tab or **UDP** tab, you can see Address A, Port A and Address B, Port B.

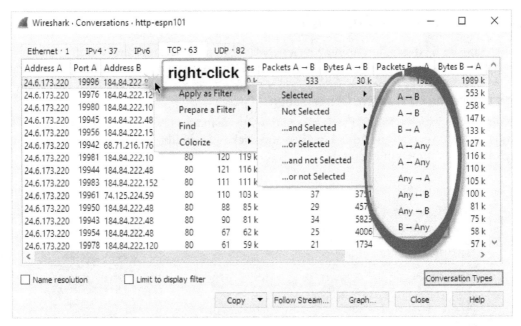

Figure 96. Right-click on any conversation to apply a filter, prepare a filter, find a packet in the conversation, or to build a coloring rule for the conversation. [http-espn101.pcapng]

TIP

Remember to expand the Conversations Window. There are some very important columns (relative time, duration, and bits per second) hidden from view on the right side when this window opens.

5.2. Locate the Top Talkers

When you are trying to determine why a network or link is saturated with traffic, take a look at which hosts are using the most bandwidth (based on bytes, not packets).

Sort to Find the Most Active Conversation

To determine which IPv4 or IPv6 conversations are using up the most bandwidth, select **Statistics | Conversations | IPv4** or **IPv6** and click twice on the **Bytes** column to sort from high to low, as shown in Figure 97.

Wireshark · Conversations · http-espn101									— ☐ ✕

Ethernet · 1   IPv4 · 37   IPv6   TCP · 63   UDP · 82

Address A	Address B	Packets	Bytes	Packets A → B	Bytes A → B	Packets B → A	Bytes B → A	Rel Start
24.6.173.220	184.84.222.88	1,855	2020 k	533	30 k	1322	1989 k	9.726479000
24.6.173.220	184.84.222.48	720	649 k	265	43 k	455	605 k	0.322923000
24.6.173.220	184.84.222.120	613	628 k	195	14 k	418	614 k	6.716176000
24.6.173.220	184.84.222.10	371	382 k	119	7502	252	374 k	7.950911000
24.6.173.220	184.84.222.152	303	286 k	110	25 k	193	261 k	3.261301000
24.6.173.220	68.71.216.176	127	134 k	38	7147	89	127 k	0.168701000
24.6.173.220	74.125.224.59	142	115 k	51	9643	91	105 k	2.843065000
24.6.173.220	184.84.222.16	41	36 k	15	1768	26	35 k	7.951909000
24.6.173.220	184.84.222.75	36	33 k	12	1602	24	32 k	5.377013000
24.6.173.220	138.108.7.20	31	24 k	11	1675	20	23 k	5.436636000
24.6.173.220	68.71.216.171	29	24 k	12	1007	17	23 k	5.192672000
24.6.173.220	75.75.75.75	180	22 k	90	6973	90	15 k	0.000000000
24.6.173.220	68.71.216.157	132	20 k	66	3672	66	16 k	21.802866000
24.6.173.220	184.84.222.137	30	19 k	14	1638	16	17 k	3.270647000

☐ Name resolution   ☐ Limit to display filter   Conversation Types

Copy ▼   Follow Stream...   Graph...   Close   Help

*Figure 97. Sort on the **Bytes** column under the **IPv4** tab or **IPv6** tab to identify the most active conversations in the trace file. [http-espn101.pcapng]*

Right-click on the top conversation line to apply or prepare a filter based on these top talkers, find a packet in the conversation, or build a coloring rule for the conversation.

Sort to Find the Most Active Host

We need to go to another statistics window to find the top single talker on the network. Close the Conversation window, select **Statistics | Endpoints | IPv4** or **IPv6**, and click twice on the **Bytes** column to sort from high to low, as shown in Figure 98. Since the top talker is generally based on bandwidth usage, the **Bytes** column is the best column to use.

If you are interested in the most active transmitter on the network, sort the **Tx Bytes** column from high to low.

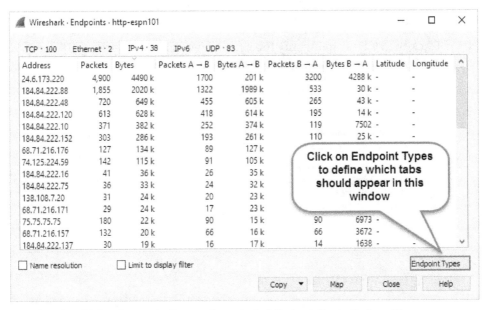

*Figure 98. Sort from high to low on the **Bytes** column to find the top talker in the trace file.* *[http-espn101.pcapng]*

Wireshark displays tabs based on the traffic in the trace file. You can define which tabs appear in this window by clicking on the **Endpoint Types** button.

TIP

The **Map** button is only active when you are looking at the IPv4 and IPv6 tabs. This button can be used to plot the IP addresses on a map of the world. You will get a chance to enable/disable this feature and use this skill in Lab 32.

▢ Lab 31: Filter on the Most Active TCP Conversation

Pulling out the most active conversation is a common network analysis task when trace files contain tens or even hundreds of conversations.

Step 1:   Open *http-misctraffic101.pcapng*.

Step 2:   Select **Statistics | Conversations**.

Step 3:   Click on the **IPv4** tab to examine the two IPv4 conversations in this trace file. Based on the bytes count, the most active IPv4 conversation is between 24.6.181.160 and 107.6.133.250.

Step 4:   Click the **TCP** tab to identify the most active TCP conversation. Click twice on the **Bytes** column heading to sort from high to low.

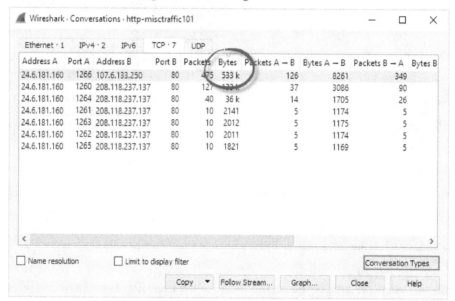

We can see the most active TCP conversation is between 24.6.181.160 on port 1266 (a dynamic port number) and 107.6.133.250 on port 80.

Notice that clients use a dynamic port number when they communicate with an HTTP server. In this case, the client has selected port 1266. If you'd prefer to see resolved port names rather than port numbers, you must enable transport name resolution and check the **Name resolution** check box on this screen.

Step 5: Right-click on the most active TCP conversation and select **Apply as Filter | Selected | A ←→ B**. Wireshark automatically creates and applies a display filter for this TCP conversation.

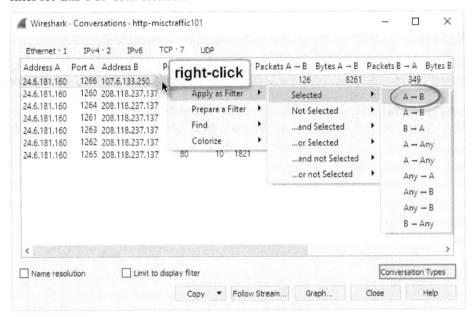

The result of this filter is shown below. There are 475 packets that match this filter.

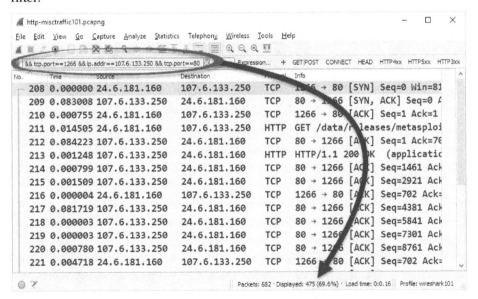

Step 6:   Click the **Clear** button ⊠ to remove your display filter before continuing. Toggle to the Conversations window and click **Close**.

!TIP

You can add other conversations to your filter easily by returning to the Conversations window, right-clicking on another TCP conversation and selecting **Apply as Filter | ...or Selected**. Spend some time becoming proficient using this method for conversation filtering. You can also click the **Copy** button in the Conversations window to buffer the current Conversations view in CSV format. You can then paste the information into a text file, name the file with a .csv extension and open it in a spreadsheet program to further analyze the information.

Lab 32: Set up GeoIP to Map Targets Globally

Wireshark can use the MaxMind GeoLite database files to list the country, city, AS (Autonomous System) number, latitude, and longitude of an IP address and map IPv4 and IPv6 addresses on a map of the earth. In this lab, you will configure Wireshark to use this database and map IP addresses seen in a trace file.

Step 1:   Open *http-browse101c.pcapng*.

Step 2:   Visit *www.maxmind.com* and download the free legacy GeoLite database files (geo*.dat files). These files can be found by clicking the link to the GeoIP databases and services link and looking for the GeoLite database files link.[43]

Step 3:   To enable the GeoIP feature, create a directory called *maxmind* on your drive and place the *maxmind* files in that directory. Now select **Edit | Preferences | Name Resolution** and click the GeoIP database directories **Edit** button.

Click the **Add** button + and browse to your *maxmind* directory. Click **Select Folder**. Click **OK** to close the GeoIP Database Paths window and **OK** to close the Wireshark Preferences window.

Step 4:   Select **Statistics | Endpoints** and click on the **IPv4** tab. You should see information in the **Country**, **AS Number**, **City**, **Latitude**, and **Longitude** columns.

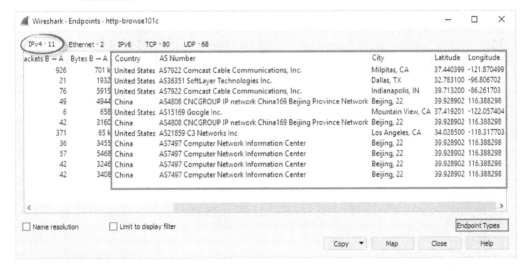

---

43   At the time this book was written, the direct link to the MaxMind GeoLite database files was *dev.maxmind.com/geoip/legacy/geolite/*, but this may change. Just look around their web site for any reference to the free GeoIP database and the free GeoLite binary/gzip files.

Step 5:   Click the **Map** button. Wireshark will launch a global view in your browser with the known IP address points plotted on the map. This process uses ActiveX, which may require that you allow the ActiveX process to run. Click on any of the plot points to find more information about the IP address.

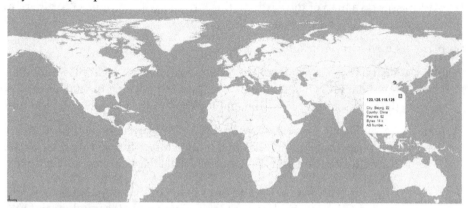

Step 6:   **LAB CLEAN-UP** Close the browser window when you are finished. Spend some time capturing your own traffic and mapping it globally. Learn where your packets are traveling.

GeoIP mapping is very helpful when you are concerned about the external destination of your traffic. For example, if you work at a facility that should not have outbound traffic leaving the country, GeoIP maps can help identify unwanted external targets.

5.3. List Applications Seen on the Network

If you are concerned about the type of traffic flowing over a network (perhaps you suspect a host is compromised), use Wireshark to characterize TCP- and UDP-based applications.

View the Protocol Hierarchy

Select **Statistics | Protocol Hierarchy** to determine which protocols and applications are in a trace file. In Figure 99, we opened *http-browse101b.pcapng*. We can see this trace file contains IPv4 and IPv6 traffic. There is only UDP traffic running over IPv6 and only TCP traffic running over IPv4.

You cannot sort or reorder items in the Protocol Hierarchy because of the hierarchical structure of the list.

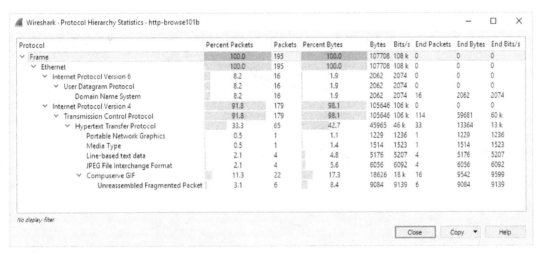

Protocol	Percent Packets	Packets	Percent Bytes	Bytes	Bits/s	End Packets	End Bytes	End Bits/s
∨ Frame	100.0	195	100.0	107708	108 k	0	0	0
∨ Ethernet	100.0	195	100.0	107708	108 k	0	0	0
∨ Internet Protocol Version 6	8.2	16	1.9	2062	2074	0	0	0
∨ User Datagram Protocol	8.2	16	1.9	2062	2074	0	0	0
Domain Name System	8.2	16	1.9	2062	2074	16	2062	2074
∨ Internet Protocol Version 4	91.8	179	98.1	105646	106 k	0	0	0
∨ Transmission Control Protocol	91.8	179	98.1	105646	106 k	114	59681	60 k
∨ Hypertext Transfer Protocol	33.3	65	42.7	45965	46 k	33	13364	13 k
Portable Network Graphics	0.5	1	1.1	1229	1236	1	1229	1236
Media Type	0.5	1	1.4	1514	1523	1	1514	1523
Line-based text data	2.1	4	4.8	5176	5207	4	5176	5207
JPEG File Interchange Format	2.1	4	5.6	6056	6092	4	6056	6092
∨ Compuserve GIF	11.3	22	17.3	18626	18 k	16	9542	9599
Unreassembled Fragmented Packet	3.1	6	8.4	9084	9139	6	9084	9139

No display filter.

Figure 99. Wireshark creates a hierarchical view of the protocols and applications seen in the trace file. [http-browse101b.pcapng]

Right-Click to Filter or Colorize any Listed Protocol or Application

To perform further research on any type of traffic shown, right-click on a line and select **Apply as Filter** or **Prepare a Filter**. You can also use right-click to build a coloring rule based on a protocol or application.

Look for Suspicious Protocols, Applications or "Data"

This is a great window to examine when you think a host may be compromised. For example, this window would help you identify unusual network applications, such as (1) Distributed Computing Environment/Remote Procedure Call (DCE/RPC) traffic directly under TCP, (2) Internet Relay Chat (IRC) traffic, or (3) Trivial File Transfer Protocol (TFTP) traffic, as shown in Figure 100. When you see this suspicious traffic, right-click to filter on the traffic and examine the traffic to determine if it is malicious[44].

"Data" listed directly under TCP or UDP in the Protocol Hierarchy window indicates that Wireshark could not apply a dissector to the traffic because it does not recognize the port number and no heuristic dissector matched the packets.

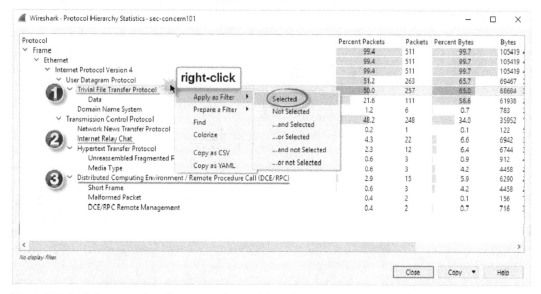

Figure 100. Look for unusual applications or the word "data" directly under TCP or UDP.
[sec-concern101.pcapng]

---

44   The only way to really know what is "unusual" is to know what is usual. Capture and analyze your traffic to learn what applications are typically seen on your network.

📖 Lab 33: Detect Suspicious Protocols or Applications

When you are concerned that there may be a security issue in your trace file, open the Protocol Hierarchy window first. Look for suspicious applications or protocols and the dreaded "data" directly under IP, UDP, or TCP.

Step 1:   Open *general101c.pcapng*.

Step 2:   Select **Statistics | Protocol Hierarchy**. This trace file contains some traffic of concern. We see Internet Relay Chat and Data under the TCP section.

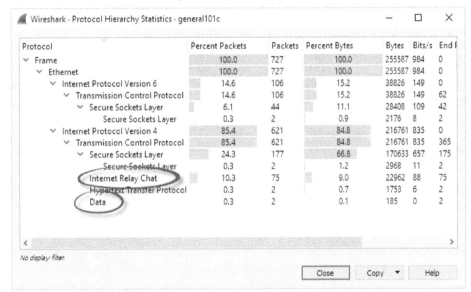

Step 3:   Right-click on the **Internet Relay Chat** line and select **Apply as Filter | Selected** to examine it further. Expand the Internet Relay Chat section in the Packet Details pane to learn more about the communications. Look for the user name and the target IRC server. Perform the same steps to examine the traffic listed as "data." In Chapter 6 you will revisit this file to reassemble the communications for further analysis.

Step 4:   **LAB CLEAN-UP** Click the **Clear** button ☒ to remove any display filters. Toggle back to the Protocol Hierarchy window and click the **Close** button.

Remember to use the Protocol Hierarchy window first when you suspect malicious traffic on the network. It's a quick way to find breached hosts.

5.4. *Graph Application and Host Bandwidth Usage*

Although you can use the Protocol Hierarchy to determine the percent of total bytes or packets that an application uses, a graph can help you analyze the flow of applications in a trace file.

Export the Application or Host Traffic before Graphing

One of the easiest ways to determine how much bandwidth an application or host is using is to filter on that traffic type and export the traffic to a separate trace file. For example, *http-download101e.pcapng* contains traffic to and from a single host, 24.6.173.220. This trace file was created by exporting a host's traffic from a larger trace file.

Note: *This is a large trace file (168 MB) and may be slow to load.*

Select **Statistics | I/O Graph** to plot all the traffic in the trace file based on packets or bits. By default, Wireshark plots the packets per second (Y axis). When we categorize the bandwidth usage of an application, we talk about bits per second or megabits per second. In Figure 101, we changed the Y axis to **Bits/s**. This gives us a clear view of the traffic to and from that single host. This download process averages 5 Mbps.

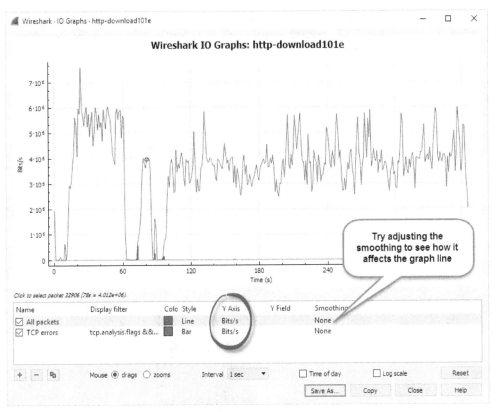

Figure 101. The IO Graph shows the flow of traffic in a trace file. [http-download101e.pcapng]

If you want to compare application usage in an IO Graph, define the application traffic in the filter areas. When you graph TCP-based applications, be sure to base your filter on a port number (`tcp.port==80`) rather than the application name to make sure you capture the connection setup and acknowledgments. For UDP-based applications, such as DNS, you can filter based on the application name (`dns`) or port number. If you are graphing a protocol, such as ICMP, simply filter on the protocol name (`icmp`) and export the packets to a new trace file. We will cover applying port filters to IO Graphs after we examine applying IP address filters to IO Graphs.

Apply `ip.addr` Display Filters to the IO Graph

If your trace file contains several IP conversations, you can use display filter syntax to graph the conversation for you.

On the IO Graph, click the **Add** button ⊞ and enter your IP address filter in the **Display filter** area. Click the **check box** in front of your new graph item to activate it.

In Figure 102, we opened *tr-twohosts.pcapng* and graphed two IP addresses using `ip.addr==` filters for 192.168.1.72 (Paige) and 192.168.1.119 (Scott). We disabled the **All packets** graph item and the **TCP errors** graph item. We also used two different styles to differentiate the graphed items.

This IO Graph indicates that traffic flowing to/from Paige's machine is much more steady averaging approximately 1,100 packets per second. The traffic to/from Scott's machine appears to be sporadic with highs around 2,200 packets per second and lows of 0 packets per second. You can use this type of filtered graph to compare the traffic rates of two or more hosts.

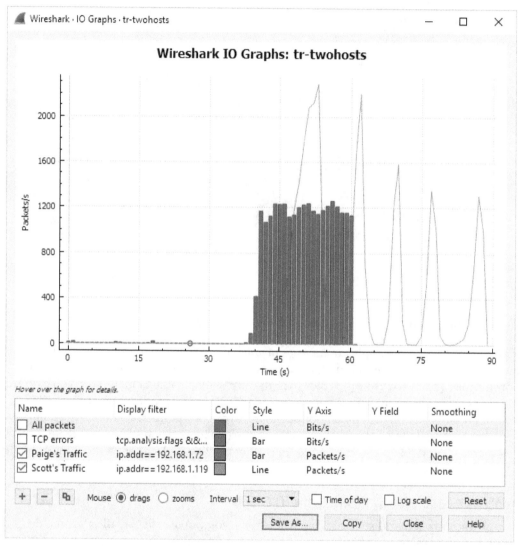

Figure 102. Use the IO Graph to identify trends in traffic to or from separate hosts. [tr-twohosts.pcapng]

Apply `ip.src` Display Filters to the IO Graph

If you want to graph unidirectional traffic, use an `ip.src`, `ip.dst`, `ipv6.src` or `ipv6.dst` display filter.

For example, in Figure 103, we opened *http-download101e.pcapng* and launched the IO Graph. We added two graph lines using the `ip.src` filter with the IP address of a client downloading a file (Jill at 24.6.173.220) and the IP address of a server that is sending a file to this client in the trace file (199.255.156.18). We changed the Y axis to Bits/s.

This graph indicates that Jill's machine is more active at the very beginning of the trace file (as it communicates with other servers and resolves addresses).

Approximately 10 seconds into the trace file, however, we see the majority of the traffic is transmitted by the server (199.255.156.18). In fact, traffic from the server accounts for almost all the bits/s graphed.

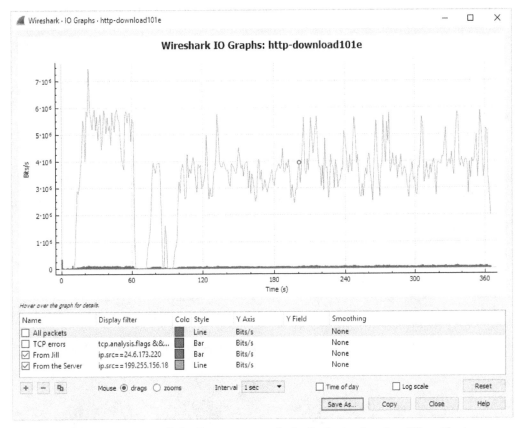

Figure 103. Using `ip.src`*, we applied a filter to compare the traffic flowing from two different hosts.* [http-download101e.pcapng]

Apply `tcp.port` or `udp.port` Display Filters to the IO Graph

If you want to compare the bandwidth use of numerous applications in a trace file, simply filter on the port number for TCP-based applications or on the application name or port number for UDP-based applications.

In Figure 104, we launched the IO Graph while we were running a live capture. We set the Y Axis to Bits/s. To find out how much bandwidth was in use by HTTP traffic on port 80, we added a display filter (`tcp.port==80`) as our third graph item. We added a filter for HTTPS traffic as the fourth graph item (`tcp.port==443`). We disabled the **All packets** and **TCP errors** graph items. Our graph indicates that port 80 traffic appears to peak around 27 seconds into the trace process while port 443 traffic appears to peak approximately 36 seconds into the trace process.

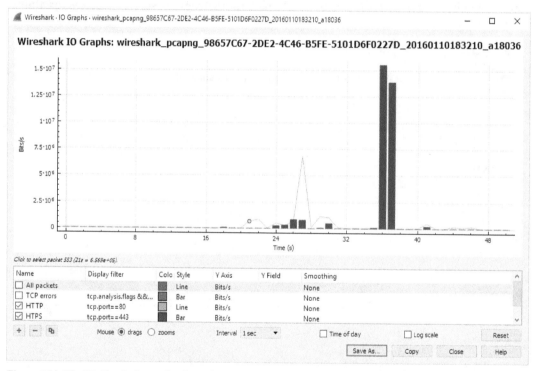

Figure 104. The IO Graph shows the flow of traffic during a live capture process or when opening a saved trace file. [live capture process]

Lab 34: Compare Traffic to/from a Subnet to Other Traffic

In this lab you will compare all the traffic to or from subnet 184.0.0.0/8 to all other traffic. To do this, you will use two IP address filters—one inclusion filter and one exclusion filter.

Step 1:   Open *http-espn101.pcapng*.

Step 2:   Select **Statistics | I/O Graph**.

Step 3:   Unselect the **check boxes** in front of the **All packets** and **TCP errors** graph items. We will not be using them in this lab.

Step 4:   First we will work with an inclusion filter. Click the **Add** button ⊞ and enter `ip.addr==184.0.0.0/8` in the Display filter field. Set the graph style to **Line**. Set the Y Axis to **Bits/s**.

Click the **check box** in front of the name field (which we cleared) to enable the graph item.

Step 5:   Now we will work with an exclusion filter. Click the **Add** button ⊞ again and enter `!ip.addr==184.0.0.0/8` in the Display filter field. Set the graph style to **Bar**. Set the Y Axis to **Bits/s**.

Click the **check box** in front of the name field (which we cleared) to enable the graph item.

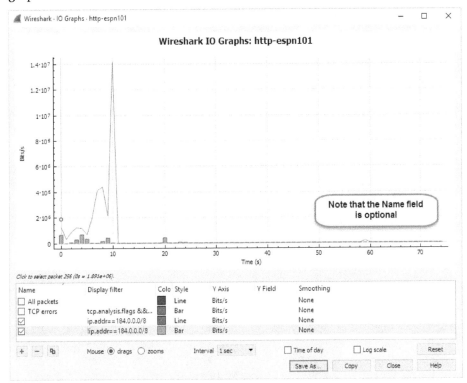

Step 5:   **LAB CLEAN-UP** Close your IO Graph before you move on.

It is easy to graph traffic to or from various subnets. Consider capturing traffic on your network to determine where it is flowing.

5.5. Identify TCP Errors on the Network

Wireshark understands many types of TCP network errors, such as packet loss and receiver congestion. When Wireshark sees packets that indicate network problems have occurred, it makes a note in the Expert System.

Use the Expert Information Button on the Status Bar

We will leave the IO Graphing for a moment to view the Expert window. The Expert Information button is on the far left side of the Status Bar. Click the **Expert Information** button ⊘ to open the Expert Information window. The Expert classifies information into five categories. The color on the **Expert Information** button indicates the highest layer of Expert detail seen:

- Error: red
- Warn (Warning): yellow
- Note: cyan
- Chat: blue
- Comment: green

In Figure 105, the Expert Information button is yellow, which indicates that there are no Expert errors, but there are warnings in *http-espn101.pcapng*.

Figure 105. The Expert Information button is color-coded to let you know the highest level of Expert detail seen. [http-espn101.pcapng]

Examine Expert Severity Levels

In Figure 106, we clicked on the **Expert Information** button and we see six items listed. Each item is color-coded. These are the colors that will appear on the Expert Information button. In this trace file we do not see the Errors level – we just see Warn (Warnings), Note, and Chat.

Generally, I focus only on Errors and Warnings.

The Group column further classifies the items. "Malformed" means that a Wireshark dissector did not fully dissect a field or protocol. This could be an indication of a non-standard packet structure, out-of-date packet structure or field use, out-of-date dissector, or perhaps just a broken dissector.

Sequence group items relate to problems in sequential communications, such as TCP (as also indicated in the Protocol column).

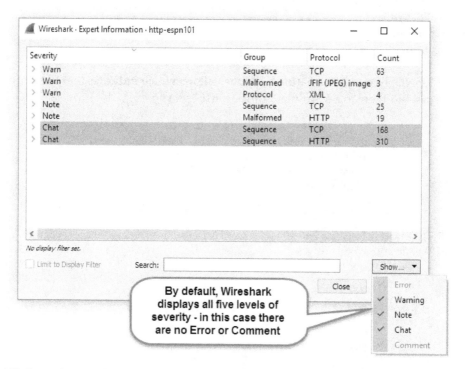

Figure 106. Expert items are broken up into separate severity levels and groups. [http-espn101.pcapng]

In Figure 107 we have expanded the top Warn group to examine the types of issues Wireshark detected. It appears we have several indications that there is a receive buffer problem in the trace file (zero window condition). Each line begins with the packet that triggered the warning. You can use the Expert to move quickly around the trace file. If you click on the second item listed, Wireshark jumps to packet 256 in the trace file.

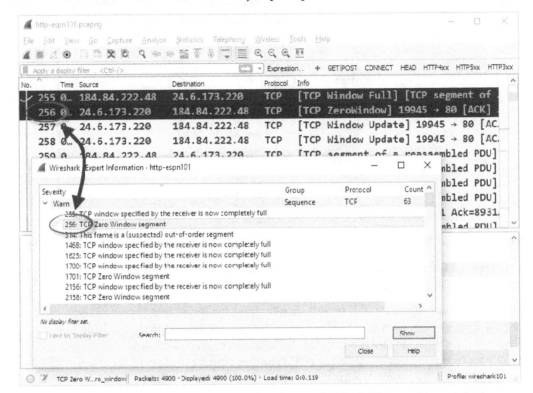

Figure 107. The Warnings area indicates that a host has run out of receive buffer space (Zero window). [http-espn101.pcapng]

Filter on TCP Analysis Flag Packets

You can quickly obtain a count of the individual TCP analysis flag packets by right-clicking on an item listed in the Expert and selecting **Apply as Filter** or **Prepare a Filter**. In Figure 108, we opened *challenge101-5.pcapng* and launched the Expert Information window. We right clicked on Packet 8 under the Warn tab, selected **Apply as Filter | Selected**.

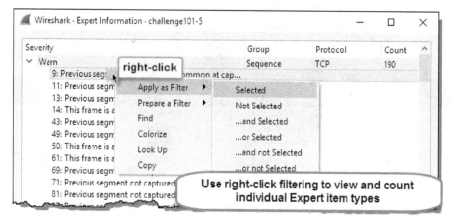

Figure 108. You can use right-click filtering inside the Expert Information window. [challenge101-5.pcapng]

This created a filter for `tcp.analysis.lost_segment`. There are 172 instances of this warning in *challenge101-5.pcapng*.

Alternately, you could simply type in a display filter for `tcp.analysis.flags`. If you are only interested in viewing TCP problems in the trace file, explicitly exclude the Window Update packets by filtering for `tcp.analysis.flags &&` `!tcp.analysis.window_update`. TCP Window Update packets are marked with a TCP analysis flag, but they are not a problem. They are an indication that a host has just increased its advertised receive buffer space.

5.6.   Understand what those Expert Information Errors Mean

Wireshark can detect many network problems, but it does not tell you what causes those problems. Understanding the causes of the errors, warnings, and notes will help you figure out what may be affecting network performance.

This section lists the most common causes of the various Expert errors, warnings, and notes.

Packet Loss, Recovery, and Faulty Trace Files

Before looking for application problems, check to see if there are TCP errors in the trace file. No application can perform well when the underlying network is falling apart.

Previous Segment Not Captured (Warnings)

This warning indicates that Wireshark did not see the previous packet(s) in a TCP communication. Wireshark tracks the packet ordering based on TCP Sequence Numbers and can therefore easily detect when packets are missing. Packet loss typically occurs at an internetwork device, such as a switch or a router. Compare the sender's TCP Sequence Number in a packet marked this way to the sender's previous packet to see how many packets were lost.

ACKed Segment that Wasn't Captured (Warnings)

This warning indicates that Wireshark saw a TCP ACK, but it did not see the data packet that is being acknowledged. If you were capturing on a spanned switch, the switch may be overloaded and unable to forward all the packets to Wireshark. A trace file containing numerous ACKed Segment that Wasn't Captured warnings should not be used for analysis. You do not have a complete view of traffic.

Duplicate ACK (Notes)

These notes indicate that a TCP host receiving data from another host believes a packet is missing. This is, in essence, a complaint requesting a missing packet. When the sender receives three ACKs requesting the same data packet (as noted in the Acknowledgment Number field of the ACKs), it should resend the missing packet. These are part of the packet loss recovery process and are likely caused by a switch or router dropping packets.

Retransmission (Notes)

These notes occur when Wireshark sees two data packets with the same sequence number. A sender will retransmit a packet when it doesn't receive a timely acknowledgment for a data packet that it sent. This is another part of the packet loss recovery process (which is most likely caused by a switch or router dropping packets).

Fast Retransmission (Notes)

These notes occur when Wireshark sees the data packet that someone requested through duplicate ACKs within 20 ms or within the Initial Round Trip Time (iRTT) of one of those duplicate ACKs. This is another part of the packet loss recovery process (which is also most likely caused by a switch or router dropping packets).

Spurious Retransmission (Notes)

These notes occur when Wireshark sees the data packet being resent after it has witnessed the ACK for that data packet. From Wireshark's perspective, the sender of the retransmission is not behaving properly. In truth, however, perhaps you are capturing traffic closer to the receiver and the ACK simply did not arrive at the sender of the data packet. In that case, we may see the ACK, but it never made it to the sender of the data packet. They should retransmit the data packet in that case.

Asymmetrical or Multiple Path Indications

Asymmetrical paths are indicated when packets travel one path outbound and another path inbound. Multiple paths are indicated when the individual packets of a data stream can be separated and travel different routes to the target. This can cause problems if one path is faster than another.

Out-of-Order (Warnings)

This warning indicates that Wireshark saw a packet that has a lower TCP sequence number than a previous packet. This may indicate that traffic flowed along different paths to reach the target. This typically is not a problem unless the receiver times out waiting for the out-of-order packet and begins to complain by sending duplicate ACKs.

Keep-Alive Indication

The TCP keep-alive process is designed to hold an idle TCP connection open for future use. However, since the connection establishment process doesn't take much time, tearing down the connection when it is idle relieves both TCP peers of the unnecessary overhead of maintaining the connection.

Keep-Alive (Warnings)

A TCP Keep-Alive packet is sent when a TCP host hasn't received any communication from a peer for a certain amount of time. If no Keep-Alive ACK is received, the connection may be terminated. The amount of time that a host waits before generating a Keep-Alive can usually be configured on a TCP host. This isn't seen as a problem.

Keep-Alive ACK (Notes)

This note is the response to a Keep-Alive packet. It is not seen as a problem.

Receive Buffer Congestion Indications

Each side of a TCP connection maintains a receive buffer (receive window) for incoming data. If an application is slow taking data out of the buffer, it may fill. When the buffer becomes full, a host advertises a zero window condition—no more data can be sent to that host on that connection until the host indicates it has buffer space through a Window Update packet.

Window Full (Notes)

This note indicates that Wireshark has calculated that the packet will fill the available receive buffer space of the target. This packet itself is not a problem, but it can be the last packet before a zero window condition.

Zero Window (Warnings)

Zero Window warnings indicate that the sender is advertising a TCP window size value of 0, meaning it has no receive buffer space available. The other side of the TCP connection cannot send more data if there is no receive buffer space available. The application running on the host that sent the zero window packet is not picking up data from the receive buffer. This can be caused by a faulty application, overloaded host, or even an intentional user-prompting process (for example, the prompt to save a file to a specific location).

Zero Window Probe (Notes)

This note indicates that a host is trying to determine if the target has any receive buffer space available. In general, this is an optional part of the zero window recovery process.

Zero Window Probe ACK (Notes)

This note indicates a host has responded to a Zero Window Probe. If the window size is still set at zero then the zero window condition continues.

Window Update (Chats)

This chat detail indicates that the sender is advertising more TCP receive buffer space than in the previous packet. This is commonly seen in TCP communications and it is the recovery packet seen after a zero window condition.

TCP Connection Port Reuse Indication

Connection reuse can become a problem if an application simply allows connection timeout at its own leisure. If the connection is not fully terminated before a host tries to use the port number again, it should receive a service refusal (TCP Reset).

Reused Ports (Notes)

This note indicates that a host is using the same port number as a previous connection between the same two hosts in the trace file. Some applications may reuse previous ports, but security scanning tools do this as well. The source of these packets should be investigated.

Possible Router Problem Indication

It seems that as routers become smarter and smarter, they also become dumber. Always test router configurations and enhancements to see if the router alters the packet in an unacceptable way, such as the issue listed below.

4 NOPs in a Row (Warnings)

This warning indicates that the TCP option value 0x01, a NOP (No Operation) option, has been seen four times in a row in a packet. Since these NOPs are used to pad a TCP header to end on a 4-byte boundary, you should never see four in a row. This is typically caused by a misbehaving router along the path.

Misconfiguration or ARP Poisoning Indication

This is an expert indication that must be investigated further to determine if you are facing an intentional or unintentional problem.

Duplicate IP Address Configured (Warnings)

This warning indicates that two or more ARP (Address Resolution Protocol) response packets offer different hardware addresses for the same IP address. This is very unusual and can either indicate that a host IP address was configured incorrectly (a static address that conflicts with the same address as a dynamically-assigned address) or a system is ARP poisoning the network.

When troubleshooting network communications, always open the Expert Information window to identify any warnings or notes. Look for any problems related to TCP before pointing at an application as the cause of poor performance.

Lab 35: Identify an Overloaded Client

In this lab we use the Expert Information window to identify the cause of poor network performance. Not only is the client overloaded in this trace file, but there is packet loss along the path as well.

Step 1:   Open *http-download101.pcapng*.

Step 2:   Click the **Expert Information** button on the Status Bar.

Step 3:   Expand the **Warn** and **Note** sections to examine the problems detected in this trace file.

Step 4:   In the **Warn** section, click on **363: TCP window specified by the receiver is now completely full**. Wireshark jumps to packet 363 in the trace file. This is where Wireshark indicates that the client is going to run out of receive buffer space.

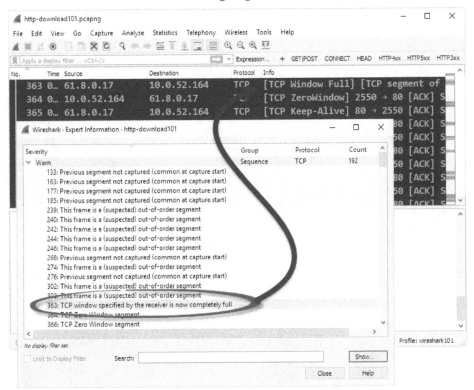

If you look past the window zero problem in this trace file, you can see the client recover with Window Update packets in frames 377 and 378. A quick glance at the **Time** column (set to *Seconds Since Previous Displayed Packet*) and you'll understand why this is a condition to watch for on your network.

Step 5:   LAB CLEAN-UP   When you are finished looking through the Expert information, click the **Close** button in the Expert Information window.

The Expert Information window is one of the first places you should look when analyzing network performance issues.

5.7. *Graph Various Network Errors*

Wireshark understands many types of TCP network errors, such as packet loss and receiver congestion. When Wireshark sees packets that indicate network problems have occurred, it tags the packets with "`tcp.analysis.flags.`"

Just as you applied IP address and port filters in the previous tasks, you can also graph all TCP analysis flags or specific flags.

Graph all TCP Analysis Flag Packets (Except Window Updates)

If you are going to graph all the TCP errors, you will need to exclude one type of tagged packet that was tagged incorrectly. A window update packet is good. It indicates a host has more buffer space available to receive data. Wireshark tags these packets with the `tcp.analysis.flags` setting. Most other items flagged this way indicate that there are TCP problems so we must explicitly exclude the window update packets when graphing TCP problems.

In Figure 109, we opened *http-download101.pcapng* and graphed All packets and TCP error packets. We explicitly excluded the window update packets in our TCP errors filter (`tcp.analysis.flags && !tcp.analysis.window_update`).

If we look closely at this graph we can see a correlation between increases in TCP errors at the points where we have a decrease in the packets/second rate. This indicates a relationship between TCP problems and throughput issues.

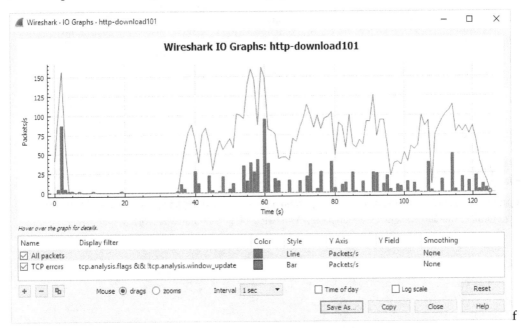

Figure 109. We graphed all the `tcp.analysis.flags` *packets while excluding the window update packets.*
[http-download101.pcapng]

Graph Separate Types of TCP Analysis Flag Packets

In Figure 110, we graphed separate TCP problems to show the relationship between them. Lost segments lead to duplicate ACKs which lead to retransmissions. In this graph we used the Stacked Bar style.

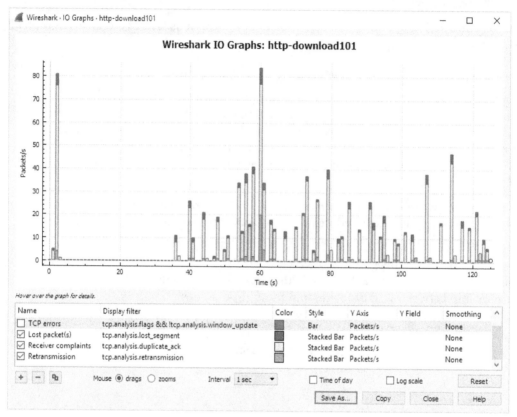

Figure 110. You can plot the separate TCP problems to observe the relationship between them. [http-download101.pcapng]

 TIP

A picture really is worth a thousand words. By graphing the TCP analysis flag packets alongside the general flow of traffic, you can see the relationship between TCP problems and drops in throughput.

Lab 36: Detect and Graph File Transfer Problems

In this lab we examine a file transfer process that takes place over TCP. Before we can consider troubleshooting the application itself, we must rule out TCP problems.

Step 1:   Open *general101d.pcapng*.

Step 2:   Click the **Expert Information** button ⬭ on the Status Bar.

Step 3:   Expand and examine the **Warn** and **Note** sections to see which problems were identified by Wireshark in the trace file.

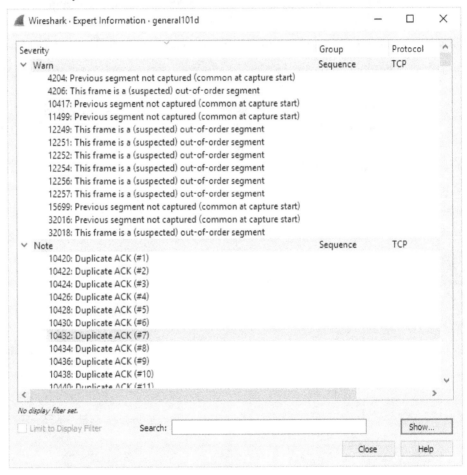

You may notice the following:

- Wireshark does not indicate a very high number of *Previous segment not captured* instances.

- Wireshark does indicate there are a lot of *Duplicate ACKs* (requests for retransmissions after packet loss).

- Wireshark indicates that there are a fair number of retransmissions in this trace file.

All of this points to significant packet loss occurring at a single time—one big chunk of data did not make it to the receiver.

Step 4:   Close the **Expert Information** window and select **Statistics | I/O Graph**.

Step 5:   Graph all `tcp.analysis.flags && !tcp.analysis.window_update` in the Graph 2 filter area.

The graph isn't very impressive at this point because we are graphing two very disparate values—the packets per second vs. these specific analysis flag packets.

One of the problems you will face over and over is the problem of graphing two very different values. When you encounter this issue, change the Y axis scale to logarithmic.

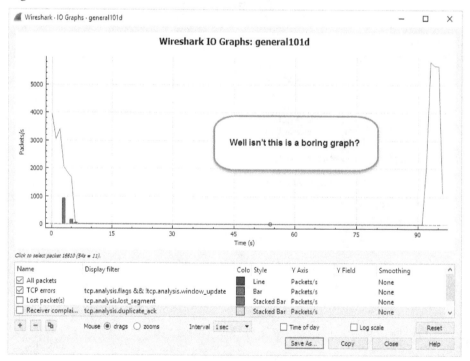

Step 6:   Click the **Log scale check box** to enable the logarithmic scale function. This will completely change the look of your graph.

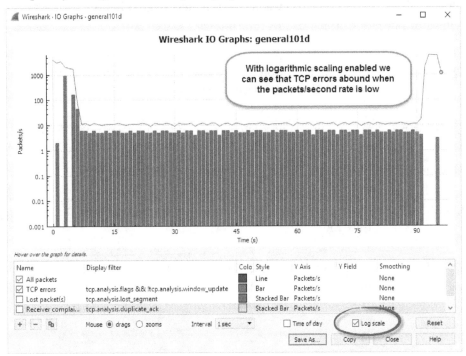

We can now see that TCP errors spiked just before the drop in throughput. When you click on any plotted point in the graph, Wireshark jumps to that spot in the trace file, allowing you to examine the situation further.

Step 7:   **LAB CLEAN-UP** Click the **Close** button when you are finished viewing the IO Graph.

You can build a graph on any display filter value. When performance problems arise, graphing TCP problems alongside all traffic enables you to find out if the TCP problems are related to throughput drops.

Chapter 5 Challenge

Open *challenge101-5.pcapng* and use the techniques covered in this chapter to answer these Challenge questions. The answer key is located in Appendix A.

Question 5-1.   Create an IO Graph for this trace file. What is the highest packets-per-second value seen in this trace file?

Question 5-2.   What is the highest bits-per-second value seen in this trace file?

Question 5-3.   How many TCP conversations are in this trace file?

Question 5-4.   How many times has *"Previous segment not captured"* been detected in this trace file?

Question 5-5.   How many retransmissions and fast retransmissions are seen in this trace file?

Chapter 6 Skills: Reassemble Traffic for Faster Analysis

Network analysis is all about the packets: what kind of story are the packets telling? Even if you speak fluent binary, you need a tool that will quickly break down the packets and the protocols/packet structure. If your login fails, what really failed? The packets will tell you. What if you are using LANDesk to capture an image and it gets so far, looking successful, then just dies. No errors. Nothing. The packets tell the story (your imaging AD account password expired...who knew?) Look at the packets first instead of "when all else fails."

Lanell Allen
Wireshark Certified Network Analyst™

Quick Reference: File and Object Reassembly Options

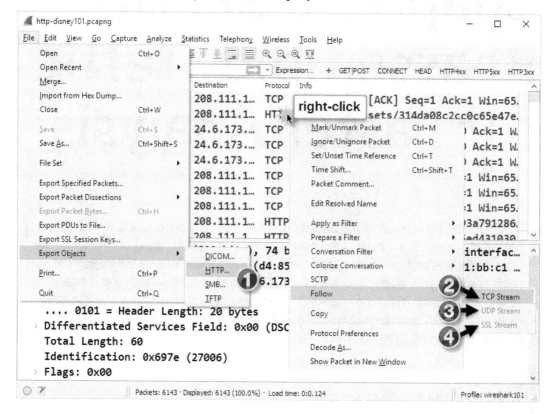

(1) Select **File | Export Objects | [DICOM|HTTP|SMB|TFTP]** to export reassembled objects[45]

(2) Right-click in the Packet List pane and select **Follow | TCP Stream**[46] (TCP stream filter)

(3) Right-click in the Packet List pane and select **Follow | UDP Stream** (UDP port numbers and IP addresses filter)

(4) Right-click in the Packet List pane and select **Follow | SSL Stream** (SSL port number and IP addresses filter)

---

[45] Be sure to enable the *Allow subdissector to reassemble TCP streams* TCP preference setting before attempting reassembly.

[46] Wireshark automatically detects if you right-clicked on a TCP, UDP or SSL stream. SSL streams must be decrypted to be reassembled and viewed.

6.1. Reassemble Web Browsing Sessions

Whether you are troubleshooting a slow web browsing session or you just want to look "under the hood" of an HTTP communication, you can use Wireshark's reassembly feature to see what's really going on by rebuilding the conversations between HTTP clients and servers.

Use Follow | TCP Stream

Right-click on an HTTP packet in the Packet List pane and select **Follow | TCP Stream**. Wireshark rebuilds the conversation without any MAC-layer, IPv4/IPv6, UDP/TCP headers or field names. The result is a clearer picture of what is being said between hosts. In Figure 111, we opened *http-browse101.pcapng*, right-clicked on packet 10 (an HTTP GET request) in the Packet List pane, and selected **Follow | TCP Stream**. The conversation is color-coded: red for the first host seen in the conversation and blue for the second host seen in the conversation[47].

Figure 111. The communications become much clearer when you follow the stream. [http-browse101.pcapng]

If you look at the display filter area, you'll note that Wireshark applies a filter based on the TCP Stream index (`tcp.stream eq 0`). This is a unique number given to each TCP conversation. This is the first TCP stream in the file, and is given stream index number 0.

TCP stream numbers are assigned by Wireshark. This field does not exist in the actual packet.

---

47   If you captured the browsing session beginning with the TCP handshake, the client communications will be in red and the server communications will be in blue.

Use Find, Save, and Filter on a Stream

There are several options available after you follow a stream.

- Click **Find** to search for a text string.

- Click on the up/down arrows on the Stream field to reassemble different streams.

- Click **Save As** to save the conversation as a separate file. The Save As feature is great if you want to export a file that was transported across a conversation.

- Select **Hide this stream** to create and apply an exclusion display filter for this stream (`!tcp.stream eq 0`). The ability to filter out conversations after examining them is crucial in narrowing down suspicious traffic on a network.

You will use the Save As function in Lab 38.

Lab 37: Use Reassembly to Find a Web Site's Hidden HTTP Message

It is not unusual to have numerous "hidden" messages sent to your browser when you hit a web site. In this lab you will analyze a trace file that contains two hidden messages. Afterwards, visit the same web site again to catch other interesting messages.

Step 1:   Open *http-wiresharkdownload101.pcapng*.

Step 2:   The first three packets are the TCP handshake for the web server connection. Frame 4 is the client's GET request for the *download.html* page. Right-click on frame 4 and select **Follow | TCP stream**.

Traffic from the first host seen in the trace file, the client in this case, is colored red. Traffic from the second host seen in the trace file, the server in this case, will be colored blue.

Step 3:   Wireshark displays the conversation without the Ethernet, IP, or TCP headers. Scroll through the stream to look for the hidden message from Gerald Combs, creator of Wireshark. It is located in the server stream and begins with *X-Slogan*.

`X-Slogan: Sniffing the glue that holds the Internet together.`

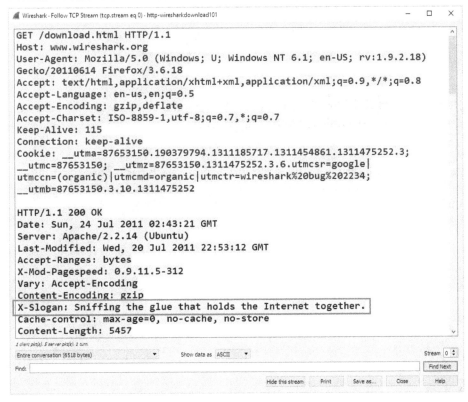

Step 4:   This isn't the only message hidden in the web browsing session. Now that you know the message begins with "X-Slogan," how could you have Wireshark display every frame that has this ASCII string?

Click the **Close** button ⊠ and then the **Clear** button ⊠ to remove the TCP stream filter.

Apply the display filter `frame contains "X-Slogan"`.

Step 5:   Right-click on the two other displayed frames and select **Follow | TCP Stream** to examine the HTTP headers exchanged between hosts. Did you find the other message?

Use stream navigation arrows to move from one stream to another.

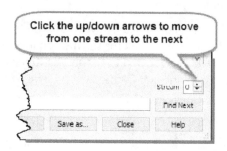

Step 6:   **LAB CLEAN-UP** Click the **Close** button on the Follow TCP Stream window when you have finished following streams.

Rather than scroll through a trace file and examine each packet one at a time, follow the TCP, UDP, or SSL streams. [48] This is a function you will use again and again in your analysis process.

---

[48]   You must configure Wireshark with a decryption key in the SSL preferences area in order to follow SSL streams and view the decrypted traffic.

6.2. Reassemble a File Transferred via FTP

Wireshark's ability to reassemble files transferred on a network might surprise some people. It should also emphasize the importance of using a secure channel or even file encryption to protect against unwanted interception and reassembly of confidential files.

FTP communications use two types of connections: a command channel and a data channel. The data channel only consists of the TCP handshake to establish the connection and then the actual data transfer itself. Using **Follow | TCP Stream** on the data channel, you can easily reassemble the transferred file into its original format.

Check your TCP preference setting to ensure *Allow subdissector to reassemble TCP streams* is enabled. This setting is required for proper reassembly.

Locate the data channel by either watching packets in the command channel leading up to it, locating "FTP-DATA" in the **Protocol** column, or looking for maximum-sized packets following the RETR or STOR command. Sometimes the FTP data channel will be established over the default port 20, but that's not required. In the command channel communications, another port number can be defined for the data channel.

To reassemble the file transferred on the FTP data channel, right-click on the data packet and select **Follow | TCP Stream**, as shown in Figure 112.

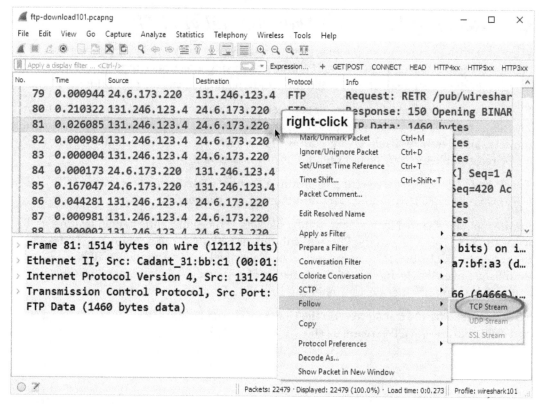

Figure 112. *Look for the FTP-DATA or full-sized packets after the RETR or STOR command.* [ftp-download101.pcapng]

Wireshark displays the communications in ASCII format, indicating the direction of the data flows using color coding (red is applied to the first communicating host while blue is applied to the second communicating host). Change the format to **Raw** (set in the **Show data as** drop-down list), select **Save As**, and name your new file based on the file name seen in the RETR or STOR command preceding this file transfer.

That's it. You now have an exact duplicate of the file that was transferred over FTP.

TIP

When you follow streams that contain a file, you can usually identify the file based on the first few bytes. For example, .jpg image files begin with JFIF whereas .png image files begin with the byte string 0x89-50-4E-47. It's good to know what format the file uses if you want to reassemble that file. Take a look at a tool called TRIDnet to identify file types (*mark0.net/soft-tridnet-e.html*).

🖳 Lab 38: Extract a File from an FTP File Transfer

In this lab you will follow an FTP data stream to reassemble the file that was transferred. First you will reassemble the command channel traffic to see the client login and file retrieval commands, and then you will reassemble the data transfer channel traffic to view the file transferred.

Step 1:   Open *ftp-clientside101.pcapng*.

Check your TCP preference setting to ensure *Allow subdissector to reassemble TCP streams* is enabled. This setting is required for proper reassembly.

Step 2:   Scroll through the beginning of this trace file. You will see numerous FTP commands used to log in, request a directory, define a port number for the data transfer, and retrieve a file.

Step 3:   Right-click on **frame 6** (USER anonymous) and select **Follow | TCP Stream**. You can easily read the commands and responses exchanged between the client and server. The client logged in (USER and PASS), requested the directory listing (NLST), set the transfer type to binary (TYPE), defined a port to use for the data channel (PORT), requested a file (RETR), and ended the connection (QUIT).

Step 4:   There are two data connections in this trace file: one for the directory list and another for the file transfer. We are only interested in the data stream used for the file transfer.

The Follow TCP Stream window is linked to the packets in the trace file. Click on the **RETR pantheon.jpg** line and Wireshark jumps to that packet. Click **Close**.

Step 5: Click the **Clear Filter** button ![X] to remove the display filter that was created when you followed the stream.

Packet 34 should be selected. Immediately following that packet you will see the start of a new TCP connection (SYN packet) in packet 35. This is the data connection used to transfer the file *pantheon.jpg*.

Right-click on packet 35 and select **Follow | TCP Stream**.

Step 6: You can view the file identifier that indicates this is a .jpg file (JFIF) and the metadata contained in the graphic file.

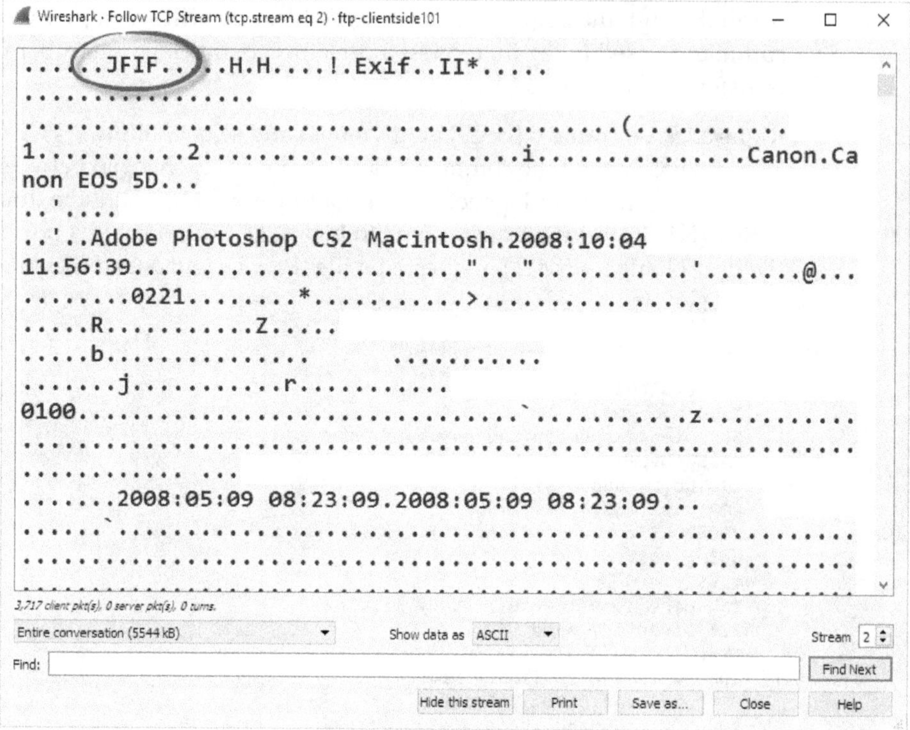

Step 7:   To reassemble the graphic image transferred in this FTP communication, first you must click the **Show data as** drop-down arrow and change the data format to **Raw**.

Then click the **Save As** button, select a target directory for the file, and set the file name as *pantheon.jpg*. Click **Save**.

```
5a02000004920a0001000000620200000079203000010000
000500000009920300010000000100000000a920500010 0
00006a020000869207000801000007202000000a0070004
00000030313030001a0030001000000fff000002a00400
010000001011000003a0040001000000600b00000ea205
00010000007a0300000fa20500010000008203000010a2
```

1,766 client pkt(s), 0 server pkt(s), 0 turns.

| Entire conversation (5544 kB) | ▼ | Show data as | Raw | ▼ | Stream | 2 ⬍ |

Find: _____   Find Next

| Hide this stream | Print | Save as | Help |

ASCII
C Arrays
EBCDIC
Hex Dump
UTF-8
YAML
Raw

Step 8:   Navigate to the target directory and open ***pantheon.jpg***. You should see the following photo:

Step 9:   ▌**LAB CLEAN-UP**▐ When you've finished examining the Pantheon image you extracted, close your image viewer. Return to Wireshark to close the TCP Stream window and clear your display filter.

It is easy to reassemble files transferred over TCP or UDP using **Follow | TCP Stream** or **Follow | UDP Stream**. When the data stream is clean (does not contain any commands), you can simply reassemble the stream and select **Save As.**

6.3. *Export HTTP Objects Transferred in a Web Browsing Session*

When analyzing HTTP communications, it can be helpful to see what individual page elements (HTTP objects) were transferred. You can reassemble html, graphics, JavaScript, videos, style sheet objects, and more.

Check Your TCP Preference Settings First!

Before beginning this process, ensure your TCP preference for *Allow subdissector to reassemble TCP streams* is enabled.

If you don't enable TCP reassembly, Wireshark cannot reassemble the HTTP objects. In fact, Wireshark will list each packet used to transfer an object rather than each object.

View all HTTP Objects in the Trace File

After capturing HTTP traffic or opening an HTTP trace file, select **File | Export Objects | HTTP**. Wireshark displays all the elements transferred in the HTTP traffic.

In Figure 113, we opened *http-espn101.pcapng* and selected **File | Export Objects | HTTP** to list the various objects transferred when someone browsed to *www.espn.com*. Note that the client connected to numerous servers when building the main view of the web site. Some of these objects were served by ad servers.

Packet	Hostname	Content Type	Size	Filename
9	www.espn.com	text/html	227 bytes	\
107	a.espncdn.com	application/x-javascript	26 kB	mbox.js
128	espn.go.com	text/html	266 kB	\
132	a.espncdn.com	text/css	74 kB	c?css=espn.teams.r4j.css
178	a.espncdn.com	text/css	309 kB	btn-toggle-tablet.css
180	ratings-wrs.symantec.com	text/xml	329 bytes	brief?url=http:%2F%2Fespn.go.com%2F&shz=1&guid=%7
291	a.espncdn.com	application/x-javascript	431 kB	espn.insider.201112021227.js,espn.espn360.stub.r9.js,espn.n
320	a1.espncdn.com	image/jpeg	491 bytes	bg_frontpage_red.jpg
325	espndotcom.tt.omtrdc.net		92 bytes	standard?mboxHost=espn.go.com&mboxSession=1325973
339	a.espncdn.com	image/png	245 bytes	social_facebook_14.png
340	broadband.espn.go.com	text/html	87 bytes	user?callback=jQuery171044244468988128804_13259732489
350	a1.espncdn.com	image/png	114 bytes	trans_border.png
351	a1.espncdn.com	image/jpeg	16 kB	bg_frontpage_elements.jpg
366	a1.espncdn.com	image/png	10 kB	header_sprite_fp.v3.png

*Figure 113. Select **File | Export Objects | HTTP** to export one or all of the objects. [http-espn101.pcapng]*

The HTTP object list window lists all the files transferred in the trace file.

- The **Packet** column indicates the last packet of each reassembled object.
- The **Hostname** column provides the *http.host* value from the GET request that preceded each file transfer.
- The **Content Type** column indicates the format of the objects. The objects may be graphics (.png, .jpg, or .gif, for example), scripts (.js, for example), or even videos (.swf or .flv, for example).
- The **Size** column indicates the size of the transferred object.
- The **Filename** column provides the name of the object requested. The request for "\" indicates a request for the default element (such as *index.html*) on a web page.

To export all the objects, select **Save All** and choose the directory where you want to save all the objects, click **Select Folder**, and be patient. This may take a long time if lots of HTTP objects are listed.

To export a single object, select the object, select the directory where you want to save the object, and click **Save**. Wireshark will fill out the file name based on the object name, so all you need to do is select an export directory.

If you don't recognize some of the file extensions shown in the HTTP Object List window (such as *.css* for Cascading Style Sheets), visit *www.fileinfo.com/help/file_extension*. You can enter the file extension in the search box to look up the file type and a list of programs that use that type of file.

▢ Lab 39: Carve Out an HTTP Object from a Web Browsing Session

In this lab, you will open a trace file that contains a web browsing session. Using the **File | Export Objects** process, you will extract one of the images transferred during the web browsing session.

Step 1:   Open *http-college101.pcapng*.

Step 2:   If you didn't already do so while reading the previous section, enable your *Allow subdissector to reassemble TCP streams* setting (**Edit | Preferences ▷ Protocols | TCP**). When you finish this lab you will disable the setting again. This setting is required for the **File | Export Objects** function.

Step 3:   You created a **Host** column in Lab 14[49]. It may be hidden, however. Right-click any column heading and enable your **Host** column. You may need to widen your **Host** column to see full host names.

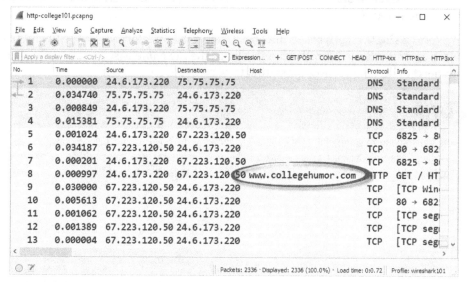

When you scroll through the trace file, you can see the user is browsing *www.collegehumor.com*. We will create a list of the HTTP objects transferred in this trace file and then extract one of the files.

In Lab 38, you used **Follow | TCP Stream** to extract a file from an FTP data transfer process. It's much easier to extract HTTP objects.

---

[49]   If you did not save your **Host** column, return to Lab 14 and follow the steps to create the column again.

Step 4: Select **File | Export Objects | HTTP**. Scroll through the list of objects to find a file called *7c7b8db9ca172221a20922a49e92a86b-definitely-real-trampoline-trick.jpg* that begins downloading in frame 307.

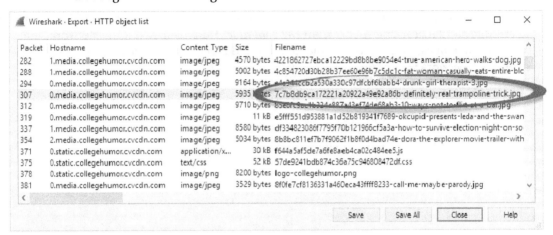

Step 5: Click **Save**, select the target directory and let Wireshark use the actual file name. Click **Save**.

Navigate to your target directory to view the saved file.

Step 6: **LAB CLEAN-UP** Close the HTTP Object List window and right-click on a TCP header in the Packet List pane and disable the *Allow subdissector to reassemble TCP streams* setting.

Wireshark's object exporting capability does a good job carving HTTP objects out of a web browsing session. It does *not* do a good job helping you look through the exported files, however. You must use an external viewer to see the files.

If you are a forensic investigator who needs to export thousands of files from traffic (also referred to as "data carving"), check out *NetworkMiner* from Netresec, a free network forensic tool that can import .pcap[50] files and carve out and display the images. You can download NetworkMiner from *www.netresec.com*.

---

[50]   As of the writing of this book, the free version of NetworkMiner could not import .pcapng files, but the paid version could process .pcapng files. To convert a .pcapng file to a .pcap file format, open the file and select **File | Save As** and choose the **Wireshark/tcpdump/... - libpcap** format. Use the .pcap extension when you name your file.

Chapter 6 Challenge

Open *challenge101-6.pcapng* and use the techniques covered in this chapter to answer these Challenge questions. The answer key is located in Appendix A.

Question 6-1.   What two .jpg files can be exported from this trace file?

Question 6-2.   On what HTTP server and in what directory does *next-active.png* reside?

Question 6-3.   Export *booksmall.png* from this trace file. What is in the image?

Question 6-4.   Reassemble TCP stream 7. What type of browser is the client using in this stream?

[This page intentionally blank.]

Chapter 7 Skills: Add Comments to Your Trace Files and Packets

Wireshark is like an X-ray machine. It gives you a look at what's going on inside (the network), but you need to develop the skills to interpret what you see and know what to look for - practice makes perfect.

Anders Broman
Wireshark Core Developer
System Tester, *Ericsson*

Quick Reference: File and Packet Annotation Options

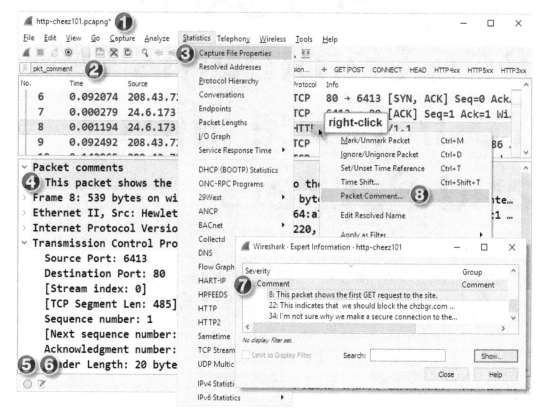

(1) **Title bar** — Wireshark adds an asterisk to the Title Bar to indicate that changes to the trace file (such as trace file or packet annotations) have not been saved

(2) `Pkt_comment` **filter** — Apply a filter for `pkt_comment` to view all packets that contain comments

(3) **Statistics | Capture File Properties** — Displays trace file information, including trace file annotations and packet comments

(4) **Packet comments section** — Packet comments are displayed above the Frame section

(5) **Expert Information button** — Click to open the Expert Information window, which contains a Comments section, as shown in (7)

(6) **Trace File Annotation button** — Click to open or edit the Capture File Properties window where you can add or edit a trace file comment[51]

(7) **Expert Information window/Comments section** — Click on a comment to jump to that packet in the trace file

(8) **Edit or Add Packet Comment** — Right-click on a packet to create/edit a packet comment

---

[51] Comments can only be saved in the *.pcapng* format. If you try to save a trace file that has comments in any format other than *.pcapng*, Wireshark will pop up a warning dialog. You must save your files in *.pcapng* format if you wish to retain trace file or packet annotations.

7.1. Add Your Comments to Trace Files

Before you hand your trace files off to another analyst, customer, or vendor, consider adding some notes on the packets that interest you or on the trace file in general. Trace file and packet comments are saved with *.pcapng* trace files and can be read in Wireshark version 1.8 and later.

To add a comment to the entire trace file, click the **Annotation** button on the Status Bar, as shown in Figure 114. Enter your text in the **Capture file comments** section and click **Save Comments**.

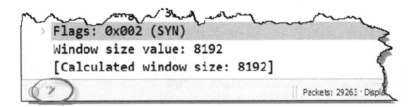

*Figure 114. Click the **Annotation** button on the Status Bar to add a trace file comment.*

Although you can type in any length comment, keep in mind that the trace file size will be affected by the note size, so don't write a novel in there. If you are going to hand this trace to other analysts who may add their own comments, consider prefacing your comment with your name, as shown in Figure 115. Wireshark does not keep track of who entered text in this window.

Remember to save your trace file after adding comments. Wireshark places an asterisk in front of the file name in the title bar if there are unsaved comments in a trace file.

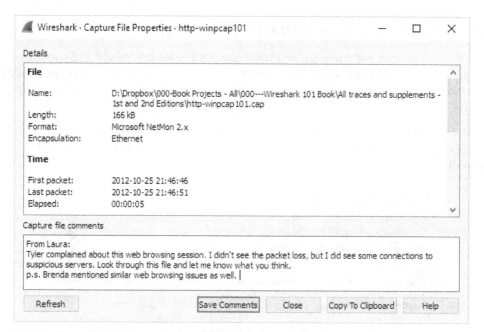

*Figure 115. Type your trace file comments and click **OK**.*

To determine if a file contains trace file comments, click on the **Annotation** button or select **Statistics | Capture File Properties**.

7.2. Add Your Comments to Individual Packets

To add a comment to a single packet, right-click the packet in the Packet List pane and select **Packet Comment**, as illustrated in Figure 116. Follow the same steps to edit a packet comment.

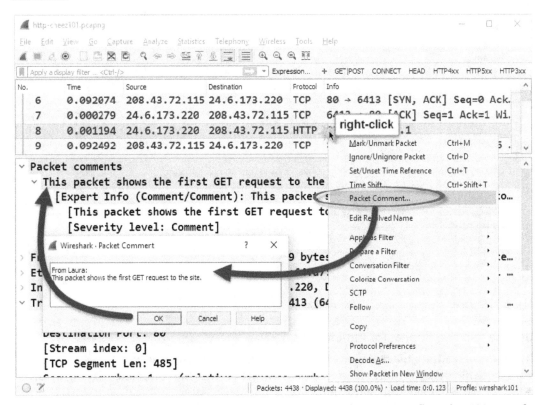

Figure 116. *If people collaborate on analysis, add your name to your packet comments. [http-cheez101.pcapng]*

Once you create a packet comment, a Packet comments section appears in the Packet Details window, as shown in Figure 117. The color code for packet comments is a bright green.

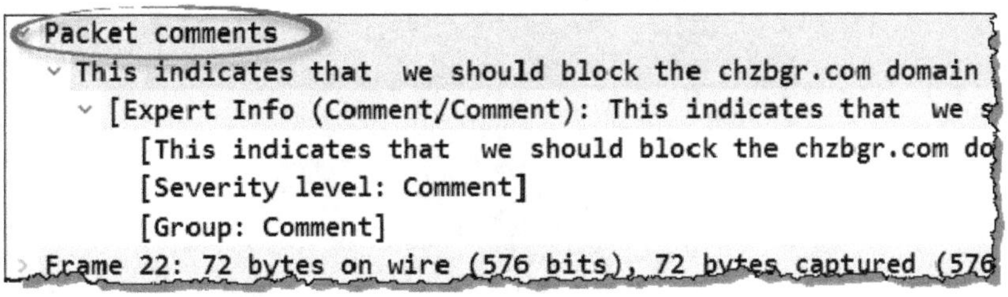

Figure 117. *Packet comments appear before the Frame section. [http-cheez101.pcapng]*

To determine if a trace file contains packet comments, click on the **Expert Information** button on the Status Bar and expand the **Comments** section, as shown in Figure 118. Click on a comment to jump to that packet.

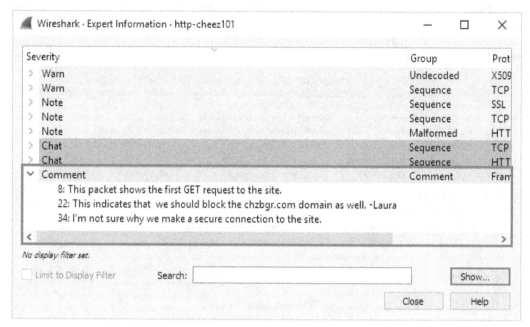

Figure 118. Packet comments are listed in the Expert Information window. [http-cheez101.pcapng]

Use the .pcapng Format for Annotations

If you opened a trace file that uses an older trace file format (such as *.pcap*), be sure to save your trace file in *.pcapng* format after adding packet or trace file comments. Saving in any other format will delete all your comments.

Add a Comment Column for Faster Viewing

To view all your comments in the Packet List pane, simply expand the packet comment section in a frame that contains a comment (frame 8 in *http-cheez101.pcapng*, for example). Right-click on the actual comment and select **Apply as Column**, as shown in Figure 119.

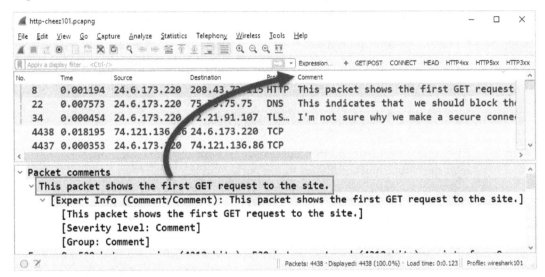

*Figure 119. Right-click on a comment and select **Apply as Column**. [http-cheez101.pcapng]*

If you add or edit comments to the trace file, click the **Save** button to save the file with your new comments.

You may need to click the **Reload** button to refresh your **Comments** column.

▭ Lab 40: Read Analysis Notes in a Malicious Redirection Trace File

It can be a blessing to have notes inside the trace file to assist other analysts (or even you) in following the traffic flow. In this lab you will examine the notes left in a trace file that contains unusual communications.

Step 1:   Open *sec-suspicous101.pcapng*.

Step 2:   Click the **Annotation** button 🖉 on the Status Bar to launch the Capture File Properties window. Read the **Capture file comments** section.

The trace file annotation recommends that you "*See packet comments for more detail.*"

Click **Close** to close the Capture file comments window.

Step 3:   Click the **Expert Information** button ◯ and expand the **Comment** section to read the individual comments in the packets in this trace file.

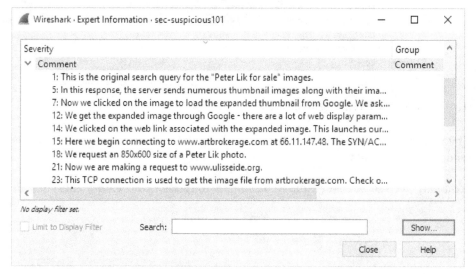

Step 4:   Click once on any of the comments to jump to that packet in the trace file. Take some time to read through the trace file and packet comments. You will see when a redirection sends the user to a malicious site.

Step 5:   **LAB CLEAN-UP** When you have finished looking through the packet comments, click the **Close** button on the Expert Information window.

Trace file annotations can be very helpful when there are many separate events happening in a trace file. In Lab 41 we will export all the packet comments in this trace file.

7.3.   *Export Packet Comments for a Report*

If you plan to create a printed report of your analysis findings, consider adding packet comments and exporting those comments into .txt or .csv format.

You can select **Statistics | Capture File Properties | Copy to Clipboard** and then paste the comment data into another program.

In Lab 41 you will have a chance to practice exporting packet comments using the **Export Packet Dissections** function. This is a function you should master to export field values.

First, Filter on Packets that Contain Comments

First, apply a `pkt_comment` filter to your trace file to view only commented packets.

Next, expand the **Packet comments** section of any displayed packet. Leave the rest of the packet compressed, as shown in Figure 120.

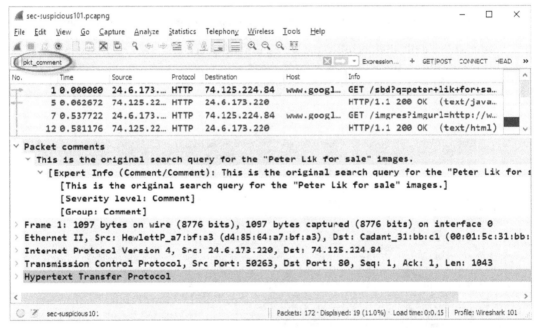

Figure 120. Filter on `pkt_comment` *and then expand the Packet comments section of a packet before your export operation. [sec-suspicious101.pcapng]*

Next, Export Packet Dissections as Plain Text

Select **File | Export Packet Dissections | As Plain Text** and choose **All packets (Displayed), Packet details (As displayed)**, as shown in Figure 121. Uncheck the Packet summary check box. Consider naming your text file with the same stem as the trace file. For example, if your trace file is *sec-suspicious101.pcapng*, name your text file *sec-suspicious101.txt*.

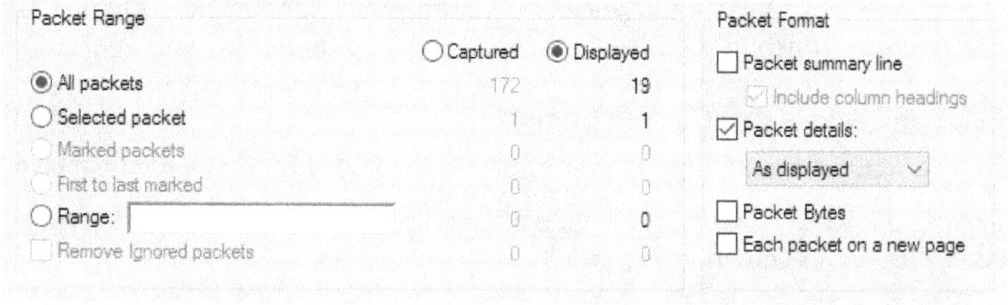
Packet Range
Captured
Displayed
All packets
172
19
Selected packet
1
1
Marked packets
0
0
First to last marked
0
0
Range:
0
0
Remove Ignored packets
0
0
Packet Format
Packet summary line
Include column headings
Packet details:
As displayed
Packet Bytes
Each packet on a new page

Figure 121. Set up your export to include displayed packets and only the Packet details "As displayed".

The result will be a file that includes packet comments preceding the Frame summary of each packet, as shown in Figure 122.

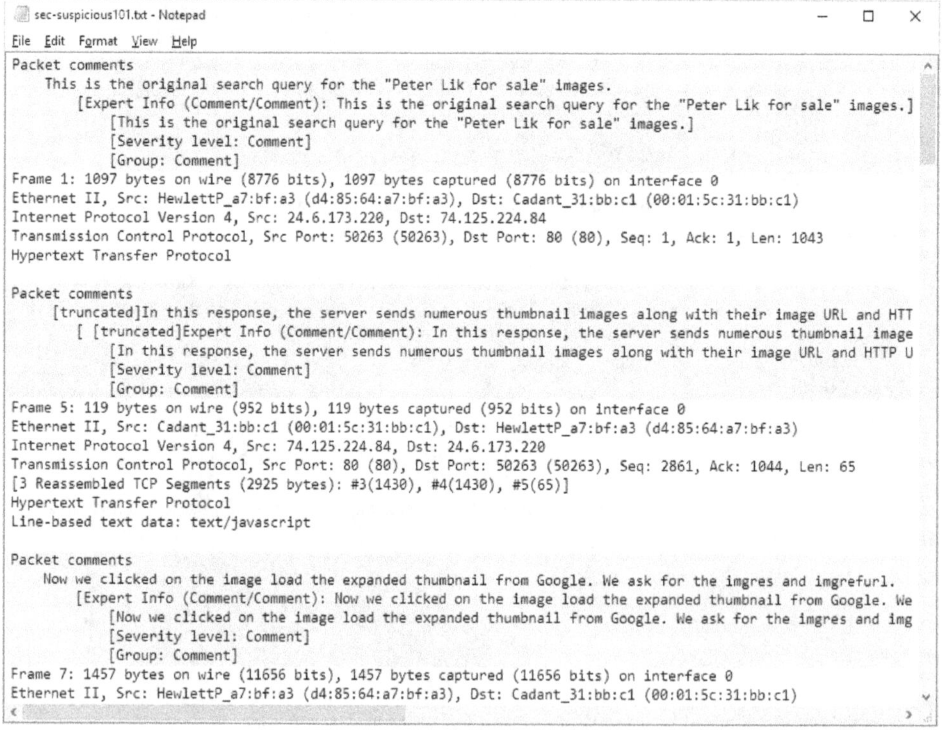
sec-suspicious101.txt - Notepad
File Edit Format View Help

```
Packet comments
    This is the original search query for the "Peter Lik for sale" images.
        [Expert Info (Comment/Comment): This is the original search query for the "Peter Lik for sale" images.]
            [This is the original search query for the "Peter Lik for sale" images.]
            [Severity level: Comment]
            [Group: Comment]
Frame 1: 1097 bytes on wire (8776 bits), 1097 bytes captured (8776 bits) on interface 0
Ethernet II, Src: HewlettP_a7:bf:a3 (d4:85:64:a7:bf:a3), Dst: Cadant_31:bb:c1 (00:01:5c:31:bb:c1)
Internet Protocol Version 4, Src: 24.6.173.220, Dst: 74.125.224.84
Transmission Control Protocol, Src Port: 50263 (50263), Dst Port: 80 (80), Seq: 1, Ack: 1, Len: 1043
Hypertext Transfer Protocol

Packet comments
     [truncated]In this response, the server sends numerous thumbnail images along with their image URL and HTT
        [ [truncated]Expert Info (Comment/Comment): In this response, the server sends numerous thumbnail image
            [In this response, the server sends numerous thumbnail images along with their image URL and HTTP U
            [Severity level: Comment]
            [Group: Comment]
Frame 5: 119 bytes on wire (952 bits), 119 bytes captured (952 bits) on interface 0
Ethernet II, Src: Cadant_31:bb:c1 (00:01:5c:31:bb:c1), Dst: HewlettP_a7:bf:a3 (d4:85:64:a7:bf:a3)
Internet Protocol Version 4, Src: 74.125.224.84, Dst: 24.6.173.220
Transmission Control Protocol, Src Port: 80 (80), Dst Port: 50263 (50263), Seq: 2861, Ack: 1044, Len: 65
[3 Reassembled TCP Segments (2925 bytes): #3(1430), #4(1430), #5(65)]
Hypertext Transfer Protocol
Line-based text data: text/javascript

Packet comments
    Now we clicked on the image load the expanded thumbnail from Google. We ask for the imgres and imgrefurl.
        [Expert Info (Comment/Comment): Now we clicked on the image load the expanded thumbnail from Google. We
            [Now we clicked on the image load the expanded thumbnail from Google. We ask for the imgres and img
            [Severity level: Comment]
            [Group: Comment]
Frame 7: 1457 bytes on wire (11656 bits), 1457 bytes captured (11656 bits) on interface 0
Ethernet II, Src: HewlettP_a7:bf:a3 (d4:85:64:a7:bf:a3), Dst: Cadant_31:bb:c1 (00:01:5c:31:bb:c1)
```

Figure 122. Export your packet comments into a .txt file to copy into a report.

In Wireshark 2.x, only 127 characters of the Packet Comments field are exported.

As mentioned earlier, you can also select **Statistics | Capture File Properties | Copy to Clipboard** to export all packet comments and basic trace file statistics. Figure 123 shows the Capture File Properties window. Simply click the **Copy to Clipboard** button to buffer the contents of this window and paste the contents into another program.

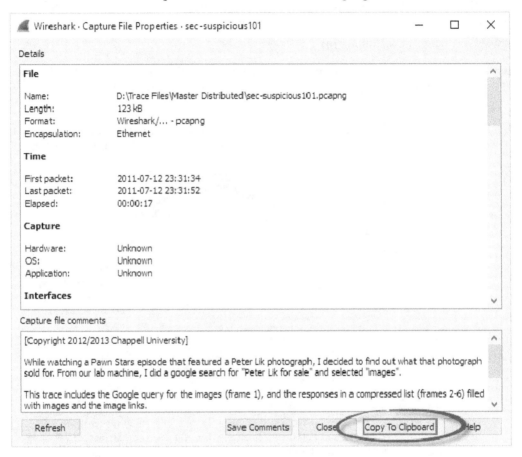

*Figure 123. To quickly export trace file and packet comments, use the **Statistics | Capture File Properties** feature and then select **Copy To Clipboard**. [sec-suspicous101.pcapng]*

Since Wireshark supports packet and file anotations, consider building your troubleshooting and network forensics reports directly in Wireshark by adding comments in the trace files. When you have finished annotating your findings, export your packet comments for quick inclusion in your reports.

🖳 Lab 41: Export Malicious Redirection Packet Comments

We will use the *sec-suspicious101.pcapng* trace file again in this lab. We will use a two-step process for comment export. First we will prepare the trace file to export the field information we are most interested in. We will export the fields in text format. Unlike in the previous section, we will export the packet comments using the Packet summary line.

Step 1:   Open *sec-suspicious101.pcapng*.

Step 2:   In frame 1, right-click on the **Packet comments** line in the Packet Details area and select **Apply as Filter | Selected**. Only 19 packets should match your display filter.

Step 3:   Now expand the Packet comments section of frame 1. Right-click on the actual comment starting with "**This is the original...**" and select **Apply as Column**.

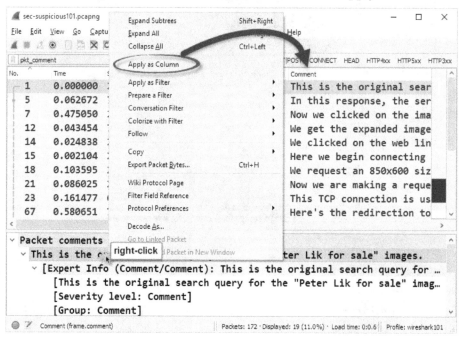

Step 4:   Select **File | Export Packet Dissections | As CSV**.

 TIP

If you find yourself building many reports detailing your analysis findings, consider looking into SteelCentral™ Packet Analyzer by Riverbed (see *Consider a Different Solution—SteelCentral™ Packet Analyzer* on page 111). This product was designed to accept comments and export the comments into a report along with charts and graphs depicting the traffic patterns.

Step 5: Navigate to the directory where you want to save your text file and name your file *sec-suspicous101.csv*. Ensure **Displayed** and **Packet summary line** are selected and **Packet details** is not selected before clicking **Save**.

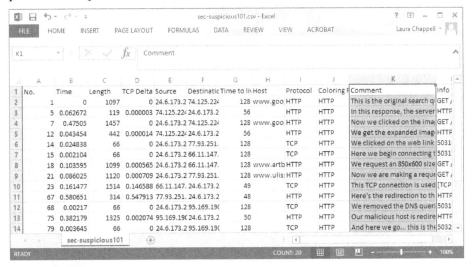

Step 6: Open your **CSV file** in a spreadsheet program to review the exported information. You will notice that your hidden columns are exported as well. This is a good reason to keep your hidden column count to a minimum. If you just have too many hidden columns, you could simply switch to a nice, clean profile and export a CSV file from there.

Step 7: **LAB CLEAN-UP** Return to Wireshark and click the **Clear** button ☒ to remove your display filter. Right-click on your **Comment** column heading and select **Remove This Column** or unselect that column from the list to hide it.

You should master the skill of adding columns to use for exported reports. Also, it's very easy to use the **Statistics | Capture File Properties | Copy To Clipboard** feature to begin building reports for your analysis sessions.

Chapter 7 Challenge

Open *challenge101-7.pcapng* and use the techniques covered in this chapter to answer these Challenge questions. The answer key is located in Appendix A.

Question 7-1.   What information is contained in the trace file annotation?

Question 7-2.   What packet comments are contained in this trace file?

Question 7-3.   Add a comment to the POST message in this trace file. What packet did you alter?

Chapter 8 Skills: Use Command-Line Tools to Capture, Split, and Merge Traffic

Network communication is a conversation. We don't usually think about the subtle rules of human conversation: what to say first, next, and when we can say that, and when it's going to be rude, impolite, and maybe cause our partner to quit talking. Once we learn the rules of the protocols and know what the calls and responses should be, we can examine what actually happened and see where things went wrong. The better we know the etymology and anthropology of the protocols, the better we understand the trace.

SYN= "Hi, Paris! I'd love to meet you!"
RST= "Sorry, I'm too sexy for you!"

John Gonder
Cisco Academy Director, *Las Positas College*

The command-line tools referenced in this chapter are included with Wireshark and are installed in the Wireshark program directory.

Quick Reference: Command-Line Tools Key Options

EDITCAP

`editcap -h`	View Editcap parameters.
`editcap -i 360 big.pcapng 360secs.pcapng`	Split *big.pcapng* into separate *360secs*.pcapng* files with up to 360 seconds of traffic in each file.
`editcap -c 500 big.pcapng 500pkts.pcapng`	Split *big.pcapng* into separate *500pkts*.pcapng* files with up to 500 packets in each file.

MERGECAP

`mergecap -h`	View Mergecap parameters.
`mergecap -w merged.pcapng files*.pcapng`	Merge *files*.pcapng* into a single file called *merged.pcapng* (merge based on packet timestamps).
`mergecap -a -w ab.pcapng a.pcapng b.pcapng`	Merge *a.pcapng* and *b.pcapng* into a single file called *ab.pcapng* (merge based on the order files are listed).

TSHARK

`tshark -h`	View Tshark parameters.
`tshark -D`	List the available capture interfaces that can be used with the `-i` parameter.
`tshark -i2 -f "tcp" -w tcp.pcapng`	Capture only TCP-based traffic on interface 2 and save it to *tcp.pcapng*.
`tshark -i1 -Y "ip.addr==10.2.1.1"`	Capture all traffic on interface 1, but only display traffic to or from 10.2.1.1.

`tshark -r "myfile.pcapng"`
`-Y "http.host contains ".ru""`
`-w myfile-ru.pcapng`
	Open *myfile.pcapng*, apply a display filter for the value ".ru" in the HTTP host field, save the results to a file called *myfile-ru.pcapng*.

8.1. Split a Large Trace File into a File Set

Wireshark can become sluggish or even non-responsive when working with large trace files. Once you get above that 100 MB size, applying display filters, adding columns, and building graphs may be too slow. Consider splitting larger files into file sets for faster analysis. File sets are groups of trace files that begin with a common stem name followed by a trace file number and a date and time stamp.

Add the Wireshark Program Directory to Your Path[52]

Use Editcap to split a large file into smaller files that are linked together. Editcap.exe is located in the Wireshark program file directory (see **Help | About Wireshark | Folders** to locate this directory). To use Editcap (or any of the included command-line tools) from any directory, add the Wireshark program directory to your path.

Once you've added the Wireshark program directory to your path, open the command prompt/terminal window and navigate to the folder that contains the large file that you want to split into a file set. Type **editcap –h** to view all Editcap parameters. You can split a file based on number of packets (-c option) or amount of time in seconds (-i option).

---

[52]   For step-by-step instructions for adding the Wireshark program directory to your path, perform a Google search for "add directory to path for *operating system*."

Use Capinfos to Get the File Size and Packet Count

Capinfos is a command-line tool that provides basic information about trace files, as shown in Figure 124. Capinfos resides in the Wireshark program directory. The basic syntax for Capinfos is simply `capinfos <filename>`. Use Capinfos to find the capture duration (seconds) and packet count of a trace file before splitting it. We will use Capinfos again in Lab 42.

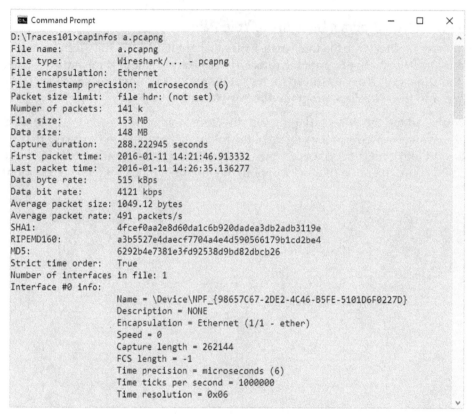

Figure 124. Use Capinfos to obtain basic trace file information before splitting the file. [a.pcapng]

Split a File Based on Packets per Trace File

In Figure 125, we typed **editcap -c 10000 a.pcapng a10000set.pcapng** to split a single trace file called *a.pcapng* into a set of files (*a10000set*.pcapng*) that contain a maximum of 10,000 packets each. The last trace file of the set will likely have less than 10,000 packets, unless the original file ended on a 10,000-packet boundary.

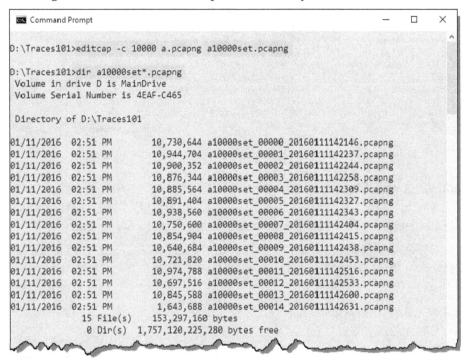

Figure 125. Use the −c parameter to split a trace file based on packet count. [a.pcapng]

Split a File Based on Seconds per Trace File

In Figure 126, we typed **editcap -i 60 a.pcapng a60set.pcapng** to split a single trace file called *a.pcapng* into a set of files (*a60set*.pcapng*) that contain up to 60 seconds of traffic each. Wireshark will not split a packet at the 60-second mark, so your files may have slightly less than 60 seconds of traffic in them.

The last trace file of the set will likely have less than 60 seconds of traffic in it unless the original file ended on a sixty-second boundary.

In our example, Editcap split our *a.pcapng* trace file into five linked trace files numbered 00000 to 00004.

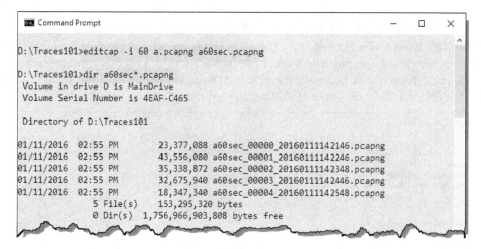

Figure 126. Use the −i *parameter to split a trace file based on number of seconds. [a.pcapng]*

Open and Work with File Sets in Wireshark

When working with file sets in Wireshark, open any file of a file set using **File | Open**. Then use **File | File Set | List Files** to switch between files of a file set quickly.

In Figure 127, we are looking at the file list for a file set that contains 15 files. Click on any file to open that file in Wireshark. If you have a display filter in place, that display filter will be applied to each file you open.

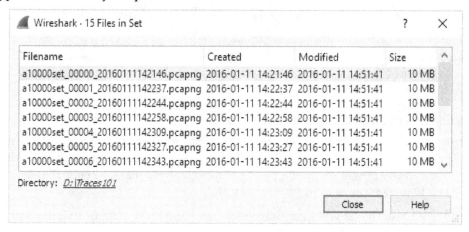

Figure 127. Click files to move quickly through the file set.

Lab 42: Split a File and Work with Filtered File Sets

You will be working with *http-download-c.pcapng* in this lab. This trace file is only 27 MB, but we will use it to practice splitting a file. After splitting the file, we will move through the file set while a display filter is applied. Wireshark automatically applies the display filter to each file as it is opened.

Step 1: Open the **command prompt** (Windows) or a **terminal window** (Linux/Macintosh).

Step 2: Navigate to your trace file directory[53].

Step 3: We are going to split this file based on the packet count. Type **capinfos "http-download-c.pcapng"**[54].

This file contains is 141,531 packets. Capinfos displays 141 k as the number of packets. We will split this trace file into a file set containing up to 20,000 packets in each file.

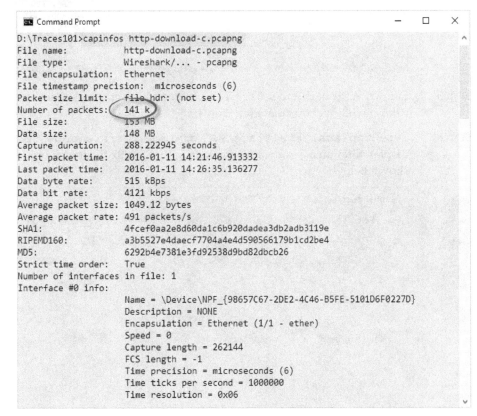

---

53 Be certain to add the Wireshark program directory to your path as mentioned on page 277.

54 You only need to use quotes around a file name if it contains spaces. Adding quotes around all file names may be a good habit to get into, however.

Step 4:   Type `editcap -c 20000 http-download-c.pcapng`
`http-download-c20000.pcapng`. Press **enter**. Wireshark will create eight
files which begin with *http-download-c20000* and contain a file number followed
by a date and timestamp, as shown below.

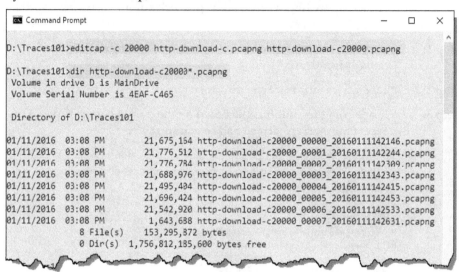

Step 5:   Launch Wireshark and select **File | Open** and select the file numbered "*_00002*"
from the file set you created in Step 4.

Step 6:   Type `tcp.analysis.flags && !tcp.analysis.window_update` in the
display filter area. None of the packets in the _00002 file match our filter, as
shown below.

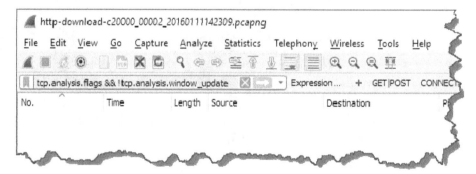

Step 7:   Select **File | File Set | List Files**. Click on each file name to browse the files.

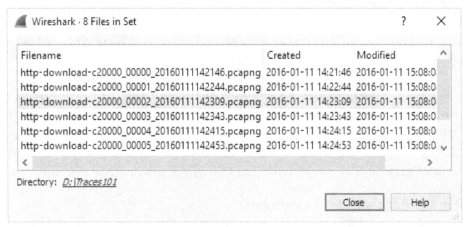

Wireshark applies the current display filter as you open the various files.

As you move through the files, look at the Status Bar to determine how many packets matched your filter in each of the trace files. Every file except for "00002" and "00007" contains these flagged TCP packets.

Step 8:   **LAB CLEAN-UP** Click the **Close** button on the File Set window and then click the **Clear** button ✕ to remove your display filter.

Since Wireshark maintains the display filter setting as you move through files within a file set, it is easy to determine how many packets matched the filter.

8.2. *Merge Multiple Trace Files*

You may want to merge several smaller files to create an IO Graph of all the traffic, save time applying display filters to look for key words, or launch the Protocol Hierarchy window to detect suspicious protocols or applications.

Ensure the Wireshark Program Directory is in Your Path

Use Mergecap to combine smaller files into one larger file. Mergecap.exe is located in the Wireshark program file directory (see **Help | About Wireshark | Folders | Program** to locate this directory).

To use Mergecap from any directory, add the Wireshark program directory to your path.

Run Mergecap with the −w Parameter

Assuming you've added the Wireshark program directory to your path, open the command prompt and navigate to the folder that contains the files you want to merge. Type **mergecap −h** to view all Mergecap parameters.

You can merge a file based on frame timestamps (the default) or use the −a parameter to merge the files based on the order in which you list them during the merge process. Use the −w parameter to write the new merged file to disk. In Figure 128, we created a file called *c.pcapng* by merging all files that have a name starting with *httpset*.

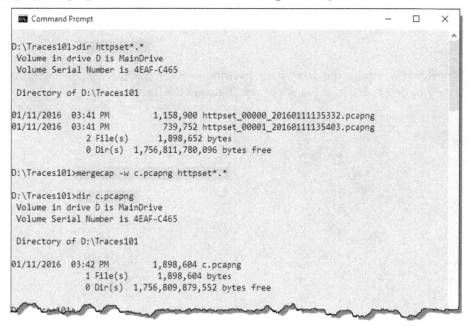

Figure 128. Use Mergecap to combine trace files based on frame timestamps. [httpset.pcapng]*

You will notice that the merged file is smaller than the sum of bytes of the separate trace files. This change in file size is because there is only one trace file header in the new file instead of the three trace file headers counted in the total bytes count before the merge.

In Lab 43 you will get a chance to try out this merging skill.

🖥 Lab 43: Merge a Set of Files using a Wildcard

In this lab you will merge the six-file *http-download-c20000*.pcapng* set that you created in Lab 42. You will use a wildcard to make this process a bit easier and less error-prone.

Step 1:   Open the **command prompt** (Windows) or a **terminal window** (Linux/Macintosh).

Step 2:   Navigate to your trace file directory. Type **dir http-download-c20000*.*** (Windows) or **ls http-download-c20000*.*** (UNIX-based systems) to view the trace files you created in Lab 42.

Step 3:   Type **mergecap -w http-downloadc2kset.pcapng http-download-c20000*.***. Press **enter**.

Type **dir http-downloadc2kset.pcapng** (Windows) or **ls http-downloadc2kset.pcapng** (UNIX-based systems) to view your new file.

```
Command Prompt                                           —    □    ×

D:\Traces101>dir http-download-c20000*.*
 Volume in drive D is MainDrive
 Volume Serial Number is 4EAF-C465

 Directory of D:\Traces101

01/11/2016  03:08 PM        21,675,164 http-download-c20000_00000_20160111142146.pcapng
01/11/2016  03:08 PM        21,776,512 http-download-c20000_00001_20160111142244.pcapng
01/11/2016  03:08 PM        21,776,784 http-download-c20000_00002_20160111142309.pcapng
01/11/2016  03:08 PM        21,688,976 http-download-c20000_00003_20160111142343.pcapng
01/11/2016  03:08 PM        21,495,404 http-download-c20000_00004_20160111142415.pcapng
01/11/2016  03:08 PM        21,696,424 http-download-c20000_00005_20160111142453.pcapng
01/11/2016  03:08 PM        21,542,920 http-download-c20000_00006_20160111142533.pcapng
01/11/2016  03:08 PM         1,643,688 http-download-c20000_00007_20160111142631.pcapng
               8 File(s)    153,295,872 bytes
               0 Dir(s)  1,756,809,842,688 bytes free

D:\Traces101>mergecap -w http-downloadc2kset.pcapng http-download-c20000*.*

D:\Traces101>dir http-downloadc2kset.pcapng
 Volume in drive D is MainDrive
 Volume Serial Number is 4EAF-C465

 Directory of D:\Traces101

01/11/2016  03:53 PM       153,295,088 http-downloadc2kset.pcapng
               1 File(s)    153,295,088 bytes
               0 Dir(s)  1,756,656,545,792 bytes free

D:\Traces101>
```

If you compare the size of *http-downloadc2kset.pcapng* to *http-download-c.pcapng*, you will notice a size difference. During the file splitting process, the trace file annotation is removed. During the merging process a new trace file annotation is created that lists the merged files as shown in the image below.

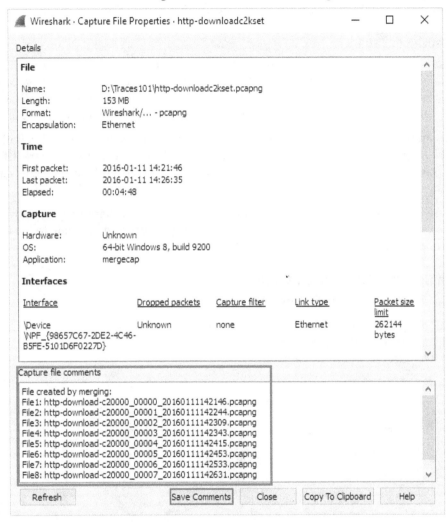

In this lab exercise, you used the default setting for the order of the merged files — merge based on packet timestamps. If you want to merge the files in a particular order, you must use the -a parameter and list each trace file in the order you want them to be merged.

8.3. Capture Traffic at Command Line

Use *dumpcap.exe* or *tshark.exe* to capture traffic at the command line when Wireshark can't keep up with the traffic (drops appear on the Status Bar), or you are deploying a streamlined remote capture host, or you are scripting an unattended capture.

Dumpcap or Tshark?

This is an interesting question. Dumpcap is a capture tool only. When you run Tshark, it actually calls *dumpcap.exe* for capture functionality. Tshark contains extra post-capture parameters which makes it a better option for many situations. If you are really struggling with memory limitations, just use Dumpcap directly. Otherwise, Tshark is the answer.

You can run either tool at the command line to capture traffic to *.pcapng* files. Both tools are located in the Wireshark program file directory (see **Help | About Wireshark | Folders | Program** to locate this directory). Both can use capture filters and various other capture settings.

To use Dumpcap or Tshark from any directory, add the Wireshark program directory to your path[55]. Open the command prompt/terminal window and navigate to the folder where you want to save trace files. Run both tools from this directory.

Capture at the Command Line with Dumpcap

Type **dumpcap -h** to view Dumpcap parameters.

Type **dumpcap -D** to view your available interfaces, as shown in Figure 129. Use the number preceding the interface name when you capture. In the image below, we can use **1**, **2**, or **3** to select an interface for capture.

```
Command Prompt                                              —    □    ×

D:\Traces101>tshark -D
1. \Device\NPF_{BD0C1124-CBA7-41BB-95BA-DB895B9631F2} (Ethernet)
2. \Device\NPF_{A12D03D0-E3C1-4622-B3C0-0986DF457AD8} (Local Area Connection* 2)
3. \Device\NPF_{98657C67-2DE2-4C46-B5FE-5101D6F0227D} (Wi-Fi)

D:\Traces101>_
```

Figure 129. Use **dumpcap -D** *to view available interfaces.*

---

[55] We keep mentioning this—have you done it yet?

Use the -c option to stop capturing after a certain number of packets have been captured. For example, dumpcap -c 2000 -w smallcap.pcapng will automatically stop the capture after 2,000 packets have been captured to a file called *smallcap.pcapng*.

Use the -a option with duration:n (seconds) or filesize:n (KB) to stop capturing after a certain number of seconds have elapsed or until your trace file has reached a certain size. For example, in Figure 130 we typed dumpcap -i3 -a filesize:1000 -w 1000kb.pcapng to automatically stop the capture as soon as the file size reaches 1000 KB.

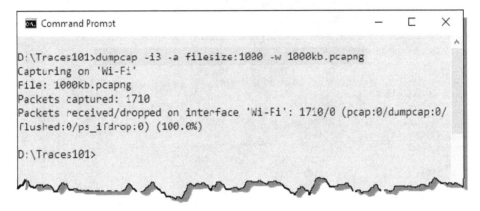

Figure 130. Use –a with an autostop condition such as filesize:1000.

Capture at the Command Line with Tshark

Tshark relies on Dumpcap to capture traffic, so when you type tshark -c 100 -w 100.pcapng, Tshark launches Dumpcap to do the actual capturing.

Tshark can be used for command-line capture, but it also offers some processing options for existing trace files. Use **tshark -h** to explore more possibilities for command-line capture with Tshark.

Use **tshark -D** to view the available interfaces. Just as you did with Dumpcap, use the number preceding the interface name with the -i parameter when capturing. Use -w to define the name of your capture file and -a with autostop parameters.

Save Host Information and Work with Existing Trace Files

Why would someone use Tshark instead of Dumpcap? There are a few advantages. For example, Tshark can use the -H <hosts file> option during the capture process. When your packets are saved to a trace file, the name resolution information contained in the <hosts file> is saved with your trace file.

Tshark can also process existing trace files. For example, you can specify an input trace file, apply a display filter, and save a new file based on the display filter. In Figure 131, we applied a dns.flags.response==1 display filter to *http-espn101.pcapng* and saved a new trace file called *dns-espn-responsesonly.pcapng*.

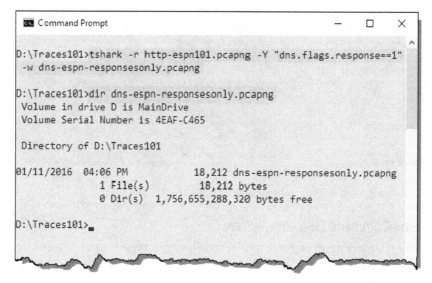

Figure 131. Tshark can be run against existing trace files. [http-espn101.pcapng]

Practice with the Tshark parameters listed when you type **tshark -h**.

▭ Lab 44: Use Tshark to Capture to File Sets with an Autostop Condition

In this lab, you will get a chance to use Tshark with various parameters. We'll define file set "next file" parameters and include an autostop condition for unattended capture.

Step 1:   Open the **command prompt** (Windows) or a **terminal window** (Linux/Macintosh).

Step 2:   Navigate to your trace file directory. Type **`tshark -D`** to view the list of available interfaces. If you aren't certain which interface sees traffic, return to the Wireshark Start Page and look at the sparklines.

Step 3:   Once you have determined which interface to use, type **`tshark -h`** to view the available parameters for saving to multiple files and setting an autostop condition.

Look at the **Capture stop conditions** and **Capture output sections**[56]. For this lab, we will switch to the next file after 30 seconds and stop after 6 files have been created.

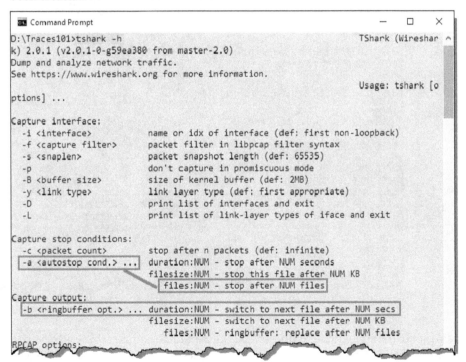

```
Command Prompt                                              —    □    ×

D:\Traces101>tshark -h                                  TShark (Wireshar ^
k) 2.0.1 (v2.0.1-0-g59ea380 from master-2.0)
Dump and analyze network traffic.
See https://www.wireshark.org for more information.
                                                         Usage: tshark [o
ptions] ...

Capture interface:
  -i <interface>        name or idx of interface (def: first non-loopback)
  -f <capture filter>   packet filter in libpcap filter syntax
  -s <snaplen>          packet snapshot length (def: 65535)
  -p                    don't capture in promiscuous mode
  -B <buffer size>      size of kernel buffer (def: 2MB)
  -y <link type>        link layer type (def: first appropriate)
  -D                    print list of interfaces and exit
  -L                    print list of link-layer types of iface and exit

Capture stop conditions:
  -c <packet count>     stop after n packets (def: infinite)
  -a <autostop cond.> ... duration:NUM - stop after NUM seconds
                        filesize:NUM - stop this file after NUM KB
                        files:NUM - stop after NUM files
Capture output:
  -b <ringbuffer opt.> ... duration:NUM - switch to next file after NUM secs
                        filesize:NUM - switch to next file after NUM KB
                        files:NUM - ringbuffer: replace after NUM files
RPCAP options:
```

---

[56]   Note that the Capture output option area implies that you must use a ring buffer. You don't. We will just use the *duration:NUM(secs)* capability of this parameter.

We will need to use the following parameters during this capture process:

- **-i 3** to capture on the 3rd interface
- **-a files:6** to automatically stop capturing after 6 files
- **-b duration:30** to create the next file after 30 seconds
- **-w mytshark.pcapng** to save to this trace file stem name

Step 4: At the command line, put it all together by typing **tshark -i3 -a files:6 -b duration:30 -w mytshark.pcapng** and press Enter.[57]

Open your browser and spend some time browsing *www.wireshark.org*. Return to Wireshark. Be patient if the capture process is still running. It may take longer than the time allocated (3 minutes in this case) for Wireshark to write all the buffered files.

Step 5: Type **dir mytshark*.*** to view your files. Notice the timestamp detail that matches your setting to switch to the next file after 30 seconds.

```
■ Command Prompt                                        —    □    ×

D:\Traces101>tshark -i3 -a files:6 -b duration:30 -w mytshark.pcapng
Capturing on 'Wi-Fi'
62493

D:\Traces101>dir mytshark*.*
 Volume in drive D is MainDrive
 Volume Serial Number is 4EAF-C465

 Directory of D:\Traces101

01/11/2016  04:19 PM         1,196,172 mytshark_00001_20160111161842.pcapng
01/11/2016  04:19 PM        28,009,924 mytshark_00002_20160111161912.pcapng
01/11/2016  04:20 PM        25,630,708 mytshark_00003_20160111161942.pcapng
01/11/2016  04:20 PM            26,944 mytshark_00004_20160111162012.pcapng
01/11/2016  04:21 PM         3,085,036 mytshark_00005_20160111162042.pcapng
01/11/2016  04:21 PM            17,388 mytshark_00006_20160111162112.pcapng
               6 File(s)     57,966,172 bytes
               0 Dir(s)  1,756,549,517,312 bytes free

D:\Traces101>_
```

Spend some time practicing with Tshark. It's best to be comfortable with the parameters and capabilities of Tshark before someone comes screaming into your office with network complaints[58].

---

[57] This command will work with or without a space between the -i parameter and the interface number.

[58] Time to get a lock on your door, eh?

!TIP

If you use the same parameters and a very long, detailed Tshark string, consider building a batch file with variables to reduce the chance of typing mistakes. For example, you might create a batch file called *t1.bat* that contains the following:

```
tshark -i%1 -a files:6 -b duration:30 -w %2.pcapng
```

To use the batch file, type **t1**, the interface number (%1 variable) and file stem (%2 variable), such as **t1 4 test1**. This will capture traffic on interface 4, create six files containing 30 seconds of traffic each, and name each file beginning with the stem *test1_00001<date/timestamp>* through *test1_00006<date/timestamp>*.

8.4. Use Capture Filters during Command-Line Capture

Use capture filters with Dumpcap or Tshark when you are capturing on a busy network or you just want to focus on specific traffic during the capture process.

Both Dumpcap and Tshark use the -f option to specify a capture filter using the capture filter (BPF) format. Use the -w option to set the name of your new trace file. For example, if you are interested in capturing all traffic running on TCP port 21, enter **dumpcap -i3 -f "tcp port 21" -w port21.pcapng**, as shown in Figure 132. You will have to manually stop the capture process (Ctrl+C).

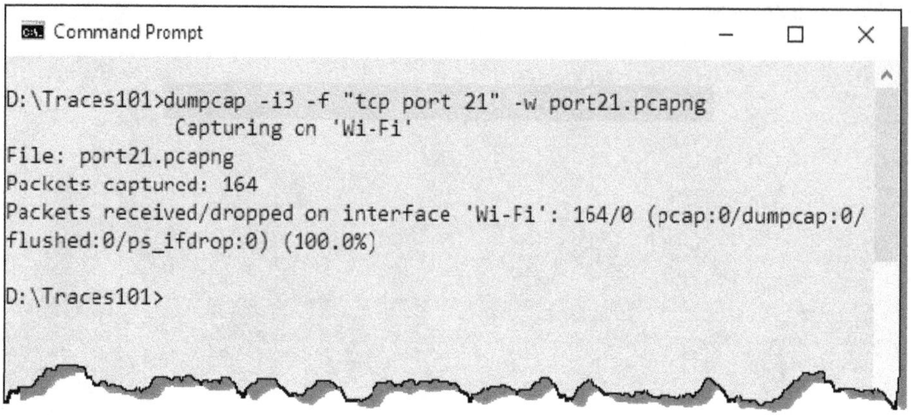

Figure 132. You will need to manually stop the capture unless you've defined a stop condition.

Capture filtering with Tshark uses the same parameters. For example, in Figure 133 we are capturing all TCP port 21 traffic to or from 192.168.44.7 to a file called *myport21.pcapng* using the **-i**, **-f**, and **-w** parameters.

The command would be **tshark -i3 -f "tcp port 21 and host 192.168.44.7" -w myport21.pcapng**.

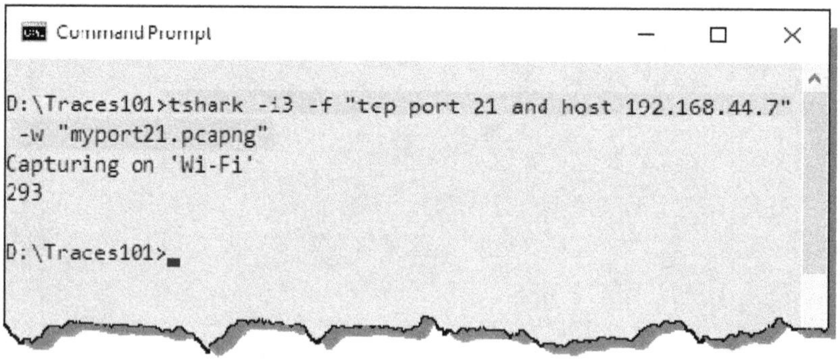

Figure 133. Both Tshark and Dumpcap use the Berkeley Packet Filtering (BPF) capture filter syntax.

TIP

Wireshark doesn't recognize capture filter names, such as NotMyMAC (created in Lab 12). Use the capture filter string and enclose the filter string in quotes. Quotes are necessary if you have spaces in your filter, as we see in Figure 133.

8.5. Use Display Filters during Command-Line Capture

Display filters have many more options than capture filters. When capturing at command line, however, there is a display filter limitation that you must be aware of. You can use display filters with the `-Y` parameter during a live capture, but you can cannot save the trace file while using that parameter.

Because of this limitation, consider capturing all traffic, saving the packets to a file (or file sets if necessary), applying display filters to the saved trace file, and saving the subset to a new trace file.

If you want to capture only packets that match the `tcp.analysis.flags` filter, for example, first use a capture filter to capture all TCP traffic and save that traffic to a file. In Figure 134, we are capturing and saving TCP traffic to a file called *tcptraffic.pcapng*. That is the first step.

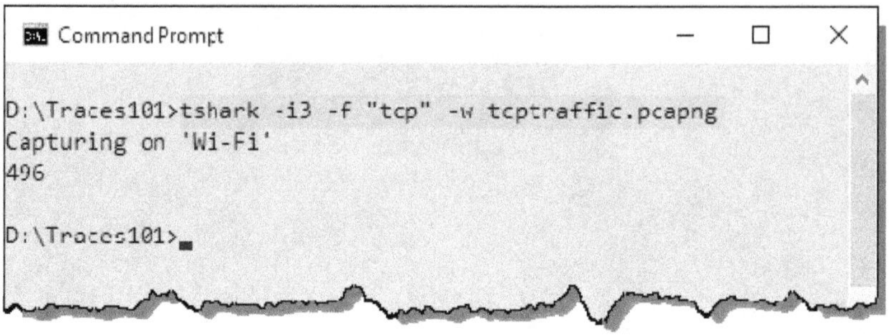

```
D:\Traces101>tshark -i3 -f "tcp" -w tcptraffic.pcapng
Capturing on 'Wi-Fi'
496

D:\Traces101>
```

Figure 134. Begin with a capture filter and save the packets to a file.

The second step is to use the `-r` parameter to read the trace file you created, the `-Y` parameter to specify a display filter, and the `-w` parameter to save a new trace file, as shown in Figure 135.

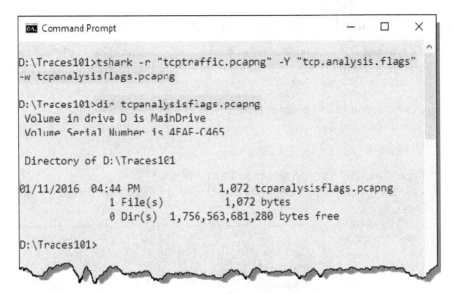

Figure 135. Use the −Y and −w parameters to apply display filters and save a subset of the packets.

In Lab 45 you will use the −Y parameter to extract HTTP GET requests from a trace file and save these GET requests in a new trace file.

🖳 Lab 45: Use Tshark to Extract HTTP GET Requests

In this lab you will use the `-r` parameter to read a trace file and then apply a display filter with the `-Y` parameter. Finally you will save a trace file that contains only the HTTP GET requests.

Step 1:   Open the **command prompt** (Windows) or a **terminal window** (Linux/Macintosh).

Step 2:   Navigate to your trace file directory.

Type `tshark -r "http-espn101.pcapng"` `-Y "http.request.method==GET" -w "httpGETs.pcapng"` and press **Enter.**

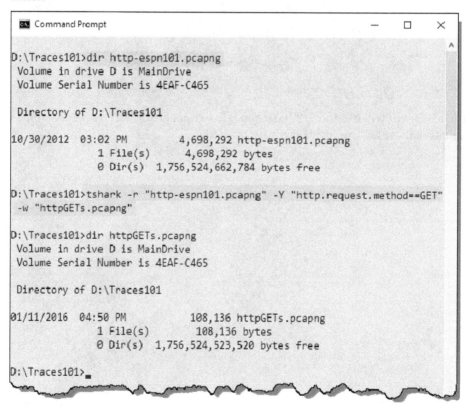

```
D:\Traces101>dir http-espn101.pcapng
 Volume in drive D is MainDrive
 Volume Serial Number is 4EAF-C465

 Directory of D:\Traces101

10/30/2012  03:02 PM         4,698,292 http-espn101.pcapng
               1 File(s)     4,698,292 bytes
               0 Dir(s)  1,756,524,662,784 bytes free

D:\Traces101>tshark -r "http-espn101.pcapng" -Y "http.request.method==GET"
 -w "httpGETs.pcapng"

D:\Traces101>dir httpGETs.pcapng
 Volume in drive D is MainDrive
 Volume Serial Number is 4EAF-C465

 Directory of D:\Traces101

01/11/2016  04:50 PM           108,136 httpGETs.pcapng
               1 File(s)       108,136 bytes
               0 Dir(s)  1,756,524,523,520 bytes free

D:\Traces101>
```

That's it. Now you can open your trace file in Wireshark for further analysis.

TIP

The best way to use display filters and Tshark is to capture and save all the traffic using Tshark and then open the trace file in Wireshark to apply display filters and perform analysis tasks.

8.6. Use Tshark to Export Specific Field Values and Statistics from a Trace File

Sometimes you may want to get a general feel for the traffic with or without capturing the traffic. This is where Tshark is the only command-line tool to use.

Run **tshark -h** to view the available options. Field export options and export statistics are listed under the Output area.

Export Field Values

You must use -T fields first. Then you can list the fields you are interested in after the -e parameter. You can combine these parameters with display filters as needed. For example, in Figure 136 we typed **tshark -i3 -f "dst port 80 and host 192.168.44.7" -T fields -e frame.number -e ip.src -e ip.dst -e tcp.window_size** to capture traffic to/from 192.168.44.7 to destination port 80 on interface 3 and display the frame number, source and destination IP addresses, and TCP window size value.

You will need to manually stop the capture process using **Ctrl+C**. If you can't manually stop the process, consider adding a stop condition to your Tshark command.

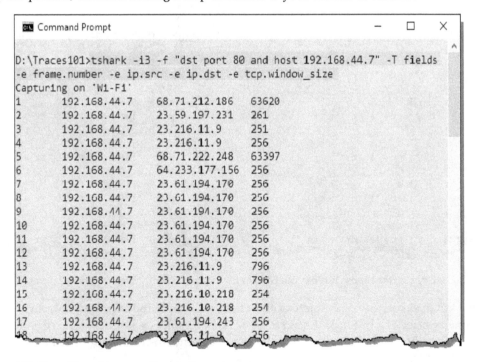

Figure 136. You will need to manually stop the capture process

Use the -E parameter to add options to make the exported information easier to read. For example, add -E header=y to add a field header.

To analyze the information in a spreadsheet, use -E separator=, to set up the exported information in comma-separated format.

You can use > stats.txt at the end of your command to save this information to a file named *stats.txt*.

Again, use **tshark -h** to view all available options.

Export Traffic Statistics

Use the -z parameter to view numerous statistics about your traffic. You might also consider using the -q parameter to quiet down Tshark from displaying each frame on the screen. For example, in Figure 137 we ran **tshark -i3 -qz io,phs** to display the Protocol Hierarchy Statistics (phs) seen on interface number 3.

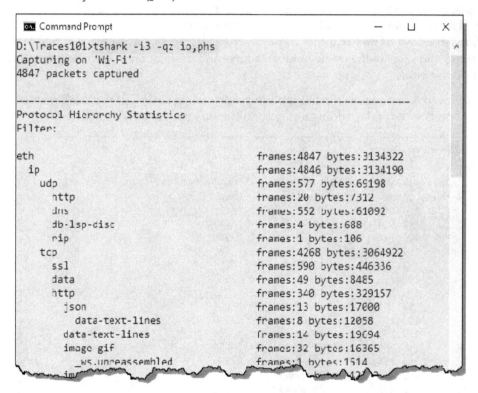

Figure 137. We can see the various protocols and applications in use without capturing traffic.

If you want to export any of the statistics to a text file, simply redirect the results to a file, as mentioned earlier. For example, tshark -i3 -qz io,phs > stats.txt. As you continue to gather statistics, use >> instead of > to append additional information to the existing text file.

One of the most interesting statistics is the list of hosts that are communicating on the network. In Figure 138, we typed **tshark -i3 -qz hosts** to extract the list of active hosts seen on interface number 3.

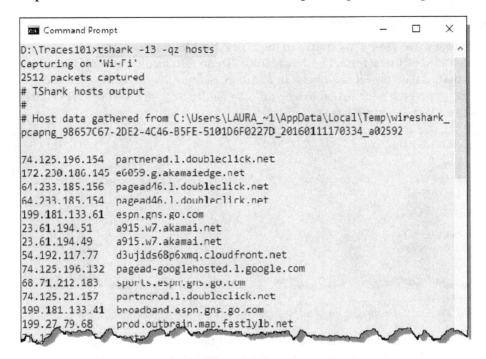

Figure 138. *It is easy to build a list of active hosts seen on the network using* `tshark -qz hosts`.

If you want to extract the Expert warnings, notes, and errors from an existing trace file, use the -r parameter. For example, in Figure 139 we typed **tshark -r "http-download101.pcapng" -qz expert,warns** to see we have packet loss and a zero window condition in the trace file.

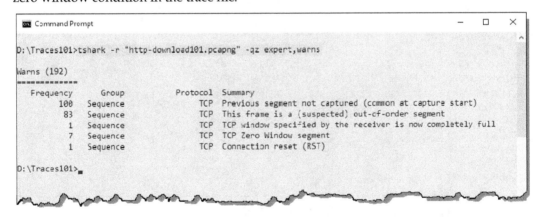

Figure 139. *Pulling the expert warnings, we can see some indications of segments not captured.* [http-download101.pcapng]

See *www.wireshark.org/docs/man-pages/tshark.html* for more details on the –z parameter.

Export HTTP Host Field Values

You can easily use Tshark to capture all the HTTP Host field values currently seen on the network and save that information to a text file. To do this, include a display filter for packets that contain the *http.host* field. In addition, define *http.host* as the exported field name and export the information to a text file. In Figure 140, we saved the HTTP Host field values to a file called ***httphosts.txt***.

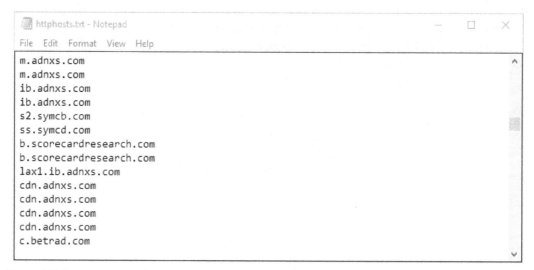

Figure 140. *We used a display filter and field value of http.host to create a host list file.*

The resulting text file only includes the HTTP Host field values, as shown in Figure 141. We could add another field parameter to save the destination IP address (*ip.dst*), as well. We will do this in Lab 46.

```
m.adnxs.com
m.adnxs.com
ib.adnxs.com
ib.adnxs.com
s2.symcb.com
ss.symcd.com
b.scorecardresearch.com
b.scorecardresearch.com
lax1.ib.adnxs.com
cdn.adnxs.com
cdn.adnxs.com
cdn.adnxs.com
cdn.adnxs.com
c.betrad.com
```

Figure 141. *You can create a list of all the HTTP Host field values seen in the trace file.*

🖳 Lab 46: Use Tshark to Extract HTTP Host Names and IP Addresses

In this lab we will use a combination of display filters and field names to create a file that contains both the IP addresses and host names of HTTP servers contacted on the network.

Step 1:   Open the **command prompt** (Windows) or a **terminal window** (Linux/Macintosh).

Step 2:   Navigate to the directory in which you want to save your new HTTP host name/address file.

Type **tshark -i3 -Y "http.host" -T fields -e http.host -e ip.dst -E separator=, > httphostaddrs.txt** and press **Enter**. Substitute the appropriate interface number for your system for "-i3."

Step 3:   Toggle to your browser and visit various web sites. After a few minutes, toggle back to your command prompt or terminal window and manually stop the capture process (**Ctrl+C** on windows, for example).

Wireshark displays the captured packet count, which is the number of host names/destination IP address sets you have in your text file.

```
🖳 Command Prompt                                    —    □    ✕

D:\Traces101>tshark -i3 -Y "http.host" -T fields -e http.host -e ip.dst
 -E separator=, > httphostaddrs.txt
Capturing on 'Wi-Fi'
39

D:\Traces101>_
```

Step 4:   Open and examine your **httphostaddrs.txt** file.

```
httphostaddrs.txt - Notepad                          —    □    ✕
File  Edit  Format  View  Help
clients1.google.com,64.233.177.102
clients1.google.com,64.233.177.102
clients1.google.com,64.233.177.102
ocsp.godaddy.com,72.167.18.239
ocsp.digicert.com,72.21.91.29
renoairport.com,216.70.107.150
regular-expressions.info,66.39.67.31
www.regular-expressions.info,66.39.67.31
```

Practice working with the fields and filters to extract just the information in which you are interested. Consider creating a batch file or script to run Tshark commands you use often.

8.7.   Continue Learning about Wireshark and Network Analysis

By this point you've covered the most important Wireshark skills and network analysis functions. You've run through 46 labs and you're about to finish Challenge 8. Once that is complete, what's next?

Here are some recommendations for continuing your education in network analysis:

- Visit *www.wiresharkbook.com* and check out the supplements for this book and other books listed on that site.

- Visit *www.wireshark.org* to sign up for the Wireshark-Announce mailing list to receive notifications when a new Wireshark version is available for download.

- Sign up for the newsletter at *www.chappellU.com* to participate in free online Wireshark events.

- Practice capturing your own traffic to become accustomed to the type of traffic that is generated when you browse web sites, send email, or log in to the company server.

- Continue customizing Wireshark by adding new profiles and new display filters, coloring rules, and Filter Expression buttons.

- Share your customized settings with other IT team members to create a master profile that improves your team's network analysis efficiency.

- If you want to validate your Wireshark proficiency, consider the Wireshark Certified Network Analyst (WCNA) certification. For information on the WCNA program, visit *www.wiresharktraining.com/certification.html*.

As you've read on the title page for each chapter, there are many benefits to becoming proficient at network analysis. Now is the time to start delving into your network traffic to spot problems and detect those network anomalies faster.

Chapter 8 Challenge

Use *challenge101-8.pcapng* and the command-line tool techniques covered in this chapter to answer these Challenge questions. The answer key is located in Appendix A.

Question 8-1.   What Tshark parameter should you use to list active interfaces on your Wireshark system?

Question 8-2.   Using Tshark to extract protocol hierarchy information, how many UDP frames are in *challenge101-8.pcapng*?

Question 8-3.   Use Tshark to export all DNS packets from *challenge101-8.pcapng* to a new trace file called *ch8dns.pcapng*. How many packets were exported?

[This page intentionally blank.]

Appendix A: Challenge Answers

Now that you know, share. Share the knowledge with others. Take five minutes to teach someone something cool that you learned that could end their networking nightmare.

I will never forget the first person that introduced me to Wireshark and I am forever grateful. Be that first for someone.

Jennifer Keels
CNP-S, CEH, Network Engineer

Chapter 0 Challenge Answers

Answer 0-1.   The Status Bar indicates this trace file contains 20 frames.

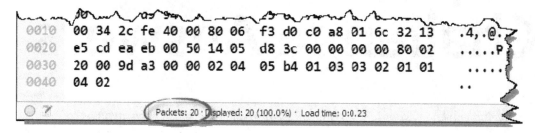

Answer 0-2.   The **Source** and **Destination** columns indicate this TCP connection is
                between 192.168.1.108 and 50.19.229.205.

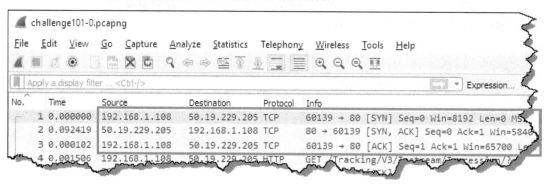

Answer 0-3.   Frame 4 is an HTTP GET request.

4   0.001506 1384 192.168.1.108 50.19.229.205 HTTP GET /Tracking/V3/Instream/Impr

Answer 0-4.   Sorting on the **Length** column (or even just scrolling through the file and looking at the **Length** column) indicates the largest frames are 1,428 bytes.

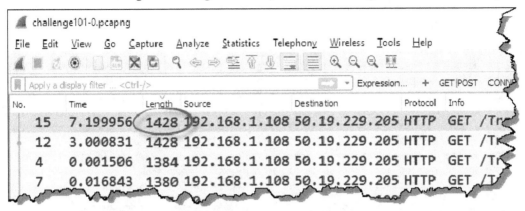

Answer 0-5.   Wireshark displays only HTTP and TCP in the **Protocol** column.

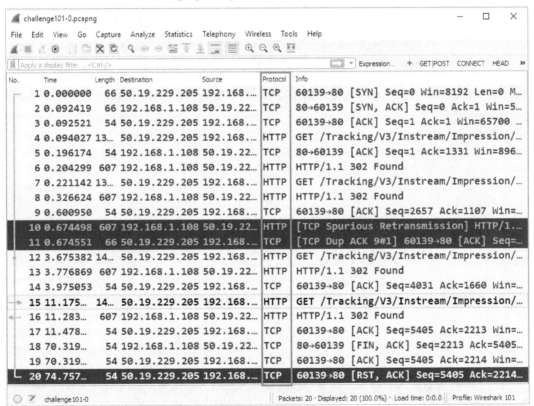

Answer 0-6.   The HTTP server sends 302 Found responses (frames 6, 8, 10, 13, and 16).

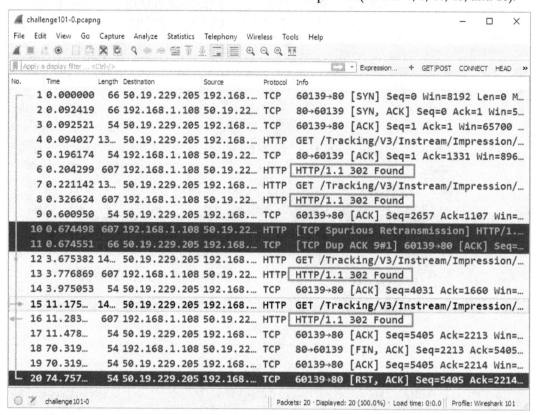

Answer 0-7.   There are no IPv6 packets in this trace file—the **Source** and **Destination** columns only display IPv4 addresses.

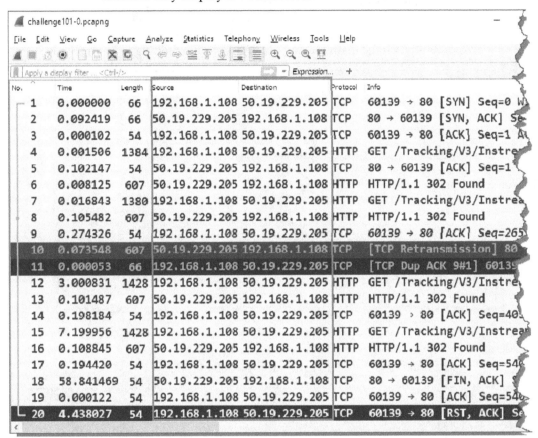

Chapter 1 Challenge Answers

Answer 1-1.   If you are running an earlier version of Wireshark (Wireshark v1.x), you must add port 87 in the HTTP preference setting (**Edit | Preferences** > **Protocols | HTTP**), as shown below. You may need to click the **Reload** button on the main toolbar to apply your new setting to the trace file.

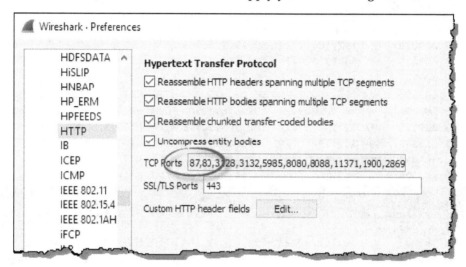

Frame 13 is the GET request for the default page.

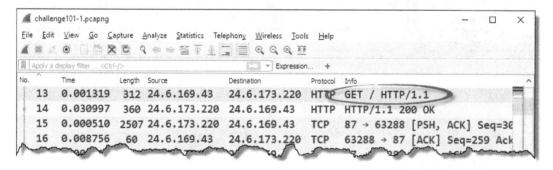

Answer 1-2. In frame 14, the server responds with 200 OK. This will appear in Frame 17 if you have the TCP reassembly feature enabled (see Lab 5).

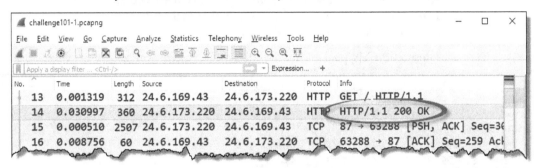

Answer 1-3. In order to view the TCP delta time, we must enable the *Calculate conversation timestamps* TCP preference (**Edit | Preferences ˃ Protocols | TCP**). Then we can right-click on the new "**Time since previous frame in this TCP stream**" line at the end of the TCP header, select **Apply as Column**, and click twice on the new column's heading to sort from high to low. Frame 285 contains the largest TCP delta time, 15.438012000 seconds.

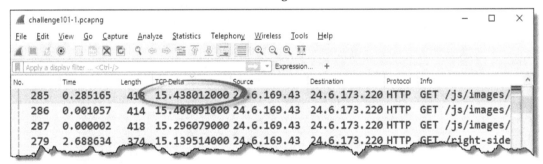

Answer 1-4.   Based on the **TCP Delta** column sorted in Question 1-3, we can look in the **Info** column and **TCP Delta** column to see how many SYN packets have a value greater than 1 second. Four SYN packets arrived after at least a 1 second delay (frames 3, 6, 2, and 5 in that order). This is a sign that there are problems connecting to a TCP peer.

These four SYN packets are denoted as TCP retransmissions, as well.

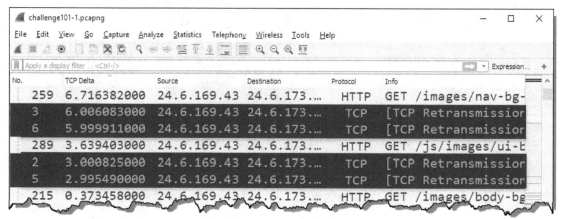

Chapter 2 Challenge Answers

Answer 2-1.   First you configured Wireshark to automatically capture only your traffic to and from TCP port 80 and save the traffic to a file named *mybrowse.pcapng*. An example Capture Options window is shown below. No ICMP traffic was captured because we were filtering on TCP.

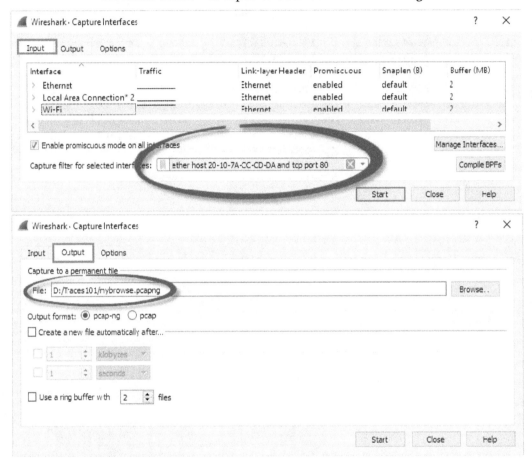

Answer 2-2.   After pinging and browsing to *www.chappellU.com*, you should only have
                   captured your traffic to or from port 80. The **Protocol** column will only list
                   TCP and HTTP traffic.

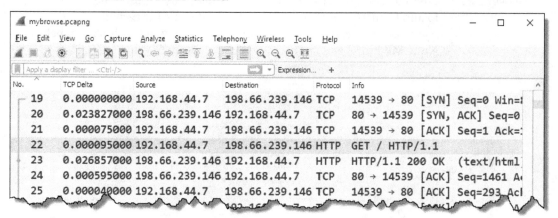

Answer 2-3.   Now you should have configured Wireshark to automatically capture and save all your ICMP traffic to a file called *myicmp.pcapng*. An example Capture Options window is shown below.

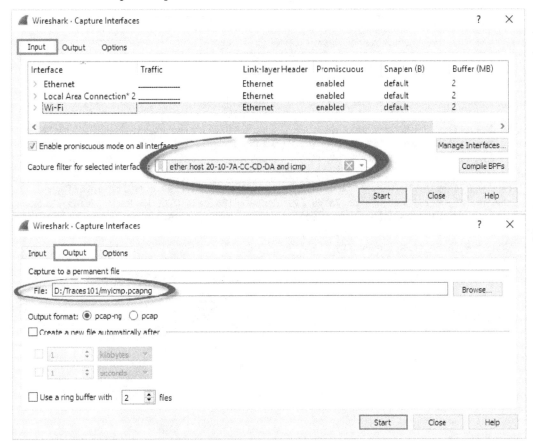

After you pinged and browsed to *www.chappellU.com* again, you should have seen that the trace file only contains ICMP traffic based on your capture filter. How many ICMP packets you captured depends on the amount of ICMP traffic generated by your ping application and any background ICMP traffic generated during your capture process.

Answer 2-4.   If you look inside the ICMP portion of the packets, you should see Type 8/Code 0 (Echo request) and Type 0/Code 0 (Echo reply). In the image below we right-clicked on the ICMP Type field and selected **Apply as Column**.

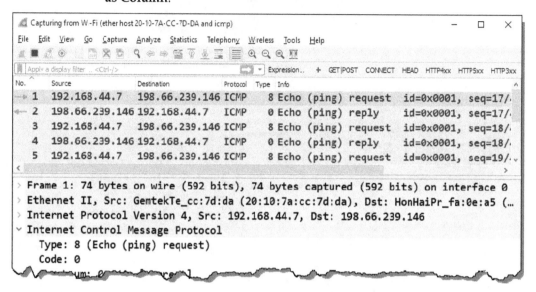

Chapter 3 Challenge Answers

Question 3-1. Using the filter `ip.addr==80.78.246.209`, we determined that 32 packets traveled to or from 80.78.246.209.

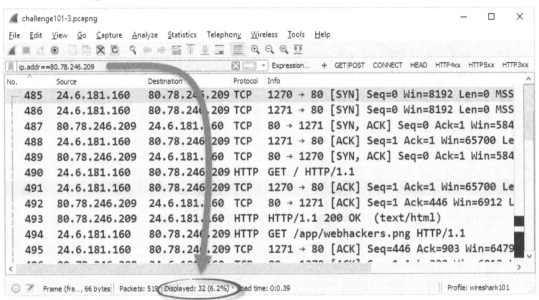

Question 3-2. Based on a **dns** filter, we determined that there are 8 DNS packets in the trace file.

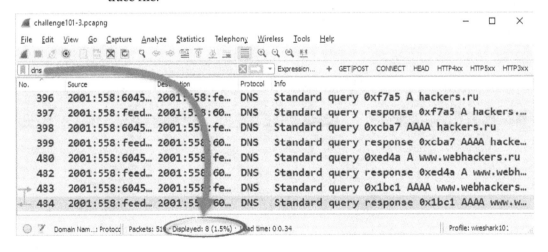

Question 3-3. Based on a `tcp.flags.syn==1` filter, we determined that there are 12 TCP packets with the TCP SYN flag set on in this trace file.

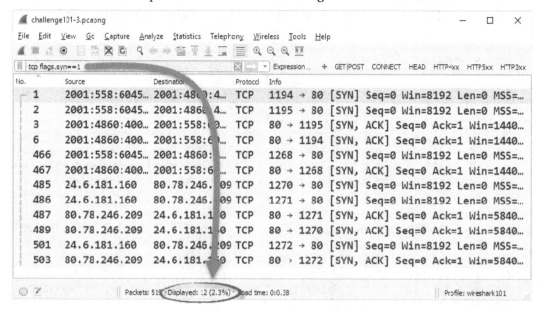

Question 3-4. Based on a `frame matches "(?i)set-cookie"` filter, we determined that three packets contained this string. We disabled *Allow subdissector to reassemble TCP streams* in TCP Preferences in order to see the response code 200 OK in frame 9.

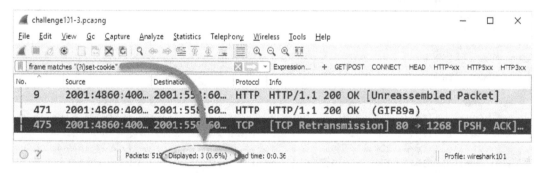

Question 3-5.   Based on a `tcp.time_delta > 1` filter, we determined that 18 TCP frames arrived with over a 1 second delay preceding them.

No.	TCP Delta	Source	Destination	Protocol	Info
369	6.926872000	2001:558:604...	2001:4860:4...	HTTP	GET /search?hl=en&rls=com.mic...
389	6.878651000	2001:558:604...	2001:4860:4...	HTTP	GET /csi?v=3&s=web&action=&ei...
392	2.620065000	2001:558:604!...	2001:4860:4...	HTTP	GET /url?sa=t&rct=j&q=metaspl...
400	55.0219050...	2001:558:6045...	2001:4860:4...	HTTP	GET /search?q=hackers.ru&sour...
472	54.2306230...	2001:558:6045...	2001:4860:4...	HTTP	GET /csi?v=3&s=web&action=&e=...
475	2.997750000	2001:4860:400...	2001:558:60...	TCP	[TCP Retransmission] 80 → 126...
477	5.958008000	2001:558:604!...	2001:4860:4...	HTTP	GET /url?sa=t&rct=j&q=hackers...
509	14.6455750...	24.6.181.160	80.78.246.209	TCP	1270 → 80 [RST, ACK] Seq=322 ...
510	15.1602640...	24.6.181.160	80.78.246.209	TCP	1271 → 80 [RST, ACK] Seq=446 ...
511	16.2138780...	2001:558:604...	2001:4860:4...	TCP	1194 → 80 [RST, ACK] Seq=5811...
512	21.3711470...	2001:558:604...	2001:4860:4...	TCP	1195 → 80 [RST, ACK] Seq=5183...
513	18.9984140...	2001:558:604...	2001:4860:4...	TCP	1268 → 80 [RST, ACK] Seq=721 ...
514	64.7993230...	80.78.246.209	24.6.181.160	TCP	80 → 1272 [FIN, ACK] Seq=728 ...
515	1.303469000	80.78.246.209	24.6.181.160	TCP	[TCP Retransmission] 80 → 127...
516	2.556541000	80.78.246.209	24.6.181.160	TCP	[TCP Retransmission] 80 → 127...
517	5.248543000	80.78.246.209	24.6.181.160	TCP	[TCP Retransmission] 80 → 127...
518	10.2856640...	80.78.246.209	24.6.181.160	TCP	[TCP Retransmission] 80 → 127...
519	20.5128190...	80.78.246.209	24.6.181.160	TCP	[TCP Retransmission] 80 → 127...

tcp.time_delta > 1

Packets: 519 · Displayed: 18 (3.5%) · Load time: 0:0.37   Profile: wireshark101

Chapter 4 Challenge Answers

Answer 4-1.   Frame 170 matches the **Bad TCP** coloring rule that looks for TCP analysis flagged packets (except Window Update packets).

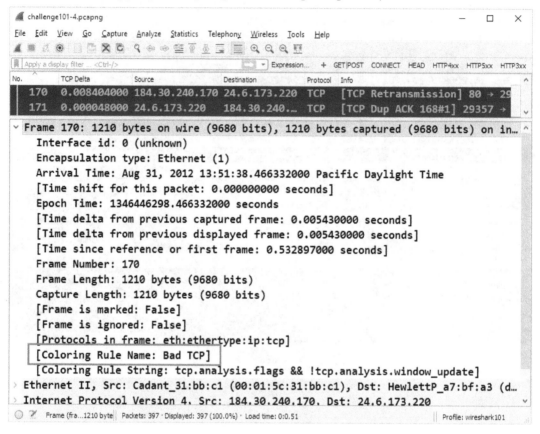

Answer 4-2.   We applied a filter for `tcp.stream==5` and then right-clicked on one line in the Packet List pane. We selected **Colorize Conversation | TCP** and selected **Color 6**. This TCP stream contains 13 frames.

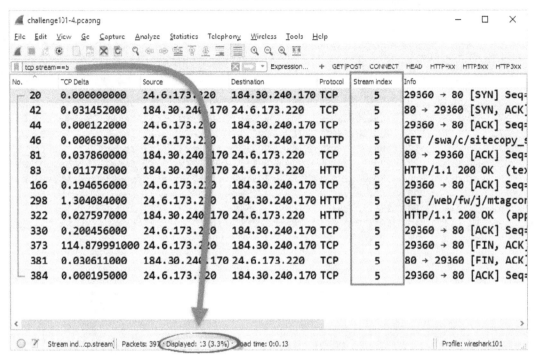

Answer 4-3.   We created a coloring rule using the filter `tcp.time_delta > 100`. We used the same string as a display filter and found 9 frames matched this filter. One packet still retained our temporary coloring rule from Question 4-2.

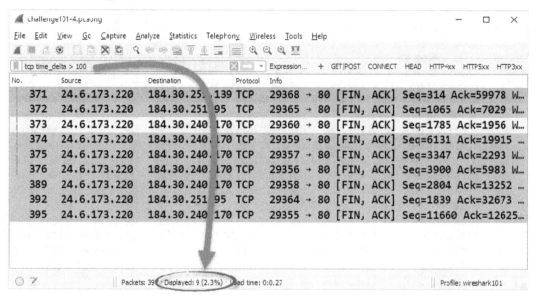

Question 4-4.   After creating a **TCP Delta** column, we selected **File | Export Packet Dissections | As CSV**. We selected to export the displayed packets and only the Packet summary line.

We opened the .csv file in Excel and determined the average value of the exported **TCP Delta** column as 115.2703762.

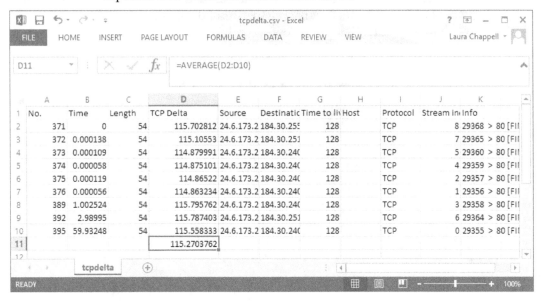

Chapter 5 Challenge Answers

Answer 5-1.   We selected **Statistics | I/O Graph** and used the default Packets/s unit in the Y axis. The highest packets-per-second value seen in this trace file is approximately 86 packets per second.

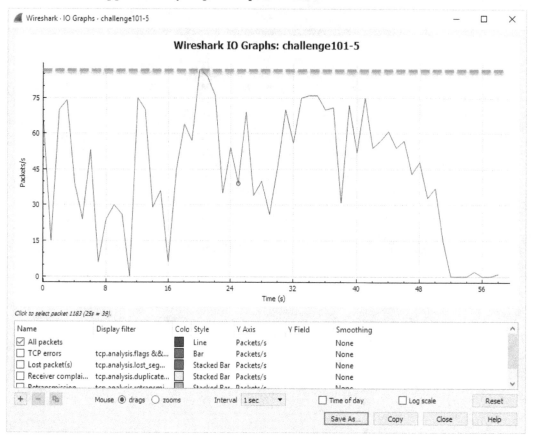

Answer 5-2.   After changing the Y axis to Bits/s, we can see the highest bits-per-second value seen in this trace file is approximately 630,000 bits per second.

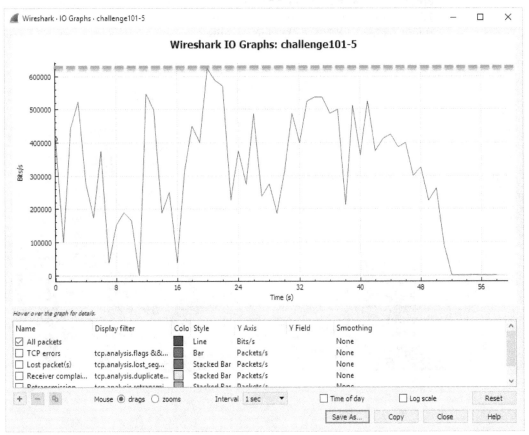

Answer 5-3:   Selecting **Statistics | Conversations | TCP**, we can see there is only one TCP conversation in the trace file.

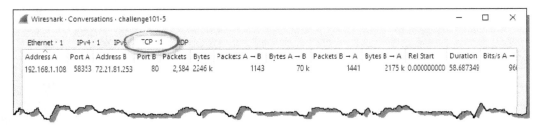

Answers 5-4.   After expanding the **Warnings** section in the Expert Information window, we can right-click on one of the *Previous segment not captured* indications and select **Apply as Filter | Selected**. . The Status Bar indicates there are 172 of these indications in the trace file. Most likely an interconnecting device along a path is dropping packets.

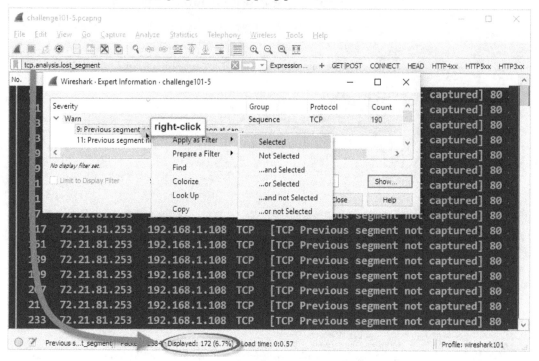

Answer 5-5.   Clicking on the **Notes** section and applying a filter for
`tcp.analysis.retransmission`, we can see there are a total of
183 Retransmissions and Fast retransmissions combined. These are the
recovery processes for packet loss.

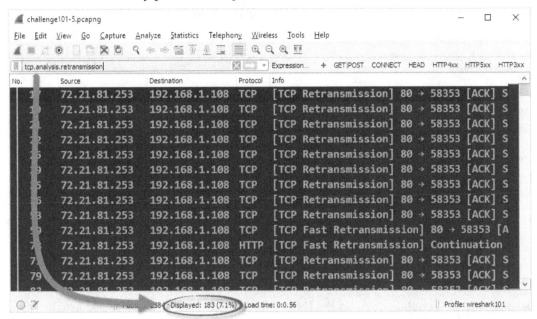

Chapter 6 Challenge Answers

Answer 6-1.   First we made certain that the TCP *Allow subdissector to reassemble TCP streams* preference is enabled. Then we selected **File | Export Objects | HTTP** to find out which HTTP objects were transferred in the trace file. The two .jpg files are *sample2b.jpg* and *featureb.jpg*.

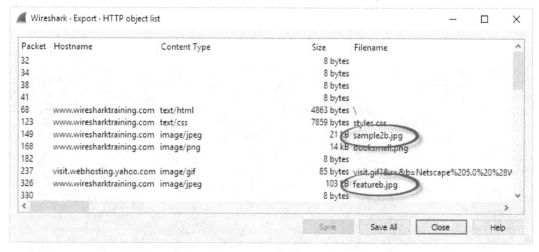

Answer 6-2.   Scrolling down in the HTTP object list, we see ***next-active.png*** listed with *arbornetworks.com*.

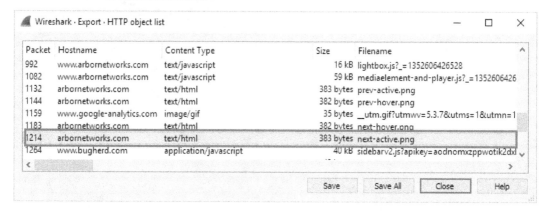

When you click on this entry to jump to packet 1,214, however, we see a 301 Moved Permanently response indicating the file is at *http://www.arbornetworks.com/modules/mod_arborslideshow/tmpl/img/icon/slider/next-active.png.*

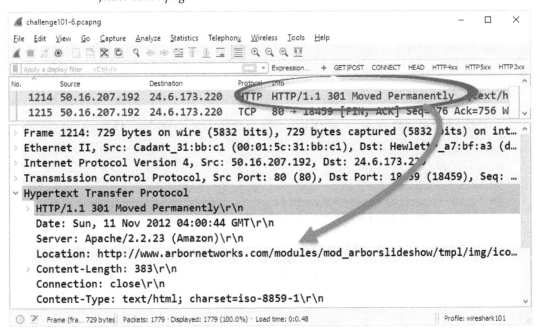

Answer 6-3.   We selected *booksmall.png* and selected **Save As**. This file depicts the top half of the *Wireshark Network Analysis* book on an orange background.

Answer 6-4.   We filtered the trace file on `tcp.stream eq 7` before right-clicking on a frame and selecting **Follow | TCP stream**. This client is using Firefox to browse *www.wiresharktraining.com* in this conversation.

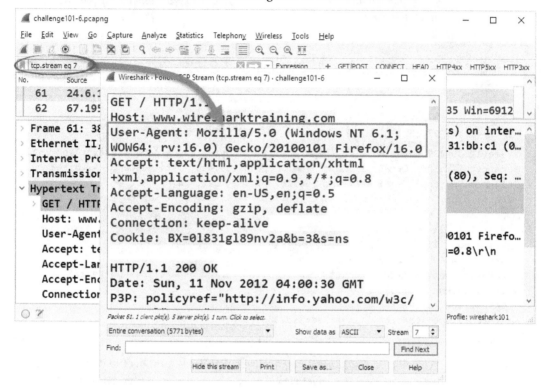

Chapter 7 Challenge Answers

Answer 7-1.   We clicked on the trace file **Annotation** button on the Status Bar to see a copyright notice and some basic information about the trace file.

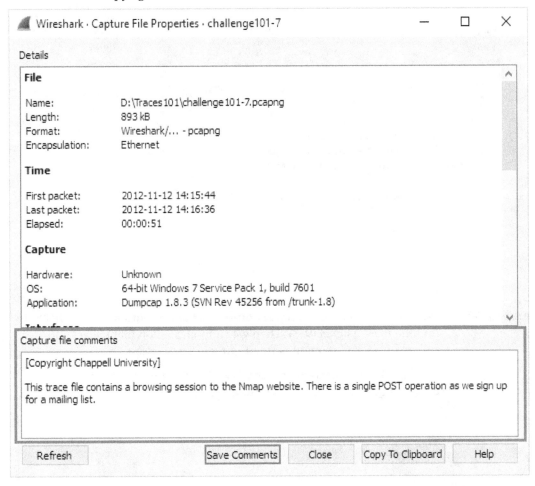

Answer 7-2.   We clicked on the **Expert Information** button on the Status Bar and expanded the **Comment** section to view three packet comments.

Answer 7-3.   We applied a filter for `http.request.method contains "POST"` to find the POST packet (938). Then we right-clicked on that packet and selected **Packet Comment** before typing in our message.

The filter `http.request.method=="POST"` or even `http.request.method matches "POST"` would have worked as well.

Chapter 8 Challenge Answers

Answer 8-1.   You should use the **–D** parameter to list active interfaces on your Wireshark system.

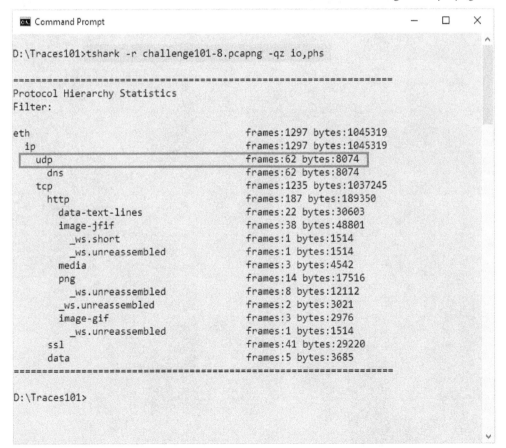

Answer 8-2.   Using **`tshark -r challenge101-8.pcapng -qz io,phs`**, we determined that there are 62 UDP frames in *challenge101-8.pcapng*.

Answer 8-3.   Using the command **tshark -r challenge101-8.pcapng -Y "dns" -w ch8dns.pcapng**, we exported the DNS traffic and found that there are 62 DNS packets. Apparently all the UDP traffic is DNS.

We could have used **capinfos ch8dns.pcapng** to obtain the packet count as well.

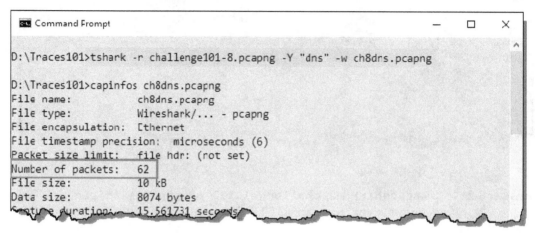

Appendix B: Trace File Descriptions

Protocol Analysis is the only way to really see how applications and networks behave. Unfortunately, the tools are only as good as the training and knowledge you gain. More practice = more knowledge.

Tony Fortunato
Senior Network Performance Specialist, *The Technology Firm*

Practice Trace Files

The book web site (*www.wiresharkbook.com*) contains all the trace files mentioned in this book. Please note the license for use below and on the book web site.

You agree to indemnify and hold Protocol Analysis Institute and its subsidiaries, affiliates, officers, agents, employees, partners and licensors harmless from any claim or demand, including reasonable attorneys' fees, made by any third party due to or arising out of your use of the included trace files, your violation of the TOS, or your violation of any rights of another.

NO COMMERCIAL REUSE

You may not reproduce, duplicate, copy, sell, trade, resell, or exploit for any commercial purposes, any of the trace files available at *www.wiresharkbook.com*.

a.pcapng

This trace file contains a download session – the client is getting the OpenOffice application. Note the server is a bit sluggish in its first response to the client. Is it experiencing performance problems? [Chapter 8]

dhcp-serverdiscovery101.pcapng

This trace file only contains DHCP traffic. Note that the display filter required to view DHCP traffic is simply bootp. [Chapter 3]

dns-nmap101.pcapng

We saved the DNS traffic from a browsing session that inclu ded an attempt to reach *www.nmap.org* and *www.insecure.org* (both managed by Fyodor, the creator of Nmap) as well as *google.com* and *dropbox.com*. It seems there are some DNS problems that will prevent us from getting to Fyodor's sites. [Chapter 1]

ftp-bounce.pcapng

This trace file depicts an unsuccessful FTP upload process. The FTP client is allowed to connect to the FTP server, send the STOR command with the file name, and even establish the TCP connection for the data transfer channel. When the client begins sending the data to the server, however, the server rudely sends TCP resets in fear of an FTP bouncd attack. [Chapter 4]

ftp-clientside101.pcapng

Wireshark is running on a client to capture the FTP command and data channel traffic seen in this trace file. The user name and password are visible in clear text. We can use Follow | TCP Stream to reassemble the file transferred in this trace file. [Chapter 3 and Chapter 6]

ftp-crack101.pcapng

We started capturing in the middle of a password cracking attempt. This is a good trace file on which to practice keyword filtering. Was the password cracking attempt successful? [Chapter 3 and Chapter 4]

ftp-download101.pcapng

The FTP banner is quite evident in the Packet List pane of this trace file. Follow the stream of the command channel to see what the client wants from the server. Practice finding the most active conversations based on bytes and applying a filter for that traffic. [Chapter 6]

general101.pcapng

This is the trace file we followed to build a picture of a network. We examined the MAC addresses and IP addresses contained in the trace file. [Chapter 0]

general101b.pcapng

An outside host (121.125.72.180) and an inside host (24.6.169.43) are trying to make a connection to a local host. Consider building a display filter for all TCP SYN packets to detect connection attempts and responses. [Chapter 3 and Chapter 5]

general101c.pcapng

We used this trace file to detect suspicious traffic on a network. Look at the Protocol Hierarchy to identify the IRC traffic and use Follow | TCP Stream to reassemble the traffic and identify commands. What is the name of the IRC server? [Chapter 5]

general101d.pcapng

This trace file contains numerous TCP problems. Open the Expert Information window to identify the problems on this network. [Chapter 5]

gen-startupchatty101.pcapng

We used this trace file to examine conversation statistics. The trace file contains 15 IPv4 conversations and 12 IPv6 conversations. Although there are only 6 TCP conversations, there are 52 UDP conversations. [Chapter 3]

http-au101b.pcapng

We used this trace file to track a web browsing session and export the HTTP Host field values. We then exported the Packet List pane columns to a CSV file for further processing. [Chapter 4]

http-browse101.pcapng

This trace file contains a web browsing session. This is a good trace file to use to practice adding columns or filtering on DNS traffic to identify web site dependencies. [Chapters 3, 4, and 6]

http-browse101b.pcapng

This trace file contains IPv4 and IPv6 traffic. We used this trace file to examine the Protocol Hierarchy window. [Chapter 5]

http-browse101c.pcapng

This trace file contains traffic between a host in the United States and hosts in China. This is a great trace file to use when practicing GeoIP mapping. [Chapter 5]

http-browse101d.pcapng

This trace file contains numerous intertwined conversations. Practice differentiating the conversations by applying temporary coloring rules to the separate conversations. [Chapter 4]

http-chappellu101.pcapng

This trace file contains a very simple web browsing session. Use this file to practice reassembling web objects. [Chapter 1]

http-chappellu101b.pcapng

In this browsing session, the user decided to open a PDF file located on the web site. Looking closely at the trace file we can see the browser used an external PDF viewing software. Checking in to that viewer site, we detected a 404 error. [Chapter 3]

http-chappellu101c.pcapng

This client browses to *www.chappellu.com* after making a DNS query to two separate DNS servers. Towards the end of the trace file we see the client performing a series of DNS queries for all the domain names contained in links on the main page. [Chapter 1]

http-cheez101.pcapng

This trace file depicts a browsing session to the infamous *cheezburger.com* site. Try opening this trace file with the TCP *Allow subdissector to reassemble TCP streams* preference enabled and disabled. You can see the difference in frame 10. [Chapter 7]

http-college101.pcapng

This is another good trace file that contains a large number of connections required to browse a single web site. Peruse through the GET requests to see some interesting .jpg file names. [Chapter 6]

http-disney101.pcapng

It's the "happiest place on Earth"… if you can get there. This trace file depicts DNS errors that are slowing down the browsing session. [Chapters 1, 3, and 8]

http-download-c.pcapng

This is a nice big trace file depicting another download of the OpenOffice suite. There are a few problems in this trace file and we notice the server is sluggish at first – just like in *a.pcapng*. [Chapter 8]

http-download101.pcapng

This trace file contains some very serious TCP problems. Use the Expert Information window to identify the errors. Pay attention to the packet time information to determine how heavily these errors affected performance. [Chapter 5 and Chapter 8]

http-download101c.pcapng

Filter on the GET requests to see what the client is downloading in this trace file. Consider creating a coloring rule based on your findings. [Chapter 8]

http-download101d.pcapng

There are numerous problems in this trace file. Create an IO Graph that compares all traffic with the TCP analysis flagged packets. [Chapter 3]

http-download101e.pcapng

Again, we have errors in the trace file that are affecting the throughput. Create another IO Graph with the TCP analysis flagged packets. You probably need to set the Y axis to logarithmic to see the relationship between TCP errors and drops in throughput. [Chapter 5]

http-errors101.pcapng

In this trace file a user is trying to load a page that does not exist. Practice setting up coloring rules for HTTP error response codes using this trace file. [Chapter 3]

http-espn101.pcapng

When you browse to *www.espn.com*, you will find that there's nothing there. This trace file shows the interdependencies between web sites. You may think you are connecting to a single site, when you are actually connecting to multiple sites. [Chapters 1, 3, 5, 6, and 8]

http-google101.pcapng

In this trace file we received IPv4 and IPv6 addresses in response to our DNS queries. Did any of our communications travel over IPv6? [Chapter 0]

http-jezebel101.pcapng

Look in the Frame section in this trace file. It was taken the day after Hurricane Sandy hit the East Coast of the United States. Numerous servers on the East Coast were knocked out by the floods. This site, *jezebel.com*, was hosted on a Datagram server that was located in a flooded basement. Reassemble the TCP streams to clearly read the responses from the temporary server to which traffic was directed. [Chapter 4]

http-misctraffic101.pcapng

Try to reassemble the executable transferred during this web browsing session. It is fully functional, but it may not be the latest copy available. [Chapter 4 and Chapter 5]

http-nonstandard101.pcapng

In this trace file we have HTTP traffic traveling over a non-standard port. You can adjust the HTTP preference settings to dissect this traffic properly. [Chapter 1]

http-openoffice101a.pcapng

This trace file depicts a slow server response. Use the **Time** column and the TCP *Calculate conversation timestamps* feature to determine the length of the delay.

http-openoffice101b.pcapng

During this OpenOffice download, the client terminates the connection to the server. It takes the server a while to receive the TCP Resets, however, so the trace file ends with a number of unacknowledged data packets. [Chapter 1]

http-pcaprnet101.pcapng

There is a noticeable delay when accessing *pcapr.net* information. Use the **Time** column and the TCP conversation timestamp details to analyze the performance of this browsing session. [Chapter 1]

http-pictures101.pcapng

We are browsing for images at *istockphoto.com*. Practice exporting HTTP objects using this file. Can you tell what search term we used on the iStockphoto site? [Chapter 3]

http-sfgate101.pcapng

This trace file contains a browsing session to *sfgate.com*, an online newspaper owned by the Hearst Corporation. Use your HTTP filtering capabilities to detect the POST message. [Chapter 3 and Chapter 4]

http-slow101.pcapng

This trace file depicts a really slow communication between an HTTP client and a server. It's a great trace file to practice your "high latency" coloring rules and display filters. [Chapter 1]

http-winpcap101.cap

This file was captured with Microsoft's Network Monitor. Wireshark can open the trace file easily using Wireshark's Wiretap Library. [Chapter 0]

http-wiresharkdownload101.pcapng

Use this trace file to compare the results of an `http` filter with a `tcp.port==80` filter. Notice the value of the **Protocol** column as you apply these filters. [Chapter 3 and Chapter 6]

mybackground101.pcapng

This trace file was taken to determine what background traffic occurs on a lab system. As we removed "normal" traffic from view, we detected an incoming connection attempt from a foreign host. [Chapter 0 and Chapter 3]

net-lost-route.pcapng

Watch what happens when the network appears to have suffered a major "glitch." Notice that the Intelligent Scrollbar can help you spot the problems quickly in this trace file. [Chapter 4]

sec-concern101.pcapng

This trace file contains some very unsettling traffic. Open the Protocol Hierarchy window and export the suspicious traffic to get a better feel for what is taking place. [Chapter 5]

sec-nessus101.pcapng

This trace file depicts a Nessus scan. You'll notice a wide range of colors applied to the packets and a very interesting Protocol Hierarchy view. [Chapter 4]

sec-suspicous101.pcapng

This browsing session illustrates a redirection to a cz.cc site. Note that in 2011, Google blacklisted all sites under the cz.cc domain stating "Over the past 90 days, cz.cc appeared to function as an intermediary for the infection of 13788 site(s) including *uniform-net.jp/, nuxi-navi.com/, flashracingonline.com/.*" [Chapter 7]

smb-join101.pcapng

This trace contains the SMB traffic from a Windows host that joins a domain. Use this trace file to test your coloring rule or display filter for SMB errors. [Chapter 3]

split250*.pcapng

This set of trace files are linked together as a "file set." Use the instructions in Chapter 2 to open and work with this file set. [Chapter 2]

tcp-decodeas.pcapng

This traffic runs over a non-standard port. In fact, Wireshark does not have a dissector for the port used. Follow the stream to figure out what the traffic is and then force a dissector using right-click **Decode As**. [Chapter 1]

tr-twohosts.pcapng

It's dueling FTP sessions. Use this trace to test your skills at comparing file transfer performance for two separate conversations. Who wins? [Chapter 5]

wlan-ipadstartstop101.pcapng

This trace file contains the 802.11 traffic from an iPad during the startup and shut down procedure. This trace file was taken with an AirPcap adapter and includes a Radiotap header. The data is not visible because the traffic is encrypted. [Chapter 3]

[This page intentionally blank.]

Network Analyst's Glossary

Note: This Glossary defines terms as they relate to network analysis and Wireshark functionality.

6to4 traffic — 6to4 traffic contains IPv6 packets embedded inside IPv4 headers. These packets can be routed through an IPv4 network to a target IPv6 host. Apply a display filter for `ip and ipv6` to detect traffic that contains both protocols.

ACK — Short for Acknowledgment, this term is used to refer to the packets that are sent to acknowledge receipt of some packet on a TCP connection. For example, a handshake packet (SYN) containing an initial sequence number is acknowledged with SYN/ACK. A data packet would also be acknowledged.

AirPcap — This specialized wireless adapter was originally created by CACE Technologies (now owned by Riverbed) to capture wireless network traffic. Designed to work on Windows hosts, this adapter can capture traffic in promiscuous mode (capture traffic sent to all target hardware addresses, not just the local hardware address) and monitor mode (capture traffic on all wireless networks by not joining any wireless network). For more information, visit *www.riverbed.com*.

Annotations — As of Wireshark 1.8, annotations, or comments, can be added to an entire trace file or to individual packets. Trace file annotations can be seen by clicking on the **Annotation** button on the Status Bar or by selecting **Statistics | Summary**. Packet annotations can be seen above the Frame section of a packet in the Packet Details pane or by opening the **Expert Information** window and selecting the **Packet Comments** tab. The display filter `comment` will show you all packets that contain comments. Add this as a column to read all comments in the Packet List pane.

Apply as Filter — After right-clicking on a field, conversation, endpoint, or protocol/application you can apply a display filter immediately using this option.

ARP (Address Resolution Protocol) — ARP packets are sent to determine if someone is using a particular IP address on a network (gratuitous ARP) or to locate a local host's hardware address (ARP requests/replies). Both the capture and display filters for ARP are simply `arp`.

ASCII (American Standard Code for Information Interchange)-ASCII is a character encoding mechanism seen in the Packet Bytes pane. When you highlight a text field in the Packet Details pane, the hex and ASCII location of that field is highlighted in the Packet Bytes pane.

background traffic — This traffic type occurs with no user-intervention. Typical background traffic may include virus detection tool updates, OS updates, and broadcasts, or multicasts from other devices on the network. Start capturing traffic on your own computer and then walk away. Let the capture run for a while to get a baseline of your machine's background traffic.

Berkeley Packet Filtering (BPF) Syntax — This is the syntax used by Wireshark capture filters. This filtering format was originally defined for tcpdump, a command-line capture tool. For more information on Wireshark capture filter syntax, see *wiki.wireshark.org/CaptureFilters*.

Bootstrap Protocol, see *BOOTP*

BOOTP (Bootstrap Protocol) — This protocol offered dynamic address assignment and is the predecessor of DHCP (Dynamic Host Configuration Protocol). IPv4 DHCP packets contain a BOOTP header and can be filtered on using the `bootp` display filter for DHCPv4 and `dhcpv6` for DHCPv6. Also see *DHCP*.

broadcast — Broadcast is a type of address that indicates "everyone" on this network. The Ethernet MAC-layer broadcast address is 0xFF:FF:FF:FF:FF:FF. The IPv4 broadcast address is 255.255.255.255 whereas a subnet broadcast would be 10.2.255.255 on network 10.2.0.0. Broadcasts to the 255.255.255.255 address are not forwarded by routers, but they are forwarded out all switch ports. Subnet broadcasts may be forwarded by a router if that router is configured to do so.

Capinfos–This command-line tool is included in the Wireshark download and can be used to obtain basic information about a trace file such as file size, capture duration and checksum value. If you are going to use a trace file as evidence of a security breach, consider obtaining file checksum values immediately after saving trace files to prove the trace file has not been tampered with. The command `capinfos -H <filename>` will generate SHA1, RMD160 and MD5 checksum values only whereas `capinfos <filename>` will generate checksum values as well as all other file information.

Capture Engine–The Capture Engine is responsible for working with the link layer interfaces for packet capture. Wireshark uses *dumpcap.exe* for the actual capture process.

capture filter — This is a filter that is applied during the capture process only. This filter cannot be applied to saved trace files. Use this filter type sparingly as you can't retrieve and analyze the traffic you drop with a capture filter. Use the `-f` parameter to apply capture filters with Tshark and Dumpcap.

capture interface — The capture interface is the hardware device upon which you can capture traffic. To view available capture interfaces, click on the **Interfaces** button on the main toolbar. If Wireshark does not see any interfaces, you cannot capture traffic. Most likely the link-layer driver (libpcap, WinPcap, or AirPcap) did not load properly.

checksum errors — When you enable checksum validation for IP, UDP, or TCP in the protocol preferences area, Wireshark calculates the checksum values in each of those headers. If the checksum value is incorrect, Wireshark marks the packet with a checksum error. Since so many machines support checksum offloading, it is not uncommon to see outbound packets marked with a bad checksum because the checksum hasn't been applied yet. Turn off checksum validation and/or disable the Bad Checksum coloring rule to remove these false positives. See also *task offloading*.

CIDR (Classless Interdomain Routing) Notation — This is a way of representing the network portion of an IP address by appending a bit count value. This value indicates the number of bits that comprise the network portion of the address. For example, 130.57.3.0/24 indicates that the network portion of the address is 24-bits long (130.57.3).

Classless Interdomain Routing, see *CIDR Notation*

Comma-Separated Value format, see *CSV format*

comparison operators — Comparison operators are used to look for a value in a field. For example, `ip.addr==10.2.2.2` uses the "equal" comparison operator. Other comparison operators include `>`, `>=`, `<`, `<=`, and `!=`.

core engine — This area of the Wireshark application is considered the "work horse" of Wireshark. Frames come into the capture engine from the Wiretap Library or from the Capture Engine. Packet dissectors, display filters, and plugins all work as part of the Core Engine.

CSV format — Saving to CSV format is available when exporting packet dissections. Using this format, Wireshark can export all Packet List pane column information for evaluation by another program, such as a spreadsheet program.

delta time (general) — This time value measures the elapsed time from the end of one packet to the end of the next packet. Set the **Time** column to this measurement using **View | Time Display Format | Seconds Since Previous Displayed Packet**. This field is inside the Frame section of the Packet Details pane (called **Time delta from previous displayed frame**).

delta time (TCP) — This time value can be enabled in TCP preferences (*Calculate conversation timestamps*) and provides a measurement from the end of one TCP packet in a stream to the end of the next TCP packet in that same stream. The field is added to the end of the TCP header in the [Timestamps] section. To filter on high TCP delta times, use `tcp.time_delta > x`, where x is a number of seconds (x.xxxxxx format is supported as well).

DHCP (Dynamic Host Configuration Protocol) — This protocol is used to dynamically assign IP addresses and other characteristics to IP clients. The capture filter for IPv4 DHCP traffic is `port 67` (alternately you can use `port 68`). The display filter for IPv4 DHCP traffic is `bootp`. The capture filter for DHCPv6 traffic is `port 546` (alternately you can use `port 547`). The display filter for DHCPv6 traffic is `dhcpv6`.

Dynamic Host Configuration Protocol, see *DHCP*

Differentiated Services Code Point, see *DSCP*

display filter — This filter can be applied during a live capture or to a saved trace file. Display filters can be used to focus on specific types of traffic. Wireshark's display filters use a proprietary format. Display filters are saved in a text file called *dfilters*. Use the -R parameter to apply display filters while using Tshark. Dumpcap does not support display filters.

dissectors — Dissectors are the Wireshark software elements that break apart applications and protocols to display their field names and interpreted values. To view the master list of Wireshark dissectors, visit *anonsvn.wireshark.org/viewvc/*, select a Wireshark version and navigate to the *epan/dissectors* directory.

DNS (Domain Name System) — DNS is used to resolve names to IP addresses and much more. We are most familiar with hosts using DNS to obtain the IP address for a host name typed into a URL field of a browser, but DNS can provide additional information, such as the mail exchange server or canonical name (alias) information. Although most often seen over UDP, DNS can run over TCP for requests/responses and always runs over TCP for DNS zone transfers (transfer of information between DNS servers). The capture filter syntax for DNS traffic is port 53; the display filter syntax is simply dns.

Domain Name System, see *DNS*

DSCP (Differentiated Services Code Point) — This feature adds prioritization to the traffic using the DSCP fields in the IP header. To determine if DSCP is in use, apply a display filter for ip.dsfield.dscp != 0.

Dumpcap — This command-line tool is referred to as a "pure packet capture application" and is included with Wireshark. Dumpcap is used for packet capture by Wireshark and Tshark. Type dumpcap -h at the command line to learn what options are available when running Dumpcap alone.

Editcap — This command-line tool is included with Wireshark and is used to split trace files into file sets, remove duplicates, and alter trace file timestamps. To see the options available with Editcap, type editcap -h at the command prompt.

Ethereal — This is the former name of the Wireshark project. On June 7, 2006, Gerald Combs and the entire development team moved from Ethereal to the new Wireshark home. This name change was prompted by a trademark issue when Gerald Combs, the creator of Ethereal, moved to his new job at CACE Technologies.

Ethernet — Developed at Xerox PARC in 1973-1974, Ethernet defines a networking technology that consists of a physical connection to a shared medium (wire), the bit transmission mechanism, and the frame structure.

Ethernet header — This header is placed in front of the network layer header (such as IP) to get a packet from one machine to another on a local network. Once the Ethernet header is placed on the packet, we refer to it as a frame. The common Ethernet header format is Ethernet II and contains a destination hardware address (6 bytes), source hardware address (6 bytes) and Type field (2 bytes). Wireshark looks at the Type field to determine which dissector should receive the packet next. There is also an Ethernet trailer that consists of a 4-byte Frame Check Sequence field. See also *Ethernet trailer*.

Ethernet trailer — This 4-byte trailer is added to the end of a packet and consists of a Frame Check Sequence field (checksum field). Upon receipt of a frame, each device strips off the Ethernet header and trailer and performs a checksum calculation on the packet content. The receiving device compares its checksum result against the value seen in the checksum field to determine if the packet is corrupt. Most NICs strip off the Ethernet trailer before handing the frame to the computer/operating system/Wireshark.

exclusion filter — This type of filter either drops frames during the capture process (exclusion capture filter) or removes the frame from view (exclusion display filter). An example of an exclusion capture filter is `not port 80`. An example of an exclusion display filter is `!ip.addr==10.2.2.2`.

Expert Information — This Wireshark window displays and links to various errors, warnings, notes, and additional information detected in the trace file. This window also displays packet comments. You can launch the Expert Information window by clicking on the **Expert Information** button on the Status Bar.

File Transfer Protocol, see *FTP*

FIN (Finish) — This bit is set by a TCP host to indicate that it is finished sending data on the connection. Once both sides of a TCP connection send a packet with the FIN bit set, each side will begin timing out the connection.

frame — The term used to define a unit of communications that consists of a packet surrounded by a MAC-layer header and trailer. Wireshark numbers each frame as it is captured or opened (in the case of a saved trace file). From that point on, however, Wireshark often refers to these frames as "packets" (**File | Export Specified Packets** for example).

FTP (File Transfer Protocol) — FTP is an established application to transfer data between devices. FTP runs over TCP using port 21 as a default for the command channel while allowing a dynamic port number to be assigned to the data channel. The capture filter for FTP command channel traffic on the default port is `port 21`. The display filter syntax is `tcp.port==21`. Although Wireshark recognizes the filter `ftp`, this filter will not display the TCP connection establishment, maintenance or tear down process.

GIMP (GNU Image Manipulation Program) Graphical Toolkit (GTK) — This is the toolkit used to present the graphical interface — the windows, dialogs, buttons, columns, etc.

heuristic dissector — A heuristic process can be considered "trial and error." Wireshark hands packets over to the dissectors that match the port in use (the "normal dissector"). If Wireshark does not have a normal dissector, it hands the packet off to a heuristic dissector. The heuristic dissector will look at the information received and, by trial and error, try to see if it fits within the dissector's definition of a certain protocol or application. If not, it sends an error to Wireshark which sends the packet to the next heuristic dissector.

hex — Short for hexadecimal, hex refers to the base 16 counting system, in which the digits are 0-9 and A-F. The Packet Bytes pane displays frame contents in hex format on the left and ASCII format on the right.

hosts file — Wireshark refers to its own *hosts* file to resolve names when network name resolution is enabled. This file is located in the Wireshark program file directory. You can place a *hosts* file in your profile directory and configure Wireshark's name resolution process to look at that file when resolving names.

HTTP (Hypertext Transfer Protocol) — This is the file transfer protocol used when you browse a web site. Typically seen over TCP port 80, you can create a capture filter using `tcp port 80` or a display filter using `tcp.port==80`. Although you could use an `http` display filter, that filter will not display the TCP connection establishment, maintenance or tear down process packets.

HTTPS (Hypertext Transfer Protocol Secure) — HTTPS is defined as the secure version of HTTP. In essence, HTTPS is simply HTTP running over SSL/TLS (Secure Socket Layer/Transport Layer Security), which are cryptographic protocols. The capture filter for HTTPS traffic is `port 443` whereas the display filter is `ssl`.

Hypertext Transfer Protocol, see *HTTP*

Hypertext Transfer Protocol Secure, see *HTTPS*

IANA (Internet Assigned Numbers Authority) — Based in Marina del Rey, California, IANA is *"responsible for the global coordination of the DNS Root, IP addressing, and other Internet protocol resources."* For network analysts, *www.iana.org* is an invaluable resource for field values, assigned multicast addresses, assigned port numbers, and more.

ICMP (Internet Control Message Protocol) — This protocol is used as a messaging service on a network. Most people are familiar with the ICMP-based ping operation. ICMP communications should always be considered when you are troubleshooting network performance. The capture filter and display filter syntax for ICMP is just `icmp`.

Initial Round Trip Time (iRTT) — The amount of time to travel round trip between TCP peers as measured in the TCP handshake process. This value is used to differentiate between a Fast Retransmission and an Out-of-Order packet.

Internet Assigned Numbers Authority, see *IANA*

Internet Control Message Protocol, see *ICMP*

Internet Protocol (IPv4/v6) — IP is the routed protocol (not the rout*ing* protocol) used to get packets through an internetwork. The capture filter syntax for IPv4 and IPv6 are `ip` and `ip6`, respectively. The display filter syntax for IPv4 and IPv6 are `ip` and `ipv6`, respectively.

Internet Storm Center (ISC) — Created by SANS, the ISC offers daily information on security risks and vulnerabilities. For more information, visit *isc.sans.edu*.

IP address — This address identifies a single host, group of hosts, or all hosts on a network. To create a capture filter based on an IPv4 address, the syntax is `host x.x.x.x`. The syntax of an IPv4 display filter is `ip.addr==x.x.x.x`. To create a capture filter based on an IPv6 address, use `host xxxx:xxxx:xxxx:xxxx:xxxx:xxxx:xxxx:xxxx`. For an IPv6 use `ipv6.addr==xxxx:xxxx:xxxx:xxxx:xxxx:xxxx:xxxx:xxxx`.

ISATAP (Intra-Site Automatic Tunnel Addressing Protocol) traffic — ISATAP is a method to encapsulate IPv6 packets inside IPv4 headers to be forwarded through an IPv4 network.

key hosts — We use the term "key hosts" to refer to the devices that are critical on the network. They may include the server that maintains the customer database or the CEO's laptop. You define which host should be tracked and analyzed as a key host.

libpcap — This is the link-layer driver used for packet capture tools, such as Wireshark. There are numerous other tools that use libpcap for packet capture. For more information, see *sourceforge.net/projects/libpcap/*.

link-layer driver — This is the driver that hands frames up to Wireshark. WinPcap, libpcap, and AirPcap are three link layer drivers used with Wireshark.

logical operators — These operators are used to expand filters to determine if a value is matched in some form or another. Examples of logical operators are `&&`, `and`, `||`, `or`, `!`, and `not`. An example of logical operator use is `tcp.analysis.flags && ip.addr==10.2.2.2`.

MAC (Media Access Control) address — This address is associated with a network interface card or chipset. On an Ethernet network, MAC addresses are 6 bytes long. Switches use MAC addresses to differentiate and identify devices connected to switch ports. They use these addresses to make forwarding decisions. To build a capture filter based on a MAC address, use the syntax `ether host 00:08:15:00:08:15`, for example. To build a display filter based on a MAC address, use `eth.addr==00:08:15:00:08:15`, for example.

***manuf* file** — This Wireshark file contains a list of manufacturer OUI (Organizational Unit Identifiers) as defined by the IEEE (Institute of Electrical and Electronics Engineers). These three-byte values are used to distinguish the maker of a network interface card or chipset. In Wireshark, MAC name resolution is on by default so you will see these OUI values in the MAC addresses (such as Hewlett-_a7:bf:a3). This *manuf* file resides in the Wireshark program file directory.

Maximum Segment Size, see *MSS*

Media Access Control address, see *MAC address*

Mergecap — This command-line tool is used to merge or to concatenate trace files. If you have a set of trace files, but you want to create a single IO Graph of all the communications in those trace files, consider using Mergecap to combine the files into a single file before opening an IO Graph. To identify the options available with Mergecap, type `mergecap -h`.

metadata—This is basically "extra data." In Wireshark, we see metadata in the Frame section at the top of the Packet Details pane. Using the *.pcapng* format, you can also add your own metadata through trace file annotations and packet annotations.

MSS (Maximum Segment Size)—This value defines how many bytes can follow a TCP header in a packet. During the TCP handshake, each side of the conversation provides their MSS value. A common MSS value on an Ethernet network is 1,460.

multicast—This is a type of address that targets a group of hosts. At the MAC layer, most multicast addresses begin with 01:00:5e while IPv4 multicasts begin with a number 224 through 239 in the first IP address byte location. An example of an IPv4 multicast is 224.0.0.2, which is targeted at all local routers. IPv6 multicasts have the preface ff00::/8 (the "8" signifying that the first 8 bits are the bits we are interested in).

name resolution—This feature is used to associate a name with a device, network interface card/chip, or port. Wireshark supports three types of name resolution: MAC name resolution, transport name resolution, and network name resolution. MAC name resolution is on by default and resolves the first three bytes of hardware addresses to a manufacturer name (such as Apple_70:66:f5). Transport name resolution is on by default and resolves port numbers to port names (such as port 80 resolved to http). Network name resolution is off by default and resolves an IP address to a host name (such as 74.125.19.106 resolving to *www.google.com*). In Wireshark, when you enable network name resolution, Wireshark may generate a series of DNS Pointer queries to obtain host names. Wireshark can be configured to look at a *hosts* file for network name resolution, rather than generating DNS Pointer queries. You can even have a separate *hosts* file for each profile.

NAT (Network Address Translation)—NAT devices alter the IP address of hosts while maintaining a master list of all the original IP addresses and the new addresses in order to forward traffic back to the correct address. NAT is often used to hide internal addresses from the outside world or enable an organization to use simple private IP addresses, such as 10.2.0.1.

NetBIOS (Network Basic Input/Output System)—This is the session-level protocol used by applications, such as SMB, to communicate among hosts on a network, typically a Microsoft-product network. In Wireshark, you can apply a display filter for nbss (NetBIOS Session Service) or nbns (NetBIOS Name Service).

Network Address Translation, see *NAT*

Network Basic Input/Output System, see *NetBIOS*

network interface card (NIC)—This card, which is typically just a chipset, offers the physical connection to the network. NICs now offer greater capability than just applying a MAC header to the packets. Some hosts now support task offloading, which relies on the NIC for various functions such as segmenting TCP data and applying IP, UDP, and TCP checksum values. See also *Task offload*.

Nmap—This network mapping tool was created by Gordon Lyon (Fyodor) to discover and characterize network hosts. For more information, visit *nmap.org*.

Packet Bytes pane — This is the bottom pane displayed by default in Wireshark. The Packet Bytes pane shows the contents of the frame in both hexadecimal and ASCII formats. When you click on a field in the Packet Details pane, Wireshark highlights those bytes and the related ASCII characters in the Packet Bytes pane. To toggle this pane between hidden and displayed, select **View | Packet Bytes**.

packet comments (aka packet annotations) — As of Wireshark 1.8, you can right-click on a packet in the Packet List pane and choose **Add or Edit Packet Comments**. This feature is only supported in trace files saved in the *.pcapng* format. Packet comments are shown above the Frame section in the Packet Details pane. To view packet comments, open the **Expert Information** window and click on the **Packet Comments** tab. You can export all trace file and packet comments using **Statistics | Capture File Properties | Copy to Clipboard**.

Packet Details Pane — This is the middle pane displayed by default in Wireshark. This pane shows the individual fields and field interpretations offered by Wireshark. When you select a frame in the Packet List pane, Wireshark displays that frame's information in the Packet Details pane. To toggle this pane between hidden and displayed, select **View | Packet Details**. This is likely a pane you will use very often in Wireshark because you can right-click on a field and quickly apply a display filter or coloring rule based on that field.

Packet List pane — This is the top pane displayed by default in Wireshark. This pane shows a summary of the individual frame values. When you select a frame in the Packet List pane, Wireshark displays that frame's information in the Packet Details pane. To toggle this pane between hidden and displayed, select **View | Packet List**. This is likely a pane you will use very often in Wireshark as you can right-click on a frame and quickly apply a conversation filter or reassemble communications using **Follow | TCP stream, Follow | UDP stream**, or **Follow SSL stream**.

packet — This is the term used to describe the elements inside a MAC frame. Once you strip off the frame, you are looking at a packet. We use this term loosely in analysis. Although Wireshark displays frames, we often refer to them as "packets".

.pcap (Packet Capture) — This trace file format is the default format for earlier versions of Wireshark (before Wireshark 1.8). This format is also referred to as the tcpdump or libpcap trace file format.

.pcapng, also .pcap-ng (.pcap Next Generation) — This trace file format is the successor to the .pcap format. This new format facilitates saving metadata, such as packet and trace file comments, local interface details, and local IP address, with a trace file. For more information about the *.pcapng* format, see *wiki.wireshark.org/Development/PcapNg*.

PCRE (Perl-Compatible Regular Expressions) — Regular expressions is a search-pattern language used to match strings of characters, numbers, or symbols. "Perl-Compatible" defines the flavor of regular expressions that Wireshark supports. See also *Regular expressions (regex)*.

Perl-Compatible Regular Expressions, see *PCRE*

Per-Packet Interface, see *PPI*

Pilot, see *SteelCentral™ Packet Analyzer*

port spanning—This process is used to configure a switch to copy the traffic to and from one or more switch ports down the port to which Wireshark is connected. Not all switches support this capability. Some people refer to this as port mirroring. Note that port spanned switches will not forward corrupt packets to Wireshark. See also *Tap*.

PPI (Per-Packet Interface)—PPI is an 802.11 header specification that provides out-of-band information in a pseudoheader that is prepended to the 802.11 header. Used by AirPcap adapters, the PPI pseudoheader includes channel-frequency information, signal power, noise level, and more.

preferences **file**—This file contains the protocol preference settings, name resolution settings, column settings, and more. Each profile has its own *preferences* file, which is contained in the personal configurations folder.

Prepare a Filter—This task can be performed by right-clicking on a packet in the Packet List pane. **Prepare a Filter** creates, but does not apply, a display filter based on the selected element. See also *Apply as Filter*.

profiles—Profiles contain the customized configurations for Wireshark. There is a single profile available on a new Wireshark system—the *Default* profile. The current profile in use is displayed in the right side of the Status Bar. To switch between profiles, click on the **Profile** area in the Status Bar. To create a new profile, right-click on the **Profile** area.

Protocol Data Unit (PDU)—This is a set of data transferred between hosts. In Wireshark, you will see [TCP segment of a reassembled PDU] when you allow the TCP subdissector to reassemble TCP streams. In essence, these packets contain segments of a file that is being transferred.

Protocol Hierarchy window—This window breaks down the traffic according to the protocols in use and provides details regarding packet percentages and byte percentages. This window is available under the Statistics menu option. Watch for unusual protocols or applications or the dreaded "data" under TCP, UDP, or IP. This designation means that Wireshark does not recognize the traffic, which is unusual considering the number of dissectors included in Wireshark.

protocol preferences—These preferences define how Wireshark handles various protocols and applications. Protocol preferences are set by right-clicking on a protocol in the Packet Details pane, by selecting **Edit | Preferences** from the menu or by clicking the **Edit Preferences** button on the main toolbar.

QoS (Quality of Service)—This term refers to a method of prioritizing traffic as it travels through a network. QoS settings can be defined on interconnecting devices (forward web browsing traffic before email traffic, for example) or by an application. When defined by an application, the DSCP bits can be set to prioritize the traffic over other traffic. See also *DSCP*.

Quality of Service, see *QoS*

Regular Expressions (regex) — Regex is a search-pattern language used to match strings of characters, numbers, or symbols. Wireshark uses Perl-Compatible Regular Expressions (PCRE) when you use the `matches` operator in display filters. For more information on regular expressions, see *www.regular-expressions.info*. See also *PCRE*.

relative start (Rel.Start) — This value is shown in the Conversations window and indicates the first time this conversation was seen in the trace file. You may need to expand the Conversations window to see this column. The time is based on seconds since the first packet in the trace file.

remote capture — This term describes the process of capturing traffic at one location and analyzing it at another location. WinPcap includes a remote capture tool (*rpcapd.exe*) that Wireshark can access through the Capture Options window (Manage Interfaces).

RST (Reset) — This bit is set by a host to terminate a TCP connection. Once this bit has been set in an outbound packet, the sender cannot send any further data on that connection. In a typical TCP connection termination process, each side of the connection sends a packet with the RST bit set and the connection is immediately closed.

Server Message Block, see *SMB*

***services* file** — This file contains a list of port numbers and service names. All TCP/IP hosts have a *services* file and Wireshark has its own *services* file as well. This file resides in the Wireshark program file directory. When transport name resolution is enabled, Wireshark replaces port numbers with service names. For example, port 80 would be replaced with "http." You can edit this file if you do not like the service names displayed.

Simple Network Management Protocol, see *SNMP*

SMB (Server Message Block) — Also referred to as Common Internet File System (CIFS), SMB is an application layer protocol used to provide network access, file transfer, printing, and other functions on a Microsoft-based network.

SNMP (Simple Network Management Protocol) — This device management protocol requires that a managed device maintain a database of managed items. Managing hosts view and/or edit that database. You may see SNMP traffic flowing between network hosts and network printers, which often have SNMP enabled to track information such as ink levels, paper levels, and more. To filter on SNMP traffic use the capture filter `port 161 or port 162` or the display filter `snmp`.

Snort — Snort is a Network Intrusion Detection System (NIDS) that was created in 1998 by Martin Roesch and is currently maintained by Sourcefire. Snort relies on a set of rules to identify and generate alerts on network scans and attack traffic. For more information, see *snort.org*.

SteelCentral™ Packet Analyzer — The traffic visualization tool created by Loris Degioanni and available from Riverbed. SteelCentral™ Packet Analyzer can open, analyze, and visually represent very large trace files with ease. In addition, SteelCentral™ Packet Analyzer can build reports based on the charts and graphs, and export key traffic elements to Wireshark for further analysis. For more information on SteelCentral™ Packet Analyzer, visit *www.riverbed.com*.

Stream index number — This number is applied to each TCP conversation seen in the trace file. The first stream index number is set at 0. When you right-click on a TCP communication in the Packet List pane and choose **Follow | TCP stream**, Wireshark applies a display filter based on this Stream Index field number (for example, `tcp.stream==3`.

stream reassembly — This is the process of reassembling everything after the transport-layer header (TCP or UDP) enabling you to clearly read through the requests and replies in a conversation. Communications from the first host seen are colored red; communications from the second host seen are colored blue.

subdissector — This is a dissector that is called by another dissector. You will see this term when you view TCP preferences (*Allow subdissector to reassemble TCP streams*). In the case of web browsing traffic, the HTTP dissector is a subdissector of the TCP dissector.

subnet — This term defines a subset of a network and is applied by lengthening network masks. For example, if you want to create two subnets out of a single network, network 10.2.0.0/16 for example, lengthen the subnet to /24 (24-bits) and assign 10.2.1.0/24 to some hosts and 10.2.2.0/24 to other hosts. The network mask indicates that we have two networks now.

SYN (Synchronize Sequence Numbers) — This bit is set in the first two packets of the TCP handshake to synchronize the initial sequence numbers (ISNs) from each TCP peer. You can use a display filter based on this bit to view the first two packets of each handshake (`tcp.flags.syn==1`) which can be used to determine the round trip time between hosts.

TAP, aka tap (Test Access Port) — These devices are used to intercept network communications and copy the traffic down a monitor port. Basic taps do not make any forwarding decisions on traffic and offer a transparent view of network communications. NetOptics is a company that makes network taps (see *www.netoptics.com*). See also *port spanning*.

task offload — This process offloads numerous processes to the network interface card to free up the host's CPU for other tasks. Task offload can affect your analysis session when checksums are calculated by the network interface card on a host upon which you are running Wireshark. Since checksum values haven't been calculated yet, they are incorrect at the point of capture. If you enable IP, UDP, or TCP checksum validation, or you have the Checksum Errors coloring rule enabled, you may see numerous false positives caused by task offload of the checksum calculation.

TCP/IP (Transmission Control Protocol/Internet Protocol) — This term refers to an entire suite of protocols and applications that provide connectivity among worldwide computer systems. The term "TCP/IP" refers to more than TCP and IP, it refers to UDP, ICMP, ARP, and more.

Teredo IPv6 traffic — Teredo is a tunneling method that encapsulates an IPv6 header inside a UDP packet. This technology was developed to assist with crossing Network Address Translation (NAT). Teredo is covered in RFC 4380, *Teredo: Tunneling IPv6 over UDP through Network Address Translations (NATs).*

TFTP (Trivial File Transfer Protocol) — This file transfer protocol runs over UDP offering minimal file transfer functionality. Most commonly, TFTP uses port 69, but you must keep in mind that many applications can be configured to run over non-standard port. Unexpected TFTP traffic can be a symptom of a security breach on your network.

Time to Live, see *TTL*

Trivial File Transfer Protocol, see *TFTP*

trace file — This general term refers to all files that contain network traffic, regardless of the format of the file. Wireshark currently uses the *.pcapng* trace file format, but it can understand most other common trace file formats. Trace files generally include a file header (which contains information about the entire trace file, including the indication of the trace file format in use) and packet headers that include metadata (such as comments) about individual packets.

Transport Layer Security, see *TLS*

TLS (Transport Layer Security) — TLS is a cryptographic protocol based on Secure Socket Layer (SSL). When analyzing TLS traffic, you can look at the initial TLS handshake packets to identify connection establishment problems. To decrypt this traffic, you must have the appropriate decryption key. TLS preferences are configured under the SSL preference area in Wireshark. To capture TLS/SSL-based traffic, use a port-based capture filter, such as `port 443`. The display filter syntax for TLS/SSL-based traffic is `SSL`.

Tshark — This command-line tool can be used to capture, display, and obtain basic statistics on live traffic or saved trace files. Tshark relies on Dumpcap to actually capture the traffic. By far the most feature-rich version of the command-line capture tools, you can type `tshark -h` to find the list of available Tshark parameters.

TTL (Time to Live) — This IP header field is decremented by each router as it is forwarded along a network path. If a packet arrives at a router with a TTL value of 1, it cannot be forwarded because you cannot decrement the TTL to zero and forward the packet. The packet will be discarded.

UDP (User Datagram Protocol) — This connectionless transport protocol is used by many basic network communications, including all broadcasts, all multicasts, DHCP, DNS requests, and more. The capture filter and display filter syntax to capture UDP is `udp`.

Uniform Resource Indicator, see *URI*

URI (Uniform Resource Indicator) — This term defines the actual element being requested in an HTTP communication. For example, when you analyze a web browsing session, you might see a request for the "/" URI. This "/" is a request for the default page (*index.html*, for example). To build a display filter to show any packets that contain a URI, use `http.request.uri`.

User Datagram Protocol, see *UDP*

WinPcap (Windows Packet Capture) — This Windows-specific link-layer driver is used by Wireshark to capture traffic on a wired network. Originally created by Loris Degioanni. WinPcap is the industry leading utility for various network tools. For more information, see *www.winpcap.org*.

Wiretap Library — This library gives you the raw packet data from trace files. Wireshark's Wiretap Library understands many different trace file formats and can be seen when you select **File | Open** and click the drop-down arrow next to **Files of Type**.

WLAN (Wireless Local Area Network) — This term describes networks that rely on RF (radio frequency) media to communicate between hosts. Wireshark contains dissectors for various WLAN traffic elements. The AirPcap adapter is a great adapter for capturing WLAN traffic.

Index

Want to learn more?
Register for the All Access Pass (AAP) Online Training

Register Online	Log in at **https://www.lcuportal2.com**.
Enroll in Classes	View available course information (including credit hours) and register for your online courses. You can enter a course immediately after registering.
My Classes	View the list of courses for which you are registered and your status (completed or in progress).
My Transcript	Print or email your training transcript (in progress and completed courses) including course CPE credits and completion dates.
AAP Special Events	Register for live AAP events or access AAP event handouts from past or upcoming events.

SAMPLE COURSE LIST

- Core 1-Wireshark Functions & TCP/IP
- Core 2-Troubleshoot/Secure Networks with Wireshark
- Combo Core 1 and 2 Update
- Wireshark Jumpstart 101
- Hacked Hosts
- Analyze and Improve Throughput
- Top 10 Reasons Your Network is Slow
- TCP Analysis In-Depth
- DHCP/ARP Analysis
- Nmap Network Scanning 101
- WLAN Analysis 101
- Wireshark 201 Filtering
- New Wireshark Features
- ICMP Analysis
- Analyzing Google Secure Search
- Slow Networks - NOPs/SACK
- TCP Vulnerabilities (MS09-048)
- Packet Crafting to Test Firewalls
- Capturing Packets (Security Focus)
- Troubleshooting with Coloring
- Tshark Command-Line Capture
- AAP Event: Analyzing the Window Zero Condition
- Trace File Analysis - Set 1
- Trace File Analysis - Set 2
- Trace File Analysis - Set 3
- Whiteboard Lecture Series 1
- Translate Snort Rules to Wireshark
- …and more

We also offer customized onsite and online training. Visit *www.chappellU.com* for sample course outlines and more information. Contact us at *info@chappellU.com* if you have questions regarding your All Access Pass membership.

Printed in the USA
CPSIA information can be obtained
at www.ICGtesting.com
LVHW070447221223
767132LV00007B/703